Two Badges

THE LIVES OF MONA RUIZ

THE EXCHANGE

What happens when your loyalty is divided?

*This book is dedicated to God Almighty,
who blessed me with a father who taught me how
to dream, and to two fellow officers
who helped me make my dreams become reality,
Lt. Felix Osuna and retired officer Billy Brown.
They are truly Santa Ana's finest.*

INTRODUCTION

Two Badges: The Lives of Mona Ruiz is the true story of a woman's struggle to escape gang life. Mona Ruiz grew up in Santa Ana, California during the 1970s and 1980s. She was the second child in a family of eight. She had a loving family and a special connection to her father. Mona's father hated gang members and one of his greatest fears was that Mona would get involved in a gang.

During the 1960s the image of gangs was not all negative. Gangs offered a sense of belonging and brotherhood. They had a code of behavior and respect. They did not commit violent acts in places like churches, shops, or movie theaters. If an enemy was walking with an older family member, they were left alone. Gang leaders provided support to their members and also took on the role of increasing pride in their communities.

The image of gangs began to get worse by the late 1970s and the 1980s. There were many different Latino gangs that controlled Santa Ana. Drug addiction and violence became serious problems. Shootings became more common. The gangs in Santa Ana earned new **reputations**. The gang lifestyle became known as a life filled

Key Concepts

reputation *n.* how people are seen and judged by others with danger and crime. Staying out of a gang became more difficult to do. Younger kids often turned to gangs for protection from other gangs. Once a person became a gang member, it was nearly impossible to escape. This was the kind of gang life that Mona experienced when she joined F-Troop. F-Troop was one of the biggest and most powerful gangs in Santa Ana. Violent crime and death were common in F-Troop. Many young gang members lost all hope for a better future.

Gangs in Santa Ana continued to be a huge problem in the 1990s. The police created Community Oriented Policing (COP) to help stop gang violence. Police officers worked with the community in the COP program. They learned gang secrets from community members. Officers used this information to arrest gang leaders. COP decreased gang violence and crime in Santa Ana. This program continues today.

Mona suffered because of her loyalty to her gang. Her father disowned her. She lost confidence and was depressed. But she refused to give up hope. She dreamed of being a police officer. But how could she ever make that dream come true with the shame of gang life hanging over her? Mona was determined to triumph over the struggles of her youth. She worked hard to change her life. And she did.

After her struggle, Mona wanted to help others who were stuck in the gang lifestyle. Mona read the book *Always Running* by Luis Rodriguez. This book tells the story of the author's life as a gang member. The events in the book reminded Mona of her own life.

Key Concepts

shame *n.* feelings of guilt, embarrassment, and unworthiness

determined *adj.* strongly decided about something

triumph *v.* to be victorious or successful

A SHARED CONNECTION

The first time Geoff Boucher saw the policewoman Mona Ruiz, he noticed her tattoo and knew that it was a gang mark. Geoff, a reporter who specialized in writing stories on gangs, wanted to learn more about Mona. Geoff found her story fascinating and inspiring. When she decided to write a book, she asked Geoff for help. Though they came from different backgrounds, they shared an understanding of gangs. They also shared loss. Mona saw friends die because of gangs. Geoff lost his sister when a gang member robbed and killed her. Mona and Geoff agree that the only true, lasting solutions to end gangs must come from the communities themselves.

She was inspired to tell her story. Mona hoped that her book would show others that it is possible to change your life.

Growing up, Mona was warned about what being in a gang could do to her life. Why did she join F-Troop? Why was she always in **conflict** over her chosen lifestyle and her dream of being a police officer? *Two Badges: The Lives of Mona Ruiz* details how Mona reacted when her loyalties where being questioned, and how she discovered who she wanted to be loyal to.

Key Concepts

conflict *n.* feelings of confusion over different ideas or interests

9

FROM THE AUTHOR

Many of the names of people depicted in this book have been changed. Talking about my past, my barrio and the circle of friends that I grew up in is difficult because there has been so much pain and loss. For many of them, the fact that I wear a police uniform now is a betrayal of sorts. I hope that this book will help them understand that I have never turned my back on the past—just the opposite, I believe I have dedicated my life to facing it and dealing with it. I never left my barrio, I never ran away. I stayed and I'm trying to make a difference.

I want to be clear, too, about my feelings for the Santa Ana Police Department. I am proud to wear a SAPD badge, and I am deeply grateful to the department for allowing me the opportunity to do so. In this book, as I describe my feelings at different stages in my life, especially my youth, I express some hostility and fear of police officers. That was how I felt then, and I think it would be wrong to say otherwise. Still, my father always told me that police officers were figures of respect, and deep down I always wanted that to be true. These days, as a patrol cop, I strive to make it true.

I also talk about police officers whom I have seen act (in my personal opinion) inappropriately, along with other officers who were distrustful or hurtful when I tried to join the force. Again, I think it would be wrong to pretend these things did not happen. At the same time, I want to be clear that the vast majority of my fellow officers in Santa Ana are clearly professional, dedicated and honorable men and women. For every negative encounter I have ever had, there have been, literally, hundreds of positive examples. The troubles or lapses in the department's history only show what a complicated, difficult mission it has taken on.

~ Chapter One ~

GHOSTS

The **war paint**. It had been years, almost a decade, but my hands still knew **the ritual**. First the pancake makeup, so thick it made my skin look like a pale seashell. Then the lipstick. The gang girls liked to use bright crimson for their lips, or a brown color that looks like an old bloodstain. Heavy eye shadow and mascara, too, so much it looked as if we were wearing little black masks. We applied the eyeliner in a streak that pulled back from the corner of our eyes, back toward our scalp, like a racing strip on a muscle car. It seemed silly, looking back, but we loved it then. The makeup made us feel older. The mask smoothed away signs of weakness and gave us power. When I was a teen, it was a sign that I belonged to the streets. At age thirty-two, staring into the peeling mirror in the locker room at the police station, it was a **disguise**, a way to hide my badge and my job. I couldn't pretend, though, that I wasn't feeling strange seeing myself in the war paint again. Behind my busy hands, I saw the face of my past staring at me in that mirror.

....

war paint makeup that I wore to identify myself as a gang member
the ritual exactly what to do
disguise costume; way to hide who I was

The undercover operation was my first, and I was nervous as hell. I was a **rookie** on that day in 1990 and feeling in over my head, but I wasn't going to let anybody know it. Anything could go wrong, everything could go wrong, and in Santa Ana that means somebody might die. I pulled a red wig out of a plastic bag and tugged it down tight over my own dark hair. I needed one more touch: Blue-green eyeliner dabbed with a wet tissue gave me a passable imitation of a teardrop tattoo beneath my right eye, the street symbol for prison time. So many symbols of the street are of sadness and death. The teardrop was the way *veteranos* announced they had **done time in the *pinta***, but there was reason for everyone in the grip of the gangs to cry, really.

The morning shift was already out on the streets of Santa Ana, and I almost wished I were with them as usual, enjoying the security of a black and white. I had always wanted to work Narcs, and I was grateful for the chance to try it in my first year on the force. They had told me my background, my life running the city's streets with a gang, made me an ideal operative, a natural for the assignment. Now, looking at my reflection, I couldn't stop thinking about the things that could go wrong. What if someone recognizes me?

I glanced at my watch and then remembered to take it off. It was a little too fancy for a *chola* making a street heroin buy. I stuffed it into my gym bag. Not much time left. I stood and inspected my reflection and tried to remember the way I walked and talked when I was in the gang. I was satisfied that my 9-millimeter and vest were hidden by the folds of my worn-out Raiders jersey. The bogus

---

rookie new police officer
veteranos older gang members
done time in the *pinta* been in prison
chola gang girl (in Spanish)

teardrop tattoo, along with the very real and very visible tattoo on my wrist, would make me appear to be a homegirl, just a local barrio girl looking to score drugs. A lot of my old friends still looked like this, wearing the look of a teen *chola* and hanging with the new generation of gangs. Most do it because they can't get away from the drugs, but others just want to relive those days when they felt they owned the streets. If anything, the streets owned us.

I took a deep breath and tried to clear my mind. I gathered my stuff and glanced in the mirror one more time. I was as ready as I was going to get.

In the hallway I passed by our department's chief and he **did a double take**, probably wondering if I had just strolled out of an unlocked holding cell. I offered a casual hello and his eyes widened. The chief was walking with Lt. Felix Osuna, a mentor and friend who had helped me **realize my unlikely dream of wearing a badge**. He had known me in the 1980s when I **ran with** F-Troop, at the time the largest, most powerful gang in Santa Ana. Osuna smiled when he recognized me, shook his head. After I walked by, I could hear Osuna explaining me to the chief, and I managed a smile despite my raw nerves.

In the Narcs office, Cpl. Ann Vickers rushed to greet me with more words of encouragement. "Nice getup! I knew you were ready for this." Vickers, my partner and supervisor at the time, had paved the way for my first undercover duty. A fifteen-year veteran cop, she had earned a level of respect that is difficult for any female in the traditionally male world of law enforcement. Her expertise

....

did a double take looked at me in surprise; tried to figure out if he knew me

realize my unlikely dream of wearing a badge become a police officer

ran with was a member of

15

was in Narcotics, and she had been telling me for weeks that my background and knowledge of the barrio made me especially effective. I hoped she was right: I had always aspired to work in Narcs or the Gang Unit, and this was a chance to prove myself.

Standing next to Vickers was Muñoz, a regular Narc investigator and my partner on **the buy**. Sgt. Messmer was the leader of the operation and, as soon as everyone was **on hand**, he ran through the plan once more. The scenario was a simple curbside buy in a heavy gang area, not far from **my stomping grounds** when I was a member of Santa Ana's F-Troop. I listened as he ran through the radio channels we would use, but part of my mind kept drifting off to the same thought as I studied the grid map of the buy area. It's amazing, the voice in my head was saying, how **far you can come** without ever leaving home.

❖ ❖ ❖

"This is 896 . . . we're in position, over," Muñoz muttered into the pac-set in his lap. He had the radio tucked down out of the view of anyone who glanced at our undercover car, a dented and dirty Monte Carlo. I moved my mouth, pretending to talk, so if anyone saw us they'd think we were carrying on a conversation. Muñoz was an old-timer, a longtime cop who didn't look like it in his disguise as a street tough. He had a goatee and his hair was close to his head in small, jet-black curls and he had a short, stocky build that suggested strength. I didn't know his background—whether he once ran the streets like me—but I would have guessed that he had, just because of his voice. I could hear a lot of street experience in his raspy words,

---

the buy the assignment of pretending to buy drugs

on hand there, ready

my stomping grounds where I used to spend time

far you can come your life can change so much

the same voice the gang *veteranos* spoke with if they were lucky enough to make it into their thirties. I would have asked him about his past, but I didn't dare. That would mean talking about my own history.

With a crackle of static, **our backup units chimed in**, one by one, that they were also in position. For the buy, we would have three marked units cruising the area, each ready to converge on the site if the deal **went sour.** I didn't want to think about that happening, but it was hard not to. A hundred different things could go wrong, and every one of them was crowding into my head as Muñoz glided the big car to the curb at the corner of Mark and Wood streets.

We were a few blocks from Myrtle Street, the target area. Gang activity throughout this barrio was high, and already I could see **a trio of homeboys kicking back** in one of the yards down the street. Most of the houses on Wood had grate fences and barred windows, barricades that residents hoped would protect them from the burglaries that supplied the gangs with income. Santa Ana was a small quiet town, rows of wood-frame houses dotted by orange groves and surrounded by clear skies when I was born, but by the 1980s, whole strips of the city looked like a Third World country. Crime was a daily part of life and the gangs were a problem in nearly every school. From the Monte Carlo, I watched two toddlers playing with a pile of Budweiser cans in a yard of dirt and weeds, and I wondered what kind of future Santa Ana promised for them.

Over the radio, the Eyes were checking in. We had one Eye, a sergeant in another undercover car, sitting at the mouth of Myrtle

....

our backup units chimed in other police officers told us
went sour did not happen as planned; became dangerous
a trio of homeboys kicking back three gang members from the neighborhood relaxing

Street and keeping tabs on the half-dozen dealers who were stalking the sidewalk, sweating beneath the afternoon sun and waiting for their **drive-through clientele** to pull up with twenty-dollar bills. A second Eye, a cop named Rubalcava, was looking down from one of the dozens of apartment windows facing the street. Rubalcava was dark-skinned and wearing ragged old clothes and carrying a bag. He had passed by the dealers disguised as an old man in the neighborhood to visit some stateside family. The homeboys ignored him as he ambled past. No one thought twice as he climbed the stairs and unlocked one of the vacant rooms with a key provided by the cooperative landlord. Once in the room, he pulled his binoculars and a radio from the bag. He had a gun tucked in his waistband. If things started to unravel, it was Rubalcava who would **call in the cavalry**.

After everyone checked in, Muñoz switched his pac-set off and then crammed it beneath his seat, stopping first to push aside the crinkled soda cans and empty potato chip bags that littered the floor. The undercover units were always a mess, partly to make them look more believable, but also because Narcs **live out of a car during long surveillances**.

"You nervous?" Muñoz was looking straight ahead, but I knew he could sense my anxiety.

"Yeah."

"First time is always that way. Let's go over the plan again: When we go in, you make a lot of eye contact with the dealers so they know we're looking to buy. They'll come up to the passenger side, ask how much, and you ask for twenty *blanca* and twenty *negra*."

....

drive-through clientele customers who wanted drugs
call in the cavalry send more police officers to help
live out of a car during long surveillances spend a lot of time in the car when watching a criminal

The terms were familiar to me. In Santa Ana, *blanca* is cocaine and *negra* is black tar heroin. Buyers who use the wrong terms announce that they are outsiders, and probably not to be trusted.

"Take mental notes of the guy," Muñoz continued, "like what he's wearing and where he's standing. Every little detail matters. You have to write this up later, and the more specific you can be, the **more solid the collar** is when it goes to court. You have to be like a camera."

I nodded and Muñoz handed me the buy money. "Keep it in your right hand, folded up small but big enough for the dealer to see it. And relax . . . **I got your back**."

"Right, nice and simple." I saw my face reflected in the passenger side mirror, and I was again surprised. How did I get here? Muñoz pulled away from the curb and we glided north on Wood. I did a quick mental inventory of my weapon, the buy money, the radio beneath my seat . . .

"We're going off air now," Muñoz said into the pac-set before shoving it under his seat. He turned on the car radio, some oldies, and he looked over at me. He pulled off his thick, wraparound black sunglasses and handed them to me.

"Here, wear these. If anything goes wrong, if you **get a bad vibe off** someone or anything, take off the glasses. That'll be our signal. You take those off and I'll get us out of there."

I felt better with the sunglasses on. We rolled up on Myrtle, like I had done dozens of times when I was an F-Trooper. Gang generations **come and go** in a handful of years, so the faces were

....

more solid the collar stronger the case
I got your back I will help you and protect you
get a bad vibe off question, mistrust
come and go change

different now, but I knew all the players anyway. The roles were unchanged: The **lookout network**, the ten and twelve year olds on their bikes, maybe cutting school to tag along with a big brother or cousin, making a game of spotting cops. Then there are the runners, the fast-talking middlemen who run to the car window like a waitress to take orders of heroin and coke, maybe even methamphetamine if slow business demands they **stock low-cost inventory**. The runners ferry the cash back to the next highest rung on the Myrtle ladder, the holder. The holder is in a hallway or doorway, waiting with the drugs while the front-line runner—always a juvenile in case they get popped by the cops—does the **dirty work**. Somewhere else, maybe up the stairs or next door, the actual dealer is sitting back while his paid workers each **take the gamble of** operating the drive-through. The teens are a buffer and the whole system serves, sadly, to teach the trade to the next generation.

As we headed west on Myrtle, I could see the Old English-style graffiti stripped down the concrete columns of the apartment buildings. A boy kicking a sagging basketball locked eyes with me as we closed in on the stretch of sidewalk where the street's dealers and bangers clump. The kid was a lookout, but we passed his inspection. If we didn't, he would have flashed a signal or yelled "One time!" or "Five-O" to his friends down the street.

My fear was gone. As a gang member or as a cop, I always found that the nerves melt away once you've committed yourself to a street mission. There's no time for panic, and knowing that has always been my strength. I know some part of me must crave the excitement, too,

....

lookout network kids that watched for the cops
stock low-cost inventory sell cheaper drugs
dirty work most dangerous job
take the gamble of risk getting arrested while

and I don't know if that's a good or bad thing.

I had my window down and the breeze felt good. I had my arm out the window, **a deliberate position** that made the tattoo on my right wrist visible. How many cops have tattoos? That's what I was hoping the lookouts would think to themselves.

As we **hit the market**, two runners nodded at us as Muñoz slowed the big car. I made eye contact with a runner at mid-block. We each nodded, barely, just enough to acknowledge that he was selling and I was buying. Before Muñoz could pull over, he was hanging on the door. His eyes ran over Muñoz and me and back to the empty street behind the Monte Carlo.

"How much?" he asked in Spanish.

Muñoz leaned over and said, "*Ese*, you got any *negra* and *blanca* for my old lady and me?"

The runner nodded and looked at the money in my hand. I tried to make my voice as blank as his.

"Twenty *negra*. Twenty *blanca*."

He said something but I couldn't hear it. All I heard was the blood pumping in my ears. My hand started to move toward the sunglasses and I was thinking about my gun. Should I give the signal? Everything was turning to slow motion. Behind the runner, stepping off the curb, I saw what my mind told me must be a ghost. It was Little John. The tall figure's clothes were in rags. The elaborate peacock tattoo—It was Little John!—did not hide the track marks, the pocked scars and scabs of a longtime **junkie**. He was filthy, with dirt in the lines of his face. He looked like he hadn't eaten in days.

....

a deliberate position purposely placing it in a way
hit the market approached the place where the drugs were sold
Ese Hey, man; Hey, homeboy (in Spanish)
junkie drug user

His wild eyes jumped out from his dark, sunburned face.

My worst fears were coming true, and everything seemed to **be hanging**. **In a heartbeat**, those eyes told me he recognized me. Does he know I'm a cop now? I didn't want to **scrap the buy for a false alarm**—everyone had guns these days, and you can never guarantee a safe escape. The street was narrow and cars and bullets flying around could be messy.

"Let me see the money," the runner insisted. I could feel Muñoz stiffen in the seat next to me.

"Yeah, here."

I flashed the bills already in my hand, but my stare was locked on Little John. He smiled and his calloused, stained hands went to his mouth to hide a chuckle. He stood there for a minute and then turned and walked away.

The runner never saw him and took off in fast walk to a doorway. He met a girl there, and, after she glanced at our car, she reached into a pocket and pulled out two small packets, one with heroin and one with cocaine. Then she casually joined a group of girls sitting on the apartment steps. The runner walked back, passed the baggies to me for inspection, and I pressed the cash into his cupped hand. He took off again, and Muñoz pulled away. The buy was a success.

I was still scanning the crowd, trying to find Little John, but he had vanished. How many years had it been since I had seen him? Once, he was among the circle of leaders of my old gang, the circle that included my cousins, the feared Elizaldes. It flashed in my head: We're only a few blocks from the house where Little John once lived,

....

be hanging be uncertain; be getting more dangerous
In a heartbeat Without a doubt
scrap the buy for a false alarm stop the undercover operation if nothing was wrong

at one time the **party central** for the gang. He looked homeless now, though, a street hype living just **for the needle**, a slow and painful death.

We rounded the corner and I pulled the radio from under my seat. "It's a go," I said to the radio in my lap. "Pick up young male Hispanic, dark blue shirt and jeans, short black hair, and female Hispanic in white sweatshirt, black jeans with a brown purse."

Muñoz looped around a block as our backup pulled in fast and **took the two into custody**. Two others, observed by the Eyes as working lookout, were also taken in. Muñoz was talking again, congratulating me. "You did good. The next one will be easier."

I smiled and handed him his sunglasses back. I could see the blue lights flashing on Myrtle and I wondered how far Little John had gotten, whether he was already ducking into the nearby concrete flood channel, down under the bridges where the hypes built fires to fight off the junkie chills. Or maybe he was a ghost, as I had thought at first, a ghost who wanted to remind me of what my life could have been if I had **stuck with an earlier path**. Maybe he just wanted to laugh at me for daring to wear the war paint again.

....

party central favorite place to party
for the needle to do drugs
took the two into custody arrested the two people
stuck with an earlier path
still been a gang member

BEFORE YOU MOVE ON...

1. **Evidence and Conclusions** Mona was thankful that she changed her life and was not in a gang anymore. Give 2 examples from pages 14–16.

2. **Inference** Reread pages 19–20. Why did gang generations change so quickly?

LOOK AHEAD Read pages 24–46 to find out how Mona's family was involved with gangs.

~ Chapter Two ~

THE SOLDIERS

I was probably just four years old when my father first showed me **the Soldiers of Christ**. The images are a jumble in my mind now, vivid and lasting, but dreamlike when it comes to the details. The moment seems almost magical now. We lived on Golden West, in a house with a wide porch and a huge tree that my sisters and I climbed almost every day. Our home was an old wood-frame house. The rooms stayed cool in the long summers beneath a shady elm that towered above it and stretched its branches over the entire yard. My father and I were inseparable in those days. Each afternoon, as a hazy dusk would start to cool off the neighborhood, my father would return home from work. I would be waiting for him, sitting on the front steps and watching the corner for the first glimpse of his hulking 1955 Buick, a red and white **beauty that was his pride and joy**. My father, Raymond Sandoval, was a construction worker in those days, and he **filled my world like a giant**.

On one late afternoon, my father and I walked up Golden West

....

the Soldiers of Christ the police
beauty that was his pride and joy car that he loved
filled my world like a giant was the most important person
in my life

toward the corner market to buy an ice cream. I remember my father held my hand as we walked. His fingers were rough from work but the grip was always gentle. Ahead, we saw a commotion. A car, one of the barrio's many **lowriders**, was parked at the curb and blocked in by two police cruisers, their blue lights flashing. All along the street, residents were stepping out into their yards and staring, shading their eyes from the setting sun.

There were two boys, but I don't remember them too clearly. They looked like most of the other young boys in the neighborhood with their short, black hair, white T-shirts and the baggy pants with sharp creases ironed in. There were two other men, too, but they didn't look like anyone I knew from the barrio. They were huge, they seemed to tower like trees over the boys, and their angry shouting had turned their faces beet red. Both were blond and wore uniforms and badges. Their size and voices frightened me.

"Don't be scared, *m'ija*," my father said. He was leaning down, close to me, and his hand held mine tighter. "They won't hurt you. Do you know who they are? They are the police . . ."

The word had only a vague meaning for me. I had learned by then, I think, that the police were the people who help you when you're lost and that they were friendly, but these men terrified me. The boys looked **like rag dolls** as the burly officers shoved and spun them and scolded in their deep, booming voices.

My father was still talking in hushed tones. "They have respect. They help people and they have respect, that's what's important. And they don't take anything from these . . . these stupid *cabrones*!"

....

lowriders cars that rode close to the ground
m'ija sweetheart (in Spanish)
like rag dolls weak
cabrones jerks (in Spanish)

Dad wagged his finger at the two gang members, who were now sitting on the curb with their heads hanging. Father always told me the gang members **were full of themselves**, too selfish to amount to anything good. He hated the way they strutted and showed **contempt for elders**, and through the years he would repeat his lectures about **the dead-end road offered by gangs**. I didn't understand much of that, but I solemnly nodded anyway. My father was the center of my world then, and if he said the boys were bad people, then they were bad.

"Listen, *m'ija*," he said, his strong hand clamping on my shoulder. "The police are like Soldiers of Christ. Do you understand? They do God's work here on Earth."

My father went on, talking about the example police officers set for all of us, the way they risk their lives for a just cause. I couldn't take my eyes off the two men. One of the officers was bent, his hands on his knees, and yelling into the face of one of the boys again. I wondered what the two had done, why God was mad at them.

"Police officer, it is a good job," my father said as if he were thinking out loud. The crowds on the sidewalk were thinning out. The street show was almost over, but my father and I did not move.

"I always wanted to be a police officer, *m'ija*. But someone like me . . . no, not me, I lack an education. These hands are good only for hard work, yes? But you, someday, you should be a police officer. To show people that a *Mexicana* can do a good job, too. For respect, for honor, for your *raza* . . ."

The words didn't make sense to me. Me? How could I be one

....

were full of themselves thought they were the best
contempt for elders disrespect for older people
the dead-end road offered by gangs how being in a gang
ruins people's lives

of them? Why would I want to? I couldn't even imagine talking to those fearsome men. One of the boys was getting pushed into the police car, and my eyes locked for a moment with one of the officers. I instinctively drew closer to my father's leg and he chuckled. Then Dad tugged at my hand to follow him as he walked up the street, toward the market. I looked back over my shoulder, back toward the flashing blue lights, trying to see more of these Soldiers of Christ, these brutal angels whom my father admired so much. I wondered: Were they ever children like me?

I would see many things during my years on the streets, horrifying sights of pain and despair and even death, but for some reason that first glimpse of the conflict between police and gangs has always **stayed with me**, just as my father's words did. If the police were Soldiers of Christ, what did that make gang members? And, if the cops were truly **agents of a greater good**, how could I justify the **corruption and excess** I would eventually see **among their ranks**?

It was simpler when I was a little girl sitting at the knee of my father, Raymond Sandoval. He made everything clear with his wise words, and I was the focus of his teachings. He loved all of my sisters, of course, but we shared a special bond that began when he named me Ramona Sandoval. He gave me a form of his name because I, like him, was the second born among my siblings. To be the second, he often told me, meant I had an extra responsibility to my family, just as he felt he has always carried.

My father saw his older brother, Paul, die as a teenager on a

....

stayed with me affected me
agents of a greater good doing God's work on earth
corruption and excess dishonesty and bad behavior
among their ranks in the police

stormy day. The two were working for a man who owned walnut trees in El Modena, and Paul was killed in a flash of blue when his aluminum tool grazed power lines running through the branches of a tree. The other men shouted for my father to stay back, but he ran to Paul's still form and cradled him as he died. He promised Paul he would **tend to** the family.

"I had to grow up then, *m'ija*," my father often told me in hushed tones. I would close my eyes and see him there, beneath the rolling black clouds and rustling trees, holding his brother. Paul was limp, his arms out to the sides so his body looked like a cross. To my child's mind, it was a bolt of lightning that killed this mysterious uncle, a bolt that transformed my father into a sad but strong adult. In my mind, I fully expected that someday some similar transformation would happen to me.

My father was **wrestling with the grief** of his brother's death when he left Orange County, staying for a time with his cousins in Cardiff and then moving down to Mexicali to join his own father. A year went by before he could return to California, when he met up with his sister, Jenny, in San Diego. Jenny was dating a man named Lupe, and she introduced Raymond Sandoval to Lupe's teen sister, Elvera. It was love at first sight, my father said.

Raymond was in his thirties, and while Elvera's parents allowed them to date, her father said he would forbid them from getting married. But that did not matter to my parents. They were in love. They ran off to Santa Cruz to marry and, after saving up money, they **set down roots** in Santa Ana, a city about thirty miles

....

tend to take care of
wrestling with the grief dealing with the sadness
set down roots lived; started their life together

southeast of Los Angeles.

My father raised me as if I were his son. We worked together in the musty workshop he set up in our old garage, listening to Motown music and the mariachi songs that always made me giggle. In the late afternoons, as the sweet smell of my mother's cooking signaled dinnertime, I would watch the street, waiting for that huge red car to round the corner.

We were always a big family. My oldest sister was Maryann, and after me there was Lydia, Roni and Sandra. I was born in 1959, and in the sixties my four sisters and I watched the world from our barrio in central Santa Ana. (Later, as I was nearing adulthood, there would be more siblings—Margie, Isabelle and Raymond, Jr.—to **bring the household to** ten.) I was always closest to Lydia, bounding off together for some new adventure while the rest of the sisters played with dolls. But while I was a tomboy, more comfortable **roughhousing than playing house**, Lydia enjoyed being at my mother's side, learning cooking and all the difficult, endless skills it takes to keep a large household going. I was mesmerized by car engines and tree climbing, while Lydia's daydreams were devoted to motherhood and her own family. Maryann was bookish and quiet, always the smart one, and always fascinated with the ceremony and solemn magic of church. As she grew older, she talked a lot about becoming a nun. And, in those days when I was a youngster, Sandy was always the baby, the **target** of our teasing and, maybe because of that, always a little spoiled by Mom and Dad. We were all different, even in appearance. Maryann was slender and dark with frizzy hair

....

bring the household to make a family of
roughhousing than playing house playing like a boy than pretending to be a mother and wife
target victim, object

and almond-shaped eyes. I always had light skin and reddish hair, while Lydia had dark skin and wavy, black hair to match her black eyes. Roni looked just like Mom, with caramel-colored skin and big, brown eyes.

Lydia and I were happiest climbing and swinging on the huge tree that dominated our home's lot. The tree was the center of our games, the finish line and the starting point. We would play hide-and-seek around the trunk and the branches would play games with the echoes, making us wonder where everyone else was. We would wrap our arms around it to see if we were growing, testing and resting ourselves against it.

Lydia and I loved to wrestle, even with our male cousins, Edward and Andy Elizalde. Many afternoons were spent going toe-to-toe with these two, the youngest of the Elizalde brothers, and their family was a **fixture in** our lives. Each weekend, they were either at our house or we would make the five-minute drive to their home. Eddie and Andy had two older brothers, who seemed huge and **intimidating** to us in those days. Their names were Ricky and Jesse James Elizalde, and they were far too **wrapped up** in their teenage concerns to spend much time with their young cousins. Eddie and Andy would tease and tangle with us, but Ricky and Jesse seemed to belong to a different world with their glowering faces, slicked-back hair and **sullen expressions**. Later, I would learn much about that world.

Everything in my youth revolved around family, both our household and the extended family that seemed to reach throughout

....

fixture in big part of
intimidating scary
wrapped up involved
sullen expressions angry looks

the city. My sisters and I were all different, but all close, brought together by two hard-working parents who strived to give us the best they could. It was not easy. We never had much money.

My mother was always the organizer of our household, **keeping tabs on** our finances and, remarkably, finding ways to stretch my father's paycheck to cover the cost of the whole family. She was also a master of making time for all of us in those days, juggling the duties of the house with tending to her girls. Looking back, I don't know how she did it.

I knew little beyond Santa Ana. Although I lived only a fifteen-minute drive from the beaches in Huntington or Newport, we rarely went. That was a different world, a white world, mostly. We did go down to San Diego each summer, a big Fourth of July vacation for us to visit my mother's family. I remember my sisters and me, all ponytails and summer clothes, piling into the car for the drive, which was less than three hours but felt impossibly long to a group of children. Going to San Diego would always feel like a dream: We would leave so early that my mother would dress us all and my father would carry each of us, sleeping, to the brown station wagon, like sagging bags of flour in his arms. Later, maybe about 6 a.m., I would wake up in the back seat, speeding down Interstate 5, well on the way. I'm sure my parents preferred it when we were sleeping. While Maryann would play quietly with her paper dolls or comic books, Lydia and I **invariably would** get bored and turn to tormenting poor Roni, staring or poking at her until she **collapsed into tears**. My father would get so angry, he'd threaten to take us all back

---

keeping tabs on carefully watching
invariably would would always
collapsed into tears began to cry

home. We'd turn our attention to coloring books for awhile, but two freeway exits later we'd be back to trouble.

My mother always dressed us to match. One year, I remember, we had bright yellow outfits, cool cotton with bell-bottom pants and a garish daisy floral pattern. We went to the big fair they had in Solano Beach, and I can still recall my sisters weaving through the noisy crowd and past the rides in those bright yellow clothes.

On the way home, weary from sun and all the hot dogs, we were far quieter. We would whine about leaving San Diego, but then it was always such a relief to get home. It always felt like we had been gone for months.

Our neighborhood seemed so vibrant and alive in those days, and so very different from what it would become **in the decades since under the eroding pressures of crowding and crime**. But it would be many years before I ever detected those woes. When I was a child, my worries went only as far as my yard and could all be solved by the wave of my father's hand.

I was always a **runt**. But father taught me that size is no excuse for fear or losing. He knew that our blue-collar neighborhood would eventually throw challenges at me, so he taught me how to protect myself, how to throw a punch. He also told me that God looks out for people **in the right**. If you stand up against people who do evil things, God will be on your side, so have no fear. Often, after dinner, I would sit in his lap and listen to his words about right and wrong, good and bad, held in his arms and feeling safe as I drifted off into a light sleep. Again, it was so simple to a child's mind and so

....

in the decades since under the eroding pressures of crowding and crime when crime and gangs took over

runt small child

in the right who are doing good things

reassuring. In the years to come, those lessons would seem like a bad joke to me, but as a young girl they made me brave.

As I said, my oldest sister, Maryann, was different from me. She was very bright, always finding the classroom success that eluded me, and she was shy and reserved. That made her a target for a pair of bullies down the street who tried to imitate their older brothers' **thuggery by preying on** anyone they could. I hated bullies, and when I saw them knock the books from her hand one day as she walked home from the library, I threw my books down and shoved the boy and kicked him in the shins. I was eight or nine, and the boys were ten-year-olds. But my father had taught me that boys were never supposed to hit girls, it was a rule of honor, and I was furious at the bullies for **flouting** that rule. My sister was kneeling on the sidewalk, picking up her books, as I shoved and kicked wildly at the two stunned boys. The world went red for me, washed away by my anger. I held nothing back. It would become a familiar sensation that would carry me through many fights, although afterward it often left me more frightened of myself than any **foe**.

Trips to the library or the market became a gauntlet for my sisters and me. The bullies were not deterred by my wild combat; if anything, it provoked and shamed them into teasing us more. Fighting became familiar. The fights were really just wrestling matches. No one ever got hurt, but I got used to the reality of hitting people, trying to hurt them. As bad as it sounds, I came to enjoy it. The release and the competition **suited me**, and as long as I believed I was in the right, I never felt guilty about fighting. And I was good at it.

....

thuggery by preying on crimes by attacking
flouting breaking
foe enemy
suited me felt right to me

My father's hatred for the gang members was **driven by** his belief that they were lazy, disrespectful and shamed our people. The gangs **flew in the face of** his strong work ethic and love of tradition. He proudly detailed his family history, his roots spreading back to Spain. He spoke with admiration of simple people who through sweat and dedication made their dreams come true for themselves and their children. History was sacred to him, and the gang members, the *vatos*, were all about today, the satisfaction of the desire of the moment, be it for beer or drugs or rowdiness. Raymond Sandoval was no saint during his youth, I know, but as he grew older and **shouldered the burden** of a family man, his spite for the gang members and their predecessors, the *pachucos* of the earlier generations, also grew. If his dream for me was to become a police officer, then his greatest fear was certainly that I would fall into the gang scene. It is ironic, I suppose, that both of these visions would come true.

My father told my sisters and me that the gangs promised only shame and danger for a young girl. As an adolescent, I **heeded his warnings**, the same way I listened to all his words. Still, I was mesmerized by the colorful characters who strutted through the neighborhood with an air of confidence and menace. Because my father called them evil, I would glare at them, made brave because I knew I was in the right. But it was not easy to despise them as my father did. They often seemed to do nothing wrong and their cocky antics made me curious. It was hard to hate them, too, because more

....

driven by based on; due to
flew in the face of went against
shouldered the burden had the responsibilities
heeded his warnings listened to what he said about gangs

than a few of them were family.

Nothing is more important than family, nothing is more binding than blood. If there were a lesson my father hammered into me, it was that I should do anything to protect the people who shared my name and past. I should be willing to die, he often said solemnly, sending a chill through me. But what about the cousins and uncles who clearly were on the side of the gangs? It confused me and, I knew, presented my father with a frustrating problem. He would not **turn his back on** the homeboys in our large, extended family, nor did he want his daughters to **embrace their ways**. It was a hard road for my parents to walk.

Once, when I was perhaps eight years old, loud banging on our front door and the insistent barking of our dogs, Chopper and Pandora, woke me in the middle of the night. Half asleep, I pulled myself up and padded past my sister's bed to the hallway. I made my way to the top of the stairs above the living room. Below, I could hear voices, my parents and someone else. Peeking around the corner, I saw my father helping a stumbling figure through the front door. As the man collapsed to the couch, my mother locked the door and closed the curtains hanging at the front window. As my eyes grew accustomed to the dim light, I recognized the man on the couch: It was my cousin, Jesse James Elizalde. A few years later, I would realize that Jesse was **a neighborhood celebrity of sorts**, one of the founders of F-Troop, the gang that liked to believe it ruled Santa Ana. Like his historical namesake, Jesse James was a popular rogue, an anti-hero for the youngsters who admired his cocky

....

turn his back on abandon; refuse to help
embrace their ways be like them
a neighborhood celebrity of sorts famous in our
neighborhood

troublemaking. But that night I did not know all that, I only knew that he was family and that he ran with the people my father did not like. He was bad, but he was blood.

It was hard to hear what my father was saying, but I could tell he was upset. Jesse was breathing hard and his teeth were bared, like an animal or someone in pain. My mother gasped and said something in Spanish when she saw the **large crimson stain** soaking Jesse's shirt, just above his waistline. Outside, the sound of sirens made the dogs howl even louder. Jesse rasped something about "no place to go" and my mother brought towels and water to him and started cleaning his wounds. My father began to **pace** in the room, shaking his head. I could not understand what was happening, but I sensed that Jesse was in trouble and was looking for help. I craned my neck to see what my father was doing, but then I quickly jerked back into the darkness— for a moment it looked like Jesse had turned toward me. When I worked up the courage to peek again, my cousin's head was down, watching my mother clean his wounds. Despite the blood, I could see the famous Jesse James Elizalde was now smiling.

That night, holding my breath and hiding in the shadows, it was impossible to imagine all the pain and loss that he and his friends would cause me and just about everyone I knew. Maybe my father knew, maybe that's why he had so much anger for the fun-loving gang members. To a young girl's eyes, though, Jesse and his friends seemed more and more like cool and exciting figures. I still believed

....

large crimson stain blood
pace walk back and forth

my father's warnings about the gang, but **my resolve was already slipping, giving way to a giddy infatuation**. Soon, the warnings in my mind would **evaporate altogether**. No one knew, but fate was about to strike my father down and, once he fell, his second-born daughter would also begin to tumble.

....

my resolve was already slipping, giving way to a giddy infatuation my feelings were changing, and I was becoming fascinated with gangs

evaporate altogether completely disappear

~ Chapter Three ~

STREET GAMES

My father was **overdue**. Dinner was getting cold, and his car had still not rounded the corner. It had looked like rain all day, the clouds were grey and low, but the storm never came. When the phone rang, my mother knew something was wrong, the way mothers always seem to know. **The foreman on the line** said there had been an accident, a bad one, and Raymond was in the hospital. He was alive, but he was hurt badly. My mother was trembling as she called my aunt to watch the kids and then bolted out the door, tears already welling in her eyes. My sisters and I just stared at each other, unable to understand completely what was wrong, but frightened to see our mother so upset.

The next time I saw my father, he was in Riverview Hospital and he didn't recognize us. The hospital was terrifying, all strange smells and vague images of sickness and death. I wanted to leave and take Dad with us, but all I could do was cry.

My father's crew had been working a ditch, preparing it

....

overdue late
The foreman on the line My father's boss

for a huge concrete pipe. But the supports were either **erected improperly** or not strong enough to hold back the weight of the channel's piled-up earth, and one of the ditch's banks **gave way**. My father was buried up to his throat, just inches away from certain death, a coworker explained to my mother. He had lived, but his body was badly battered. There would be operations, the doctor told my mother as she caressed my father's hand. "Three men died down in that hole," someone said. "Raymond is very lucky to be alive."

I just stared at my father's face and prayed as hard as I could that everything would go back to the way it was before. The world seemed to be collapsing in on me, like the dirt that tried to bury my father. Nothing felt safe or certain to me for a long time after that.

The months that followed the January 1961 accident were a bad time with lots of visits to the hospital. My father had major spinal surgery, then part of his stomach removed, followed by a leg operation. His kidneys weren't working right, and he was hunched over in pain from his back. Our family seemed to feel his wounds. Maryann **idolized Dad**, and her shyness seemed to stretch and swallow her up after the accident. For weeks, all she seemed to do was sleep and fight off illnesses of her own, and when she was well she seemed detached. My mother became increasingly edgy, exhausted from the emotional burden, my father's care and stress over the family finances. We had never been rich, of course, but now we **teetered on poverty**.

Dad's coworkers told us that he had complained about the sturdiness of the support beams for the ditch, but his foreman

....

erected improperly built wrong
gave way collapsed
idolized Dad loved Dad more than anyone
teetered on poverty were close to becoming poor

yelled at him and told him to go back to work. My family got a $7,000 settlement. There was also some money from the insurance companies and my father's union friends at Local 652, but still my mother found herself forced to accept the aid of relatives and the church.

The family money problems had another almost immediate impact: My mother had plans to send my sisters and me to Catholic school, but the tuition became a luxury we could not afford as the medical bills piled up. The difference between the private and public schools was night and day. The uniforms and strictly run classrooms of the Catholic campus were **in stark contrast to the chaotic scene** at the public schools. We knew a lot of the kids from the neighborhood, but we immediately became outsiders anyway.

By the time I reached Smedley Intermediate School, the bullies I had clashed with were everywhere and the gangs, which seemed to be only **a shadow element** at Immaculate Heart, had a clear presence. The students were the junior siblings of older gang members, and they loved to mimic the walk and talk of their idols.

The origins of the F-Troop gang were at Smedley and a few other junior highs that served the barrios in the city's center. Jesse and the other Elizalde brothers were mostly sixth and seventh graders when they began their tradition of kicking back in the dirt alley that ran behind the bowling alley near the park at First Street and Center. They were joined by buddies who would **form the nucleus** of a gang that would grow beyond their dreams. They drank warm Budweisers stolen from their family's refrigerators and hacked as they learned to

....

in stark contrast to the chaotic scene very different from the disorder

a shadow element around sometimes

form the nucleus become the main members

smoke cigarettes, all an attempt to look cool. Pot was the only drug they really used at first, but soon they were taking reds and speed. Heroin and PCP were a few years down the road.

In the early days, the late 1960s, the gang was all about good times and the connection that young boys seem so anxious to make with their friends. The gang bought jackets and **took collections** for keg parties, got in fistfights and, if it were a crazy night, used baseball bats and brass knuckles to scare off their foes. There were no guns then, really. Only big-time drug dealers carried pistols, and to see one was a rare event, something that would be bragged about for months. That, too, would change in the years to come.

F-Troop got its name, of course, from a ridiculous old television show, a farce about some stupid cavalry soldiers and Indians who would fight it out like the Three Stooges in the Old West. I'm not sure the gang members even knew about the show when they embraced the name to describe their **fledgling "social club."** The **gang's lore is hazy now**, some three decades later, but one version has it that a probation officer named Hallstrom coined the name. Hallstrom, known to all the neighborhood kids as Holster, supposedly told a group of the gang's founders that they were all a bunch of idiots, "like those guys on F-Troop." The *vatos* thought the name had a militaristic feel to it, the story goes, and told everyone the "F" stood for "a bad word", a sophomoric boast about their supposed sexual prowess. Others say the gang took the name because they thought they were like the Indians on the show, a bunch of dark-skinned guys who always got the last laugh on the bumbling

....

took collections gathered money
fledgling "social club" new, small gang
gang's lore is hazy now gang's history is unclear now

enemy who wore blue uniforms. Either way, when the gang started there were a lot of good times to be had for the members, who were really just tough-talking incorrigibles who liked to drink beer, smoke cigarettes and hang out behind the old bowling alley.

Gangs had been part of Santa Ana's history for decades, so there were plenty of role models for the fledgling Troopers. The *pachucos* of the 1930s and 1940s were long gone, of course, but their zoot suits and street swagger had inspired new generations. The *cholos* of the 1960s and 1970s shifted the fashion to Pendeltons and khakis, and created "social clubs" and "car clubs," and the Troopers **fell in step with** them. It was all about a good time, at least back then.

It didn't take the Elizalde brothers and their friends long to make their names known to the neighborhood. At Smedley, my connection to the Elizaldes was well known, and I began to realize that whether I liked it or not, their reputation colored the way some of my peers treated me. I liked being different, somehow special; it made me more curious about my cousins and their lifestyle.

At the same time, I was spending less time with my father. Everything had changed with his injuries. And, more than that, I was at an age where my parents' view of the world **was running head-on into** my own developing thoughts and identity. Jesse and his friends were the type of people my father always **bad-mouthed** (although not Jesse specifically: family ties made him reluctant to do that), but they didn't seem so bad to me. They were exciting.

One morning, that excitement exploded into tragedy. It was the first time I saw a dead homeboy.

....

fell in step with followed
was running head-on into began to seem very different from
bad-mouthed said terrible things about

What if that's Jesse under there? I thought. All I could see were two sneakers jutting out from beneath the white sheet, which was speckled with blood and flapping gently in the early morning October breeze. All around Lydia and me, our classmates were yelling and running around, excited and terrified by the sight of a *vato* sprawled out dead on a sidewalk right across the street from the campus.

Police and teachers were shouting and waving their arms, trying to gather up the kids who were bolting into traffic for a glimpse of the corpse. Residents in an apartment complex facing the school, awakened I suppose by the sirens and shouts, were beginning to **stream out toward the scene**, and I remember a woman leaning out of her second-floor apartment yelling, "*¡Está muerto, está muerto!*" The cops were hurriedly hanging crime scene tape from tree branches, trying to keep the crowd from getting to the body, but hysterical kids were everywhere, screeching, bawling and, in some cases, laughing.

I turned to Lydia and could tell she was thinking the same thing as me—what if that's one of our cousins or a Trooper under there? Our worst fears were quieted by a sobbing girl who ran by yelling, "Potato! It's Potato, he's dead! They killed him!" The boy beneath the sheet was a homeboy from **United Browns**. His real name was Juan, I think, but no one called him that. He was always just Potato. We heard some other voices, some boys who must have been walking to school early enough to see the body before it was covered. They were dancing around one another with imaginary knives, reliving the

....

vato guy (in Spanish)
stream out toward the scene come and look
Está muerto He is dead (in Spanish)
United Browns a different gang than F-Troop

fight. "Did you see his guts hanging out? That was cool!"

The day after Potato was stabbed, my cousin Eddie was locked up in **Juvenile Hall** for fighting and a drug charge. Inside, he met up with a fellow Trooper, a boy named Marty who had been arrested for killing Potato. He told Eddie how it had happened, and this is the account Eddie gave me:

Marty and his friend, Rooster, were driving past the school when they saw two **rivals**, Potato and Trino. They all exchanged words and, as the car passed by, Trino threw a rock that thudded into the side of the vehicle. Marty and Rooster did a quick U-turn and jumped out. Marty had his knife with him, and Rooster grabbed a hammer from the trunk. On the sidewalk, Potato had his blade out already.

The four boys were shouting insults and challenges at one another and the argument exploded into a fight when Potato threw his *fileto* at Marty, sticking him in the chest. The wound wasn't serious, and Potato had made a **grievous street-fighting error**—never lose your weapon. Marty jumped at Potato and stabbed him in the stomach, while Rooster began beating Trino with the hammer.

The fight didn't last long. Trino was down and groggy, dazed by the hammer blows to his head. Potato was already bleeding badly and Marty, perhaps frightened by what he had done, was trying to pull away from the injured *vato*. But Potato, grunting with each wound, gripped Marty's shoulders tight and refused

....

Juvenile Hall a children's prison
rivals enemies; members of another gang
fileto knife (in Spanish)
grievous street-fighting error serious fighting mistake

to let go. Sirens were getting closer. The fight was in plain view of the school and a row of houses, and someone must have called the police.

"Let go! Let go of me!" Marty was stabbing Potato over and over, but the homeboy refused to let his attacker loose. "Let me go, or I'll stab you in the neck, *chingón*!" The sirens seemed to be right on top of them, and Marty **abruptly carried out his threat**. The knife went through Potato's throat, the tip coming out the other side.

Potato finally let go, and collapsed to his knees. He looked over at the bloody face of Trino, who was still trying to **find his feet**, and held his hands out to his friend, calling his name. As the attackers jumped in their car and sped off, Potato sunk to the ground.

Potato was in the eighth grade. Marty, who had looked into the eyes of a boy while he stabbed him, was even younger, a seventh grader.

The members of F-Troop were still young, but they were beginning to grow up.

About that same time, my father had my cousins and uncles come and cut down the huge, shady tree that had always been a fixture in my yard and, really, in my childhood. The roots had grown too strong and too thick, and they reached toward the house's plumbing. The house looked so different without the **tree's canopy above** it.

....

abruptly carried out his threat suddenly stabbed Potato
find his feet stand up
tree's canopy above tree shading

I wondered what would happen to the owls that lived in its tallest branches and the squirrels we would sometimes see running around its trunk. When I was little, I thought the tree was like the magical ones in the *Wizard of Oz*. Now, it was gone, replaced by cement and empty space. When I think about my childhood ending, I think about the dead homeboy beneath the sheet and the loss of that tree, one of my oldest friends.

BEFORE YOU MOVE ON...

1. **Comparisons** Reread pages 34–35. Why did Mr. Sandoval hate gang members? How was this different from the way Mona felt?

2. **Conclusions** Why did Mona start to get more involved with the gangs after her father's accident?

LOOK AHEAD Mona punched a teacher. Read pages 47–66 to find out what happened.

~ Chapter Four ~

MAKING A FIST

It didn't take long to realize that the wide intimidating corridors of Valley High School were like the rest of Santa Ana—**carved up into distinct gang turf**. Some of it was marked with blocky graffiti but most of it was quietly claimed, making it difficult for unknowing freshmen to **navigate the campus** without stumbling into a confrontation.

Some of the crosstown schools were ruled solely by one of the city's dominant gangs. F-Troop more or less "owned" Santa Ana High, and Saddleback High was known as a Del Hi **stronghold**. But Valley was split uneasily among a handful of gangs when I arrived there in September 1974. Westside and F-Troop were dominant, but every bathroom seemed to be claimed by a different clique that waited inside, smoking cigarettes or even pot. They hassled anyone that walked in. Westside controlled the entire rear of the school, from the prized handball courts to the grassy sports fields and rickety bleachers on the west end of campus. The Troopers had a

---

carved up into distinct gang turf divided into separate areas for different gangs

navigate the campus walk around the school

stronghold controlled area

smaller territory, but it encompassed the entire front of the school, including the entrance where *vatos* would squat on the concrete steps like gargoyles watching everyone who passed. The small contingent from Santa Anita, one of the city's oldest gangs, had to settle for a chunk of the parking lot and some of the hallways. They shared the lot with the Samoans, a few black gangs (Orange County, unlike neighboring Los Angeles County, still has a small African American population, less than seven percent) and the white biker kids. The bikers were primary suppliers of reds, speed and weed for the student body.

Walking through the crowded hallways the first day, Lydia and I were silent as we took in the whole scene, noting the layout and **sizing up** the older girls who glowered at us. I had always been a quiet child, but by ninth grade my tight-lipped, wary demeanor had nothing to do with shyness. Trouble was everywhere, I knew, and I rarely relaxed in crowds or new places. I had learned to **watch my back,** say little, and keep my face hard and blank. I didn't avoid eye contact, but I also kept my head forward. Lydia **had more fire** than I, and she openly glared back at the juniors and seniors who chuckled at our attempts to find room numbers. "Assholes," she muttered, giving a nearby locker a swift kick.

Lydia and I knew that we would have to prove ourselves at the new school. Our reputations from middle school wouldn't carry over to Valley, especially with the older kids and students who had attended different junior highs, and even our link to the Elizaldes would only protect us so far.

....

sizing up trying to decide if we were tougher than
watch my back protect myself
had more fire was more passionate; was angrier

We expected to be confronted and challenged in this hostile new environment. We just didn't know it would be the very first day.

Changa and Güera **hit us up** in the morning, stepping in our path and demanding to know which gang we **claimed**. It was crowded and there were teachers nearby, so I knew there wouldn't be a fight. I also knew Lydia and I could not afford to **back down** for a moment. I just gave the pair a stony look and Lydia snapped back that, "We don't claim anybody, just ourselves, bitch!" The two Westside girls were familiar rivals from the neighborhood, foes who had crossed my sister in a dispute over some forgotten boy years earlier. One had hooded eyes and a pinched face; the other wore her hair in a mess of unruly, unwashed curls. Both talked tough, but I knew they feared Lydia. Most people did.

Lydia and I split up to attend our morning classes. At lunchtime we met up to explore our new school and we ventured into a bathroom along the breezeway near the school entrance. Before the door closed behind us, I knew we would have trouble: It was Changa and Güera again, but this time they were among a small crowd of Westside girls smoking cigarettes, teasing their hair and applying thick coats of makeup. Lydia and I turned to leave, but we did it slowly and casually so we wouldn't seem frightened. It was no surprise that they followed us. These types of confrontations were like a dance, and everyone knew the steps.

"*¡¿Y qué?!*"

Güera walked up to Lydia, stuck her nose in her face and challenged her in a squeaky voice. "Westside—*¿y qué?* Let's

....

hit us up approached us
claimed belonged to; were loyal to
back down look weak
"*¡¿Y qué?!*" "So what?" (in Spanish)

throw down right now!" I hated Güera. She was only brave when **she had numbers**, and I knew that even as she issued the challenge she was hoping we would back down. That was her favorite type of fight, the kind she couldn't lose.

I knew, though, that Lydia would answer the challenge. We were cornered and there was no sense trying to worm out. If we did, we'd be victims every day from then on. Far better to fight and lose than be **branded** a coward. As I expected, my sister didn't bother to answer Güera with words, she just reared back and punched the girl across the face, dropping her easily.

I was already stepping between Changa and her friends. "Just them, one-on-one," I yelled, holding my hands up. "I'll fight any of you, but this is just them." But Lydia was already beating Güera badly. My sister had her down on the ground and was delivering blow after blow to her face. Güera could only wail and scratch futilely at Lydia's face. Two of the Westside girls dove at my sister, shoving her off Güera and to the floor, and then all hell broke loose. It was six on two and I was punching and kicking in all directions. I remember knocking Changa to the ground with a bone-jarring punch. One of the girls got me pretty good with a few blows, but then I kicked her hard in the gut and she seemed to **deflate and crumple** to the concrete floor. Every time I would hit someone, another would come at me from a different direction.

I felt a hand grab my shoulder and I spun around, leading with my fist. The punch landed hard before I even saw whose face I had hit. It was a black man, a teacher. His head jerked back and hit the

....

throw down fight
she had numbers people were there to help her
branded known as
deflate and crumple weaken and fall

wall with a thud and his cracked glasses were bent and hanging. Suddenly the fight was over and, in the abrupt silence, everyone was staring, first at the fallen teacher, then at me. School security guards were stepping between the girls. **My jaw dropped** and I looked at Lydia, who was wide-eyed and slowly shaking her head. "Damn, Mona . . ."

Mom was furious. Lydia and I, disheveled and scratched up, were waiting in the office when she marched in, huffing from anger. She was humiliated to be called in, and I stared at the floor while the assistant principal launched into a description of the brawl. Mom surprised me by **lashing out at** the haughty school official for having a campus where new students were stalked and jumped, but the look she shot me told me that I shouldn't expect any mercy when we got home. My ribs were sore and it hurt when I turned to the side. Lydia was quiet, and I suspected she was thinking about all the things she wished she could have done to the Westside *cholitas*. We were suspended for three days, but the punishment could have—should have—been worse. Mr. Booker had believed me when I told him that hitting him was an accident. I doubt I could have faked the shock on my face, and maybe he knew that. A week or so later, I saw Mr. Booker in the hallway and I **avoided his gaze**. I **spun on my foot** and began to walk away, but then decided I should say I was sorry, something I hadn't done the day I punched him. I practically ran right into him when I reversed my direction and he smiled at me. My head hung low, I blurted out something, some kind of apology.

....

My jaw dropped I was shocked

lashing out at yelling at

avoided his gaze would not look at him

spun on my foot turned around

He told me not to worry.

"I know you didn't mean it," he said, rubbing his chin like it still hurt. "But I'm to keep an eye on you, Ms. Sandoval. No more fights, okay?"

"Okay, I'll try."

There were no more fights, at least not for a few months, and Mr. Booker, unknowingly, was the reason. Wildfire rumors had spread through school about the **mad-dog** new freshman, a wild girl crazy enough to punch a teacher and somehow manage to get away with it. The principal and assistant principals may not have heard about the infamous punch, but everyone else at Valley High did. The accounts grew more detailed and outlandish with each telling, and when I walked through the halls I even caught glimpses of people pointing at me. No one confronted me or dared get on my bad side. For the first time I knew the **heady** feeling of local fame that Jesse James and the Troopers enjoyed.

"Hey, are you that girl Rona, the one that punched that teacher?" It was a kid I had never seen before, another freshman by the looks of him.

"My name's Mona, not Rona."

"Yeah, Mona. Right. Well, did you punch that guy?"

I shrugged. **The notoriety had its benefits**, but I wasn't proud of hitting Mr. Booker. He seemed like a nice person. The kid pressed on. "Well, uh, they said it was you." He nodded toward some unseen friends.

"Yeah."

....

mad-dog crazy

heady thrilling

The notoriety had its benefits Having this reputation protected me from bullies

"I knew it! Right . . . yeah, that's cool." He ran off, content that he had made a connection with the campus celebrity of the month. I wondered how long people would be talking about the whole mess. I knew eventually it might actually bring me trouble—notoriety can make you a target just as easily as it can shield you. Word was also spreading that Lydia and I were cousins to the Elizaldes. Some of the Troopers we passed in the halls started giving us small signals—a barely noticeable nod or a grunt of recognition—just enough to let us know they knew us and our connection to the gang's founders. It was gang shorthand, sending a message that would never be said aloud: I couldn't count on the Troopers to defend me in a fight, but I could **rest assured** that I wouldn't be one of their targets unless I **crossed a member**.

The **subtle overtures** also told me that Lydia and I could probably work our way into the Trooper girl ranks, if we **set our minds to it**. All we had to do to set ourselves up for entry into their circle was date a Trooper or just start hanging out with the older Trooper girls. But neither of us were interested in that path. My father and I were increasingly distant, but I still embraced his disdain for the gangs, although my reasons had changed. He hated them for their actions, but I resisted them because I valued my independence. The only allies I wanted were my siblings and a few close friends, and I wasn't willing to become a follower. Lydia also distrusted the gang leaders and, besides, she was too busy to kick back with the homegirls. She and her beloved Sammy, a couple that had been inseparable since eighth grade, were too busy running off together,

....

rest assured feel comfortable
crossed a member made an F-Trooper angry
subtle overtures way other Troopers treated me
set our minds to it really tried

ditching school and staying out late. All Lydia wanted was a life with Sammy and a chance to start a family and a home, a scenario that would fulfill the childhood daydreams she used to act out while following my mother during chores.

With the implied support of F-Troop and our own growing reputations, Lydia and I were like a gang of our own, a gang of two. We could watch each other's backs and keep a distance from the gangs. Or at least that's what I thought would happen. That all changed when Lydia told me her news. Her dreams were coming true early, she said, and there would be **hell to pay.**

Mom knew something was going on. Lydia was up early every day, a rarity for her, and she would stay in the bathroom until my other sisters pounded on the door hard enough to make the house shake. The morning sickness wasn't the only clue. Lydia had been on her best behavior, despite bouts of moodiness, and Mom suspected she was trying to **cushion** some sort of bad news. My mother didn't wait for Lydia to **open up.**

Mom confronted Lydia with a stack of love letters she had found stashed away in a shoebox in Lydia's room. The notes were embarrassingly explicit, and I thought it was wrong of our mother to sit down and read through all of them. In a few of the notes, Sammy was responding to Lydia's suspicions that she was pregnant, and this was what my Mom questioned her about.

"Are you, eh? Are you pregnant, bringing **shame on this house**!?"

....

hell to pay consequences; serious problems
cushion prepare her for
open up tell her what was wrong
shame on this house embarrassment to this family

54

Lydia stood her ground, like she had always done in the streets. "Yeah, I'm pregnant, but Sammy loves me. We're gonna get married, he's got a job."

My mom would **have none of that, and cut her off**. "Shut up, you tramp! You think I want this bum as a son, huh? You bring nothing but shame to us!"

My mom's hand flashed out as she slapped Lydia across the face. My sister didn't move. She stood there **like a rock** as her cheek burned red.

I had to turn away. As always, whenever Mom hit Lydia, my sister would do nothing. I never understood how she could do that. When I was the target of Mom's anger I would always fight back, scream, throw things—I would do something. Not Lydia. She had too much respect for Mom. She would just take it. I admired that quality, because to me it showed supreme strength. Lydia could always find the control that I lacked. She could hide her fear and pain; I wanted to be like that.

My mom's screaming seemed to last all night. I remember my father didn't even yell once when he heard the news. "What did I do wrong?" he asked quietly, looking up for an answer that never came. I could tell it hurt Lydia more than any of our mother's blows or shouts. He shook his head and stared at Lydia for a moment before turning and going into his room. I walked by a little while later and saw him in there, sitting on the bed with his hands open and empty at his sides, staring at the wall.

I was scared for Lydia. Girls who got pregnant became outcasts

....

have none of that, and cut her off not accept what Lydia was saying and interrupted her

like a rock not moving

in our barrio, although no one ever seemed to blame the boys who were equally responsible. Some of the girls would just disappear, **shipped off to convents** or somewhere to have the baby far from home or to stay with anyone they knew. No one talked about them or their babies. Others got abortions, which also **forever marked them** as a whore in our neighborhood. Around school the girls would be labeled as tramps, and the only thing people would say to them was crude or mean-spirited. Some of the girls did eventually end up **selling themselves** on the streets, as if they began to believe all the things people said to them. I suppose they thought it was the only thing they had left.

It was terrifying. I had seen girls who broke the news to their families only to be literally turned out on the street, treated as strangers by parents who slammed the door in their faces. I felt so bad for Lydia. I promised myself that what happened to her would never happen to me. Even with the swirl of anger and resentment that filled my house after Lydia's departure to live with Sammy's parents, I couldn't help thinking about my own fate: My gang of two was no more, and that meant there was no one to watch my back. Where would I turn?

Was it Lydia's banishment or a rebellion against my parents, or maybe just the release of something that was inside me the whole time? I don't know, but a few weeks after my sister left Valley High I found myself with a rock in my hand, standing outside **a ramshackle** house. All around me, the Trooper girls were closing in on the

....

shipped off to convents sent to live with religious groups
forever marked them made people think of them
selling themselves working as prostitutes
a ramshackle an old, ruined

shabby home, stepping over the short, rickety fence and past the broken toys that littered the dirt lot. Some girls grabbed rocks as they snuck past the house's windows, which had tattered old blankets, stained and sun-faded, hanging in place of curtains.

The Trooper Girls were all dressed the same: Dark sweatshirts over jeans and heavy makeup that made black circles beneath their brows. It was the uniform the Trooper Girls donned when they went looking for trouble. That day, for the first time, I was wearing it too.

One of the girls, Angel—who likely had smoked a joint to build up some artificial courage for the day's mission—was giggling and making a lot of noise as she stumbled around, but there was no sign that anyone in the house heard her or even the barking dog next door. My own heart was beating so fast, so loud, I half-expected it to **alert someone to our presence**, but up and down the street there was no one looking our way. **My gut was tight** and I could feel a wave of heat and excitement building in the base of my back. Flies were buzzing in my face, angry that I had disturbed their yard, but I didn't even wave them away. I gripped the stone tighter and it flashed across my brain: What am I doing here?

The weeks after Lydia had **dropped out** had been tough ones. I had tried to squelch the hallway rumors that were spreading, but there was little I could do. Lydia was well-known and her abrupt disappearance was not hard to figure out, especially because everyone knew how tight she was with Sammy. Her absence made me more of a target, I knew, and defending her name put me in situations where trouble was getting harder to avoid.

....

alert someone to our presence be heard by someone and to get us in trouble

My gut was tight I was nervous

dropped out quit school

"Hey, where's your sister? I heard she's gonna have a baby . . .
Does she know who the daddy is yet?"

The howls and harsh words did not surprise me; the cruelty of
the teens in my school never did. But at the same time I could not
walk away. Lydia was family and I could not let anyone **disrespect
our name**. Sometimes it felt like the only thing we really owned.

More than once, I walked home bruised and sore, wincing at the
pain and my mother's pestering questions as I closed my bedroom
door. I really missed Lydia, too, and the anger I felt pushed me to
do stupid things. Enemies are everywhere, I began to think, and I
need help.

There was no specific day, no single moment, when I made the
decision to run with the gang and turn my back on everything I had
been taught by my father. It was more like **a series of surrenders
and lapses** that combined to deliver me into the very lifestyle I had
been raised to most despise. I wish I could point to a single decision
or event, because then it might be easier to understand and explain,
or even dismiss like **a bolt of bad fortune that strikes out of a
dark sky**, the way lightning had killed my uncle. But there had been
no lightning that day long ago. It was an accident, a careless moment
in a young life that led to quick death. And there was no great fall for
me, merely a steady slide. I chose the parties and the fighting and the
sense of acceptance I believed the gang would give me.

Chata had been my gateway to F-Troop. We had met when we
were fifteen. As I began accepting invitations to the late-night keg

---

disrespect our name say bad things about my family

a series of surrenders and lapses several bad decisions and
slowly giving up control

a bolt of bad fortune that strikes out of a dark sky bad luck

parties the gang seemed to have every week, I became one of her confidants. In some way, she even reminded me of Lydia.

"Meet me at lunch." Chata's voice had an edge of anger, even more than usual. "We got business. I got a plan."

The plan was a simple one: **payback**. A girl, a newcomer to Valley High, had dared to disrespect Chata, making time with her boyfriend and then **mouthing off**. I didn't know if the girl knew the unspoken rules of the school's gangs, but it didn't matter. She committed an offense, and no legal system was as effective as the gangs' punishment process. There was no forgiveness and no **blurry lines**—if you cross someone, expect a payback.

At lunch, we got our dark sweatshirts from our lockers, where we always kept them, and we put our hair up in ponytails. We all split up and then met back up a few blocks from the shabby, dilapidated house where the girl lived. Her name was Blanca and her parents were Mexican immigrants, people trying to find a new life in Santa Ana but still overwhelmed by the whole experience of living in the United States. Blanca, like many teens in similar households, was a wild child, far more savvy than her parents and hard to **rein in** because of it.

The house looked like it was crumbling in on itself. Chickens were scrambling in the dust in a nearby yard, upset by the barking of the neighbor's watchdog. I saw Tiny lean down to pick up a heavy stone, so I found a rock of my own near a rusted-out car parked along the street. I wasn't sure what was going to happen, but as I watched Chata charge up to the house's porch, I knew it was going

....

payback revenge
mouthing off speaking rudely to her
blurry lines uncertainness, confusion
rein in control

to happen soon.

Through a window, Blanca saw Chata and defiantly **shot her a bird**, thinking, I suppose, that Chata would not be brave enough to do anything with Blanca's parents home. She could not have been more wrong.

Chata threw a rock right through the window and charged in, with all the other girls right behind. Inside, everyone ran around screaming and grabbing at things. I remember the look of complete shock and fear on the faces of Blanca's parents. They had no idea what was happening. Chata jumped on Blanca and the two started fighting, with Blanca taking the worst of it. And then it was all over. We raced from the house, streaming into the street while yelling the name of the gang and shrieking. The house was a shambles, everything upended, and Blanca, when I saw her last, was dazed and crying. I felt like I watched the whole thing with somebody else's eyes. Was that me in the middle of all that?

The hot rush I felt during the raid quickly chilled into **a lump of anxiety in my stomach**. Sitting in math class afterward, the teacher's voice sounded **like a distant drone**. I kept watching the door, waiting for the principal or a cop or my dad to walk in and point a finger at me and yell out my name. My leg was twitching with guilty energy and I kept sweating. How could we not get caught? We didn't wear masks or gloves! The girl, Blanca, she knows us all—she must have called the cops! And that stuff the other girls took from the house and stuffed into their pockets and school lockers . . . how could we ever expect to get away with this?

....

shot her a bird made a rude sign with her finger to Chata
a lump of anxiety in my stomach worry and fear
like a distant drone very far away

For days, the face of every adult—especially my father and mother—accused me. I was sure everyone knew, that any minute everything would crash down on me and my friends.

But it never happened. Blanca never returned to Valley High. Weeks later, when I built up the courage to finally walk past Blanca's house, it was deserted, the soiled blankets replaced by sheets of plywood in the windows. The whole family had left, just moved away because they were so terrorized.

"That bitch is gone," Chata said in **a matter-of-fact** tone one afternoon as we sat in front of a mirror in her bedroom. We were getting ready to go to a Trooper party and we both buzzed on wine as we put on our makeup. An untouched cigarette smoldered in the ashtray next to Chata.

"Bitch? Who?"

"Y'know, that bitch, Blanca."

"Oh. Yeah, I know. I think she moved. Her house is all boarded up." I started brushing my hair, slow strokes through the length. My hand didn't shake anymore when I thought about Blanca. A month had gone by, and it didn't even seem real anymore.

"They moved! No way! Ha . . . You remember the looks on her parents' faces? They didn't know what was going on. Pretty funny, huh?"

I didn't answer. Neither of us talked for awhile, we just sat quietly as we got ready for the night.

"Mona, what's going on with you?"

---

a matter-of-fact an unemotional

It was Mr. Beasley, my auto shop teacher. He was one of the few teachers who seemed to **take a genuine interest in** me. At first it made me feel great, but later, when I started hanging with the Trooper Girls, it had just made things more complicated. I had skipped a few homework assignments and my late-night partying was making me groggy in his early morning class. I just wanted to get through the day, but Mr. Beasley **wouldn't settle for a shrug**.

"There's something changing. I can see it in your assignments and your attitude . . . and your new friends."

I looked up the hallway and saw Chata and the girls hovering near a bench. Chata smiled at me and I returned her gaze with a pained roll of my eyes. I was trapped, forced to squirm and listen through a lecture.

"There's no change. I just . . . I don't know . . . I'll try harder." Chata was making faces at me and I was trying to keep a giggle down. "Uh, I have to go now, if it's okay."

"Listen, Mona, you may not know it, but the decisions you make now affect your whole life. I know what it's like to be young, to want to have a good time, but don't make decisions that you'll pay for later."

Beasley shot a glare at Chata and the others and let out a deep sigh. "You're smart, so just think about what you're doing, Mona, that's all. Go ahead, you can go. Get out of here."

The inquiries didn't end on campus. My mother **was dropping snide comments about the hours I kept** and the way I was dressing. She said the makeup I wore made me look like a

....

take a genuine interest in really care about

wouldn't settle for a shrug wanted me to talk to him

**was dropping snide comments about the hours I
kept** complained about how late I came home

streetwalker. My father was less direct but more effective. A squint of his disapproving eyes told me that he suspected I was up to no good. I wondered when he would confront me.

"What is it with you, eh?" he asked me one morning as I was getting ready for school. "Your eyes say you have done something wrong. But your mouth says nothing."

"I don't know what you're talking about." I picked up my sweatshirt, draped over a chair, and tossed it out of sight, so it wouldn't betray me. Dad stood there for a minute, waiting, then just ambled away, his back injuries clearly **announced by his strained gait**.

My relationship with my father was a sore spot for me. I found myself exasperated with him and my mother, with the way they spoke and acted, their old-fashioned views. They made me feel trapped, and I would run out of the house for relief. Afterward, I'd feel regret and shame. I hated that I had begun lying to them **on a regular basis**, even though Chata once laughed at me when I told her that. But I still loved my Mom and Dad, and I knew how hurt they were by my activities, even if they didn't know exactly what I was doing. I wondered if my father missed his little girl. I knew that he did. In some ways, I missed her, too.

My sister Roni spared me from most of my parents' wrath. Roni was running with the Goldenwest gang, and she was not very successful masking her activities or her growing use of drugs. I'm not sure she even cared who knew. My sisters didn't know much about my gang ties. I kept them relatively quiet and distant from them, but Roni was just the opposite. She was **on a tear**, partying hard and

....

announced by his strained gait noticeable because of the way he walked

on a regular basis all the time

on a tear acting wild and crazy

taking the wildest risks. In stark contrast, my eldest sister, Maryann, had managed to make herself immune to the gangs. She was a "schoolie," an academic who was going to use her grades to carry her into business. The older gang members often seemed to **give a wide berth to** kids who were committed to education, more or less leaving them out of the street games that the rest of us played. The same studious kids that were victims in middle school became off-limits as we approached the end of high school. They were on a mission to **become something**, I suppose, and that **carried some weight even with the dead-end kids**.

If I was somewhere between Maryann and Roni, it only made me more confused about the life I was living. I had begun to think of myself as a bad kid, a fighter or at least someone playing that role. How had Maryann, growing up in the same house and neighborhood, gone a different route? Was it luck? Was she just smarter, better?

The eyes of my father might have had the answers in them, but I could not find them. I saw only disappointment and accusations there.

My father just stood there with the blade, which looked small in his thick, calloused palms. "What is this, huh? Why do you have a *fileto*? It is yours, no?" I kept quiet and stepped backward like a trapped animal. "Answer me, why do you have this?" His hand was on my shoulder then, squeezing hard. My father still had strength in his hands, no matter how bad his back had become. "Answer me!"

....

give a wide berth to stay away from the; not bother the
become something have a better life
carried some weight even with the dead-end kids was respected by everyone

I tried to shrug his grip off. "Yeah, it's mine." He let go and I looked up, meeting his stare for the first time. "I just use it to scare somebody if they mess with me. I have to walk alone a lot."

I didn't know what to expect. I was afraid he might hit me. It had been years since he grew angry enough to strike me, but I knew how much he hated gangs and street-fighting. The knife was evidence of what I knew my parents already suspected, that I was kicking back with the *vatos*. It flashed through my head that this might get me kicked out of the house for good. I started to **steel** myself for what was about to happen, prepared for anything. My father looked down at the knife and bounced it in his hand, as if he was trying to guess its weight. He turned quickly and headed out the front door. "Follow me," was all he said.

He walked to the garage, where he put the knife aside on a countertop and began pulling out tools. He took some scrap metal and began heating and **molding** it with a torch and the tools in his musty workshop. I had no idea what he was doing, but I remained silent. He kept his head down, focused on his work, for half an hour. Every few minutes his strong, nimble fingers would leave his work to wipe the sweat from his brow, and then he went back to it, crafting some mysterious object.

The lump of metal began to take shape, and I couldn't believe what I was seeing. It was a series of loops, I realized, as my father smoothed the object's curves and defined its edges. When he was done and the metal was cooled, he slipped it over his fingers and made a fist. He seemed satisfied with the finished product, so he

....

steel prepare
molding shaping

handed me **the set of brass knuckles** and asked me if I knew how to use them. I managed to nod. "Put them in your pocket," he said.

He turned, picked up the knife, and looked at me again. "Do not tell your mother about these things, eh? You use that, not this, if someone tries to hurt you. You don't want to kill someone." He walked back toward the house with me right behind him.

That night, I sat in my room and **shadow-boxed** with my new weapon, modeling the dull, heavy metal knuckles in front of the mirror. I imagined the sound it would make when the unforgiving edge came down across someone's jaw. I daydreamed about defiantly walking up to one of my rivals, and when they said the wrong thing, pulling my hand out of my jacket pocket and surprising them with a blow that would **lay them right out**. I swung and jabbed at the air for an hour until my wrist was sore from the heavy weight. I giggled when I thought about my father making the weapon I would use to defend the gang, and then I felt bad, real guilty, when I remembered the concern in his eyes. I knew he made the knuckles because he pictured me in danger. He still loved me, no matter what I did, and it occurred to me that every night I was out he was probably laying awake, worrying about me. I didn't know how that made me feel.

I fell asleep that night with my fingers still in the cold, hard rings, ready to fend off any bad dreams that might come before the dawn.

....

the set of brass knuckles a piece of metal I could wear on my hand in fights

shadow-boxed pretended to fight

lay them right out knock them to the ground

BEFORE YOU MOVE ON...

1. **Cause and Effect** Reread pages 52–53. How did Mona's fight affect her life at school?

2. **Main Idea and Details** Reread pages 56–58. List 3 details to support this main idea: Mona felt like she had to join a gang.

LOOK AHEAD Read pages 67–83 to find out how the new generation of gang members changed gang life.

~ Chapter Five ~

JUMPING IN

The girl with the pinched face and red hair was waving the joint under my nose and gagging on a lung full of pot. "Here, take it," she said, letting loose a cloud of smoke.

"No. I don't want any."

The girl's **brow knit in** confusion, as if I had presented her with a difficult riddle. She studied the joint, shrugged and passed the ratty-looking cigarette in the other direction. All around us, Troopers were dancing and drinking, but I was in a sour mood. My eyes were sore from all the smoke and I was coming off a rough day at school. My grades were **in a nosedive**, and I knew there would be hell to pay when report cards came out.

"Hey, is there something wrong with the *mota*? Or is there something wrong with you?"

I looked up to see a guy named Wino, one of the party associates who hung around with the Troopers and, I suspected, one of their many drug sources. He was somewhat handsome, but his eyes had a

....

brow knit in face showed
in a nosedive getting worse and worse
mota drugs (in Spanish)

dark, mean quality to them.

"There's nothing wrong with me. I don't smoke."

"Everybody else does . . . maybe you should try it, y'know? It might **loosen you up a bit**." He smiled and his eyes ran up and down me. "Don't you like to have a good time, *chica*?"

"I don't need pot to have a good time. I don't need you either."

His eyes grew even darker. "Yeah, maybe you think you're too good for us, huh?"

He walked off, muttering, and I looked for a friend and an exit. The party was lame and it was getting worse. Wino would be back, I suspected, after some more booze and pot, to push his point. I was in no mood for **his dance**. The closer I got to the Trooper core, the more problems I had with people pushing drugs on me. I had never minded drinking, but the drugs scared me. I had seen friends lose control and I had even been at a party once where a girl got so high on heroin that she didn't even know her name. Later, I heard, some of the gang members ran a train on her that night, taking turns raping her while she was too groggy to fight back or even care. The girl was humiliated, and because the gangs are **driven by a male code**, the disgrace of that night's events was pushed on her alone. The boys were only doing what was expected, the logic went, so in some twisted way she was to blame for her own attack. It made me sick. The thought of being that powerless, being that victimized, absolutely terrified me. I swore to myself I would never do drugs. It was not an easy oath to keep.

As the 1970s drew to a close, drugs were becoming more and

....

loosen you up a bit relax you
chica girl (in Spanish)
his dance an argument
driven by a male code controlled by men

more **central** to the gang's activities. Heroin was widespread, and at parties there would be a glut of lazy-eyed homeboys around the bathroom, waiting to sneak in with small bags they kept their syringes and smack in. Overdoses were becoming almost monthly events among the students at Valley High and the extended community of dropouts who had decided that school was interfering with their gang life. Mothers or girlfriends were usually the ones who found the bodies, their boy blue and still on the bathroom floor with a needle jutting out of his arm. I knew my cousins were caught up in the heroin scene and many of my friends, and I wondered when one of them would push too far.

One of the Troopers once told me heroin was a taste of the float and freedom of death, and when the taste became more **enticing than life**, you were gone.

"It's like cotton all around you, cotton and soft music," he said with a faraway look. "Nothing hurts. Nothing matters."

Heroin wasn't the only hard drug, of course. PCP came in and out of **vogue** with the homeboys, who enjoyed its rough, dizzying rush. It was the drug that led to explosions of violence and recklessness, the drug used by the boys who felt they were getting closer to the edge and didn't seem to care. Others did speed or coke or even LSD, but it was always the heroin that seemed to rule in our neighborhood. The needle was king in the Santa Ana of the 1970s.

Drugs were easier to get than ever before and the users were getting younger. By the end of my junior year at Valley, the steady flow of drugs—along with the neighborhood's quickly growing

....

central important
enticing than life important than living
vogue popularity

population—had brought about some dramatic changes in F-Troop and the city's other major gangs. The Troopers, who had begun with a handful of incorrigibles, had swelled into Orange County's largest gang, with a membership in the hundreds that went far beyond Santa Ana's city limits. They were known from Los Angeles to Riverside and down south to San Diego. As the first generation of homeboys, the *veteranos*, hit their mid and late twenties, they left the street-fighting to the younger soldiers and took up the formal business of drug trafficking. The Troopers had always done some dealing, to cohorts within the gang and others, to subsidize their activities, but now the aging *veteranos* had realized that the availability and growing user population held the promise of big bucks.

The drugs came from the south, up from Mexico and Central America, and the F-Troop *veteranos* were setting themselves up as part of the local distribution system. Many of their connections were found in prisons. When the F-Troop leaders were shuttled off to prison for auto theft, armed robbery or drug charges, they would meet up with members of the Mexican Mafia, a **shadow organization that ruled the lion's share** of the illegal drug commerce in southern California. Few people asked questions about *el Eme* or even mentioned it by name, and far fewer were willing to defy it. Folsom, San Quentin and other state prisons have long been seats of power for *el Eme*. My cousins told me about the brutal world inside the prisons, where the prisoner population was divided along racial lines. Hispanics grouped together, as did whites and blacks, and **allegiance** and strength were the qualities that kept them alive.

....

shadow organization that ruled the lion's share secret group that controlled most

el Eme the Mexican Mafia (in Spanish)

allegiance loyalty

"It's all 'Us and Them' in there," one homeboy told me. "You know how on the streets you can have friends in other barrios? Not inside. You stay with your kind and keep your head down. If you mess up, they **take you out**."

The guys who went to prison always came back different—harder and more desperate. I've heard people say the prisons are like a college for criminals, a place that will turn you into a hardened criminal if you aren't one when you go in. Guys that went in as robbers and burglars came out as killers. Others, who weren't strong enough to protect themselves, had to sell themselves sexually to keep alive inside. Some didn't make it at all, dying locked up in a box or bleeding on the pavement of a prison yard. They went in with a name, but died as a number, far from home.

Everything seemed to be **escalating as the 1980s loomed**. Guns, which had been rare sights when I was younger, now seemed to be everywhere. More drugs meant more money, more money meant higher stakes and more guns meant more opportunities for flare-ups. It all **mixed together into a vicious cocktail**. You could feel it at parties, the music pumping loud and the sounds of sirens in the neighborhood, the homeboys high and prowling for trouble. Sometimes it felt like everything was about to explode.

In the morning, the grey text of the local newspaper would spell out the consequences of the night. "Gang-related death" became a familiar phrase, and the stories would go on and on about the police and politicians urging action and promising crackdowns and calling for community help—but none of that mattered. Things were going

....

take you out kill you

escalating as the 1980s loomed getting more and more dangerous as the years went by

mixed together into a vicious cocktail led to more violence

to get a lot worse before they got better.

Little John's house was the place to be if you were a Trooper. It was the party spot that meant you were accepted by the **gang's elite**. Few associates were granted admission. Casually mentioning that you had been kicking back at Little John's would be enough to earn envy and respect on the street, and more than a few people lied about going there just to look big. I found myself a little wide-eyed when my cousins would bring me over, and invariably, if younger Troopers were there while Little John or other *veteranos* were holding court, the party would turn into a lesson in Trooper history and bylaws.

The gang had rules, but no real leader. The older members would **decide by committee** where the next party, burglary or major rumble would be, but the gang had grown so large that it was hard to call it organized. Still, the *veteranos* knew it was important to pass on gang lore and traditions. It inflated their own self-importance and it also added a sense of purpose and allegiance to the gang, vital for inspiring the younger **rank and file** to commit crimes and throw their bodies into street fights for the glory of the Troopers.

"If someone asks you who you claim, you better answer F-Troop." My cousin Andy, nicknamed Nip, was sipping a Budweiser and coaching some junior members in the ways of the gang.

A few nights earlier, we had all heard, some Troopers had been outnumbered and surrounded at the Orange County Fair by some homeboys from a nearby city. The Troopers had been challenged,

....

gang's elite leaders of the gang
decide by committee make decisions as a group about
rank and file gang members

but they backed down and said they claimed no gang. It was a surrender, shameful by the **gang code**.

"If you don't claim," Andy continued, "we'll kick your ass instead. You don't **run out on** homies and you don't run out on the barrio, right?"

Two of the boys nodded, a third just stared. They were all high school sophomores who seemed big and scary to their peers. Getting stared down by Andy, they seemed like little kids. "Respect the barrio," Andy summarized, "or it will come down."

Homeboys who flouted the gang rules often found their houses or cars trashed or, if the offense was great enough, they were run out of town amid threats of assorted mayhem. "Leave in a car or a coffin," was the simple advice they were given.

After the boys filed out, Andy chuckled at their wide-eyed fear. The tough talk was calculated to a certain extent, and the *veteranos* had fun pushing the buttons of their younger charges. Still, the old-timers had some worries about these younger generations they saw coming into the gangs. The new kids—my age group—were into guns and drugs far earlier and, after watching their older brothers and cousins play the street games, they wanted to **take it a notch higher**. A new madness authored by these younger, rabid homeboys arrived in our neighborhoods: **the drive-by**.

"Buncha punk *chavalas*," my cousin Eddie said one night, referring to some drive-by perpetrators.

A drive-by had left a woman with a bullet in her back. She had been a bystander, just minding her own business. To the *veteranos*,

....

gang code rules of the gang
run out on abandon
take it a notch higher make things a lot more dangerous
the drive-by shooting people out of moving cars

the shooting was proof that the wild new generation was ratcheting up the worst parts of gang life and leaving behind the codes of behavior that had guided the Troopers and others.

"They got no respect," he said. "You settle things by sticking a gun out a window? What does that prove? Come up and fight like a man, face to face."

It sounded hollow to outsiders, I'm sure, but the *veteranos* were convinced that they had fought for the gang with a clear set of guidelines. If, for instance, a foe was walking with his grandmother, they would **let him go unchallenged**, just as the schoolies were allowed to go unmolested. There were **breakdowns** in the code, they conceded, but at least they had one. The street game had rules, they lamented, sounding like old men, but now those seemed to be going out the window.

Hanging out with my cousins and their friends gave me a different perspective on F-Troop and also on my younger peers. Besides declining drugs, I felt at ease speaking out and talking back, which was hardly common, especially for a girl and an associate. But I felt like I had a view from above, that I could see the past and present and understand it all better. I always felt detached, apart from it all, but still right in the middle. It made me brave, even brave enough to share an unlikely dream that **bordered on treason**.

There were eight or nine of us at the ditching party, and wine and weed were making the rounds. Yogi's mom was working, so her house was the perfect place for us to gather as we skipped school. The afternoon drinking seemed to bring a quiet, almost somber

....

let him go unchallenged not attack him

breakdowns problems

bordered on treason made people wonder if I was really loyal to F-Troop

tone to the party, though. Someone asked about the future, always a **sensitive** subject among the homeboys.

One by one, around the room, each of us said what we thought the future would hold. A *vato* named Gordo, an associate with a plump midsection and fondness for marijuana, said he would be a welder, like his dad, and buy two or three cars. One Trooper with a new tattoo and a long scar winding down his arm said he expected to be dead or in prison in five years. Two homegirls giggled and said they wanted to be wives and mothers, and I suspected their quiet laughs were because they had shared this ambition with one another often and had probably already picked out their targeted *vatos*. Another boy, Wicked, said he wanted to deal drugs and get rich, which drew chuckles from everyone. When it came my turn, the answer that came out of my mouth surprised even me.

"I want to be a cop."

There was silence and then a torrent of laughter. I smiled but shook my head when they told me I had made a great joke. "No, really. Why not? I want to be a cop."

"After what you seen them do, to the homies . . . to your own *primos*? That's bullshit, man," Wicked said.

Another *vato* agreed, and took it to a new level: "Is that why you don't smoke dope? You a spy for the *jura*?"

"I'm not a spy for anybody, and I don't smoke because I don't want to, just like you don't shoot up, right? I just think . . ."

The faces were all on me now, and I wasn't sure what I thought. I was no fan of the cops—they had given me a hard time in the past,

....

sensitive difficult, depressing
primos cousins (in Spanish)
jura police (in Spanish)

and I had seen them beat my homies for no reason. But some part of me, maybe the part that still was loyal to my father, believed that being a cop was a way to make things better.

"I just think it might be cool. Never mind. I was just joking. You know, too much wine."

As the party split into smaller conversations, Gordo leaned over. "Don't listen to them. If that's what you want, then do it."

"He's right, you have to do what you think is right." I didn't know her name, but the girl had walked over and put her hand on my shoulder. "Besides, we could use some good cops around here."

Everything seemed to be **raging at a new level**. The nonstop parties kicked off Thursday night and seemed to slow down only when all the homeboys headed to Main Street on Sunday **for the ritual cruising night**, with caravans of low-riders, Impalas and Bel Airs taking lazy laps up and down the street. The gang presence in Santa Ana was nothing new, but as the city grew larger and larger, the *clicas* also got bigger and bolder. I was getting bolder, too, trying to keep pace in some ways with the furious drumbeat of the Trooper lifestyle. Many nights I wouldn't go home until morning or my mother would banish me for stumbling in drunk or bruised up from some gang scuffle. I was feeling invincible and intoxicated by the fear I saw in the eyes of others. The gang was something special and strong and, although I wasn't a formal member, I felt part of it.

My role as an associate always allowed me to shout back at my mother that I wasn't a gang member and, on some level, I could

....

raging at a new level getting crazier
for the ritual cruising night to drive up and down the street
clicas gangs (in Spanish)

persuade myself I was telling the truth. But the status did present some problems. **My strident opposition to using** drugs and my vague connection to the gang **raised the ire of** some Trooper Girls and gave others the excuse they needed to question my loyalty. Most of it amounted to nothing, though. I had fought for the gang many times, and I had fought well. That, and the Elizalde connection, was enough for most of the Troopers, and the rest knew where to find me if they still had a problem.

I knew the real reason some challenged me was my outspoken views. My father and I seemed to have little in the way of **common ground** anymore, but I still followed his teachings that I should stand up for my beliefs, no matter what. The gang was a collection of followers, mostly, so when I piped up with disagreement or refused to follow the group direction, there was often immediate resentment and suspicion.

As an associate, I felt the freedom to walk that tightrope, enjoying the gang's benefits but declaring independence when it suited me. I saw no reason to change. But, at a party one night, I realized the choice was no longer mine.

The girls were older, in their twenties. They had a hard look to them, streetwise, but also a proud beauty of sorts. Both had long hair and wore lots of makeup. One was tall and had pale skin, the other was darker and wore lots of jewelry. They were first- or second-generation Trooper Girls, the girlfriends of the Troopers from the early days, and the crowd of younger gang members spread to make way for them as they walked through the party's chaos.

....

My strident opposition to using My refusal to take
raised the ire of angered
common ground things we agreed on

They **made a beeline for** me and I pretended not to notice as they closed in. I wasn't sure if they were looking for trouble, but I doubted I could win a fight with either, much less both. I took a sip of wine from a rose-colored bottle and wondered what the hell I was going to do if they started swinging.

"You're Mona? Eddie's *prima*?" The taller one was standing right in front of me, her leg grazing mine as I sat on the side of a couch that smelled of beer.

"Yeah."

"We heard what you did over at the school," the darker one said. A week earlier there had been a fight in the parking lot at Valley. Some Del Hi *cholas* had jumped a Trooper girl I barely knew, and I ran in to help her. It was five on two, and we got our asses kicked.

"Uh-huh. I didn't do too well." I held up my arm to show a long scab along my elbow. I had hit the ground hard just before the teachers broke up the fight. I took another drink of wine and looked around. The three of us were clearly **the center of attention** at the party. I wondered where all this was going.

"It's your time," the tall one said. "You understand?"

I nodded even though I didn't. My time?

"Tomorrow, at Salvador Park. Noon. We'll see you there."

They turned and walked away, melting back into the growing crowd that was packed in and around the house. Someone dropped a beer bottle in the kitchen and the shattering sound set off a chorus of laughter. I barely registered the sound—I was still **chewing on the cryptic** conversation. My time?

....

made a beeline for walked straight towards
the center of attention what everyone was looking at
chewing on the cryptic thinking about the mysterious

Laying in bed, hours later, my mind was racing, trying to **get a grip on** this unexpected twist. The appointment at Salvador Park, the Troopers' stronghold and most public gathering place, could only be for one purpose: I had been selected to join the gang and had been scheduled for **initiation**. I would have to take an oath to lay down my life if necessary for the gang, to fight and even kill for the glory of F-Troop.

The **avalanche of** emotions I felt surprised me.

I was somewhat giddy and oddly proud. I was also terrified and slightly offended that I wasn't really given a choice in the whole matter. I had been **tapped** for membership and it was just assumed that I would accept. I had no idea what the consequences would be if I declined—I had never heard of that happening before—but I knew right away there was no chance of that. I would be there at noon and take the oath.

For a year, I had lived the Trooper life and I had come to realize that any distance I pretended existed between myself and the gang was in my mind only. The commitment had already been made, the initiation would only make it official. There was even some relief in surrendering myself completely, a sense of closure. Why deny the life I had chosen?

The feelings of relief were hard to enjoy, though. My mind was locked on the actual initiation rite, the painful price of passage into the gang. The Santa Ana gangs, once again following the example set by Los Angeles *clicas*, had by then begun a practice called "jumping

....

get a grip on understand
initiation the ceremony to make me a permanent member
avalanche of many different
tapped selected

in." It was a bloody tradition they were starting: A circle of gang members would beat the candidate senseless for several minutes, kicking and punching their hardest.

It was almost dawn and still I wasn't asleep. My appointment was hours away but drawing closer with every tick of the loud clock in the living room. It was uncomfortably hot that night, with the Santa Ana winds blowing in over the deserts to the distant southeast, and the heat made me more restless. I wished for Lydia's presence and wondered where she was, what she was doing. Giving up on sleep, I turned on the light next to my bed and grabbed a drawing pad. I turned some music on, real low, just a murmur of a tune, so I wouldn't wake anyone. Some oldies and some drawing to **ease my racing mind**. How would the fists feel tomorrow? I had been in plenty of fights, more than I could remember really, but how could I stand there and take the blows without **striking back**? I couldn't shake the grisly images that taunted me. I imagined the worst, a stray blow, maybe somebody's ring catching me across the eyes or their heel landing on a kidney or maybe my skull. The hospital, the funeral home . . . I looked down and realized that my drawing had almost filled the page without me noticing even what it was, like my brain was **on automatic**—that was something that happened to me all the time. The sketches were a way for me to express my feelings, to throw down on the page all the pain and joy I stored up during the day but usually kept guarded behind my street mask. The picture that came out that night was of a girl, her head thrown back in a scream. Her world, the objects and events in her life, were spread

....

ease my racing mind comfort me
striking back defending myself; fighting back
on automatic working on its own

throughout the wavy, dark hair that spread back from her face, as if her thoughts were visible and circling, closing in on her. There were syringes and knives, a cross and a flaming heart, a little baby, all alone, and menacing homeboys, with their cars and tattoos, posing and proud.

"This is the day you become part of *la familia*," Payasa said solemnly. Seven girls stood around me, some already clenching their fists. I was trying to size up who looked like the hardest hitter and who had the most rings on, so I knew which way to **throw up my defenses**. Not that it mattered much. There was no way to avoid an ass-whipping. I knew all I could hope to do was keep my hands and forearms up over my face and head and maybe try to crouch a little to protect my chest and stomach. I had to be sure, too, to keep **my feet**. If you hit the ground you could get **stomped**, and that was the quickest way to end up in the hospital.

I had been in a lot of fights and had knives and guns waved in my direction, but I had never been as scared as I was at that moment, standing on the basketball court at Salvador Park. One of the older girls, Payasa, which is Spanish for clown, was standing in front of me, talking on and on about the meaning of what was about to happen. She had the tone of voice you hear during church sermons, like she was letting you in on something very secret and sacred. It was hard to take anything she said seriously, though: Her face was too laughable. I and all the other homegirls followed gang style and wore thick layers of makeup—caking it on especially thick, like war

....

la familia the family (in Spanish)
throw up my defenses protect myself
my feet standing
stomped kicked and stepped on

paint, for fights, parties or special events like a jumping in—but Payasa was **in a whole other league, hence her nickname**. She had burnt-red blush and, above that, bone-white eye shadow set off with black eyeliner that stretched back in a line that ran, uninterrupted, to her hair. The effect made her look like a vampire. But any **ominous quality** she might have achieved was ruined by her fake eyelashes, which were so huge they caused her eyes to droop half-closed. I was standing there, waiting to get beat senseless, and all I could think about was how hard it must be for Payasa to see through that thicket of black lashes.

The first punch caught me in the back, and after that it was just a hailstorm of blows from all sides. Red flashed in front of my eyes when someone caught me across the chin, causing my head to jerk back. My left side was hurting bad, too, and I could feel the rage building up inside of me. I nearly lost my feet with the next blow, a strong slap just below my left ear that left a ringing echoing through my skull.

I tried to picture Lydia, the way she mastered pain and stood strong, in control, but my anger **got the better of me**—I started lashing out, fighting blindly against my attackers. A scream came out of my mouth and my attackers began backing up. A heartbeat later, I was swinging at air, moaning like a sick dog.

Payasa had yelled "Enough!" and, just like that, my initiation was over. The warm, coppery taste of blood filled my mouth and I started to sag to the ground, but my knees never reached the asphalt. My attackers, my friends, were holding me up, hugging and slapping my

....

in a whole other league, hence her nickname always wearing the most makeup, which is how she got her name

ominous quality frightening look

got the better of me took control

sore back in congratulations. Bloodied and bruised, I was now one of them.

"Homes, you're crazy . . ."

"All right, Mona!"

"¡La vida loca nomás!"

The noon sun was bright and, as I finally unclenched my eyes, it was too bright to see the faces around me. A sting—from sweat? blood?—made me squint even more. All I saw were shadows.

I tried not to cry as we began the long walk back to Chata's house.

....

"¡La vida loca nomás!" "Welcome to the crazy life!" (in Spanish)

BEFORE YOU MOVE ON...

1. **Cause and Effect** Reread pages 71–74. What caused the gangs to become more deadly?

2. **Assumption** Reread page 77. What did Mona wrongly assume about her relationship with F-Troop?

LOOK AHEAD Read pages 84–98 to see why Mona ended up in the police station.

My senior year arrived and I found myself watching the freshmen in the halls and envying their childish games and their distance from the pain I was seeing more and more. The drive-bys had quickly become a **staple** of gang life, and the more cowardly or squeamish homeboys who had once bottled up their jealousies and grudges were now letting them fly out a car window in a comfortably **sanitized substitute** for a street fight. They didn't have to get their hands bloody this way, or risk loss or injury. Just close their eyes, pull the trigger, and speed off into the night. They liked to think of themselves as cold-blooded killers, but they were far from it. They had just found a way to make death feel like a video game.

I hated the funerals. Most were to bury the overdosed homeboys, but the escalating street violence was contributing, too. Paybacks were leading to more paybacks. Funerals became almost monthly events. Death seemed to be everywhere and, sadly, a lot of the homeboys didn't seem to care. I don't know if they thought it made them seem heroic or if the future was such a dim prospect that they **resigned themselves**. Many talked as if they expected to die by twenty-one.

I remember seeing a guy I knew—they called him Conejo, or Rabbit—at a party, and he had this funny look on his face. He was a class clown kind of guy with a good street rep. I had this feeling as he walked away that I wouldn't see him again. The next day I got a call from a friend. Conejo had been on the I-5 freeway with his brother when some rivals recognized them. The carload of **bangers** pulled up alongside and fired, shooting Conejo in the head. Then, after the funeral, a couple of Troopers went over for a payback. It never

....

staple permanent part

sanitized substitute clean and easy replacement

resigned themselves stopped caring about life

bangers gang members

seemed to end.

As a form of respect to the fallen homeboy, most of the *vatos* would wear their colors: A club jacket or sweatshirt with Old English lettering spelling out the name of the gang the *vato* had exchanged his life to be a member in. Out would come the dark glasses to hide any tears. Some would wear their Sunday best, khakis with razor sharp creases. It was the uniform of the **calle**. We were all still kids mostly, and no one had told us how to dress or act, so the services often took on a sadly absurd atmosphere, with homeboys drinking beer out in front of the funeral home.

After the fourth or fifth funeral, I was numb to the pain. It was easier that way. It became like going to church. You would walk in, give your respects to the family, and then walk past the casket. I always told the family I was sorry and then ducked toward the back of the room instead of filing past the body like everyone else. I didn't want to see the dead face and folded hands. I was afraid I might crack and show emotion, and it was vitally important to me not to do that. It wasn't wise to show emotion, and I rarely did. It was the same as weakness.

The priests would always give angry sermons. I was stunned by this at the first few funerals. I thought it was mean and insensitive to give some lecture when someone had died. But as time went on, I understood. The priest would look down and see the wooden young face against the satin and then scan the crowd and see all the Trooper homeboys **itching to avenge him**, and he couldn't contain himself. He knew that the death being mourned would lead to more

....

calle street gangs (in Spanish)

itching to avenge him wanting to punish the person that killed him

deaths, and it infuriated him.

"Let the violence end here," he would practically shout. "Only God can **mete out vengeance** and justice. It is not man's to give out."

I would look around during the sermon to see how the group was reacting. Invariably, the *vatos* would be getting madder and madder. In their minds, they were already thinking about the vengeance the priest was begging them not to pursue. The message **was lost on them** or, worse, misread as a call for revenge.

The family members would be crying and screaming, and a lot of times the homeboys would have their own little kids, who would be running around wailing. The room was always cold. The worst part of it was the smell. McDougal's always smelled like death to me, it always made me want to run out as quickly as I could.

The worst for me was the closed coffin services. I'd stare at that box and wonder what the guy inside looked like, why it was too gruesome to let us even see the body.

Afterward, outside, the homeboys would be kicking back and talking about their **fallen buddy**. I hated that they partied right outside, cracking open tall boys and recounting war stories about the dead *vato*. I thought it was disrespectful, and I told them so, but they always said they were toasting their late friend, that he would have wanted it that way.

The crazy part is they were probably right.

As the younger homeboys jacked up their rivalries and violence, the disdainful *veteranos* were also locked into a pattern that promised

....

mete out vengeance give punishment

was lost on them did not affect them the way the priest wanted

fallen buddy dead friend

danger. The role of local drug lords came with hazards, of course, and a booming business meant more opportunity for clashes. One story that made the rounds through the gang was that some Trooper *veteranos* and three Mafia gunmen were responsible for a **grisly holdup** of a big-time Mexican dealer. They found the house where the dealer was staying in Orange County with his family, and they kicked the door down and held up the dealer, along with his wife and son, at gunpoint.

They threatened and beat the guy, but he denied having any drugs. He probably knew that losing **the hefty stash** would mean death from his own people, so he was hoping the *vatos* were **bluffing**. They weren't. They pistol-whipped him, stripped him naked, and bound him to a chair with duct tape. Still, he wouldn't turn over the heroin and cocaine. The robbers found an iron in the house and plugged it in. They grabbed the dealer's screaming son and held the iron a few inches from his face, threatening to burn the boy if they didn't get the stash. The dealer **relented**. He told them where the dope was hidden in the house.

There were other brutal robberies, too, as more *vatos* addicted to coke and heroin couldn't get ahold of the drugs they needed to feed their addictions or the money to satisfy their ambitions. One of the *veteranos* supposedly involved in that brutal crime and others had all of it come back at him one night in Garden Grove, a city bordering Santa Ana to the west.

It was a few months after the home invasion robbery and the

....

grisly holdup horrible robbery
the hefty stash his large drug supply
bluffing pretending to be more violent than they really were
relented stopped fighting

veterano pulled his motorcycle up to a convenience store. It was early, real early, around 5 A.M., and the *vato* wanted some coffee. He didn't see the faces in the car next to him in the empty parking lot until they had already recognized him. It was some of his former victims, some dealers who were happy to see the *veterano* **without his backup**. The *vato* jumped on his bike and gunned it out onto the street. He made a few quick turns and looked back to see if his pursuers were any closer. He looked too long. When his eyes came back to the road in front of him, he realized he was racing down a dead-end street at sixty miles an hour with no time to **pull out** before he ran up onto a sidewalk in front of a wall.

He reached out to a telephone pole, instinctively trying to stop himself, or maybe even try to spin around the pole to head back toward the street. Either way, the pole did more damage than good. He woke up on the street with an arm and an eye out of their sockets.

The school year was only a week old when I and a group of other girls were scheduled to speak to a counselor about the most unpopular subject at gang parties: the future. I was mad at the counselor before I even walked in. I had talked with her before and she always treated me and the other homegirls like we were trash, which, I guess, is exactly what she thought we were. I couldn't understand, though, why she took a job where she would be dealing with people she couldn't stand. It made no sense to me.

What really hurt, I think, is that I had come to her earlier hoping to talk about some serious issues I had been **mulling over**.

....

without his backup without other members of his gang to protect him

pull out turn around

mulling over thinking about

The **gang's allure was wearing thin** for me; I still loved hanging with my friends and I enjoyed the parties, but I could see the mindlessness of the fights, the shootings, and drugs. I had a lot of confused feelings and wanted someone to help me sort through them. I thought she might be the person, but she **shot me down cold**. She put a wall up and made it clear that I was a number on a piece of paper that went in a folder, and nothing more.

This time we were meeting for a career development class I was enrolled in. The school would place me in a part-time job, and I would leave campus early every day to earn money and class credit while learning how to do real-world stuff. It sounded fine to me. Anything that got me out of school and made money sounded great.

She was interviewing the students in the class one by one, because the kids were too rowdy to do it any other way. I had my mask on when I walked in and sat down. I glared at her, daring her to say the wrong thing. I never, never let anyone **catch me off guard** twice. She had burned me, I thought, by making me feel foolish for opening up, and it would not happen again.

"Full name?"

She knew my damn name. "Mona."

Her head bobbed up for the first time, and she peered over her glasses. "Ah . . . yes. Mona . . . Ramona Sandoval, right? Let's try to answer the questions, Mona."

A trained dog. That was how she talked to me. "Yeah, let's."

"Now, is there a career you're interested in? Hmm? Maybe a secretary or a beautician?"

....

gang's allure was wearing thin desire I had to be in a gang was weakening

shot me down cold was no help at all

catch me off guard see me be emotional

Her eyes were back on the papers in front of her. Those careers were the ones she expected all the girls to name, along with seamstress, cook, or nurse. I had planned to say mechanic. I knew cars well, thanks to my dad, and I enjoyed the precision, the finding of a problem or a part. I could do that for a living. But something in this woman's face made me hesitate.

"Mona, if you don't have an answer, I'll be happy to suggest something for you. We have some openings at a local restaurant . . ."

"Cop."

"What? Did you say . . ."

"Cop. Police officer. I want to be a cop."

She **locked eyes with me** for perhaps the first time, which might have been my goal. I wasn't sure why I said what I said. Police officer? Where the hell did that come from? The counselor was trying to find a hint in my eye that this was all some joke, but I **kept my face screwed tight**. She sighed and searched through her papers.

"I have a **spot** here . . . as a filing clerk at the police station," she said, handing me a card and putting a check next to my name on her class roll. Filing clerk? Wait, I hated clerical work . . .

Her hand was moving fast, checking off boxes on a sheet listing different levels of education and assorted types of schools. Police officers require college degrees, she was saying, and these were the types of classes I would need. College? Me? I didn't want to go to school again: I was thrilled to be almost out of the high school system. Those cops on the streets, those guys are college grads?

I started to ask questions, but she cut them off with a rigid wave

....

locked eyes with me looked right at me
kept my face screwed tight stared at her without emotion
spot job

of her finger. "Read these first." She dumped a stack of papers in my hand and looked past me, calling out the next name, the next number she couldn't care less about. I shuffled out of the room and studied the small slip of paper on top of the stack. It had my name, an address and the name of a cop, a sergeant. Across the bottom, it had a day and time. My start date was a few days away.

"What the hell have I **gotten myself into**?" I asked the hallway.

I sat down at lunch and read through the papers. I was stunned by the education requirements needed to become a cop, and I decided that I could never fulfill them. I spun the pages into a long cylinder and stuffed it in a trash can piled high with cafeteria food.

Why did I say cop anyway? It had been one of my father's dreams for me, but it was so unlikely it was **laughable**. Cops were usually white and always men, right? Even if someone like me could become a cop, I had eliminated any hopes with my decisions about the gang. If there were two sides, I had already made my loyalties clear. Besides, cops were assholes. I had seen that at the park and Little John's house when the *jura* came to break up the parties and bust heads. They were thugs with badges. I wanted no part of them.

I had been careful to pluck the job assignment sheet from the stack of papers before I trashed them. I read the information over and over as a daydream of my first day played out in my head. Why was I so excited? The idea of filing paper for a living made me ill, but there was something about going to the police station that **made my pulse race**.

For the first time since I was a little girl, I couldn't wait to get home and tell my dad about my day.

....

gotten myself into done
laughable funny; a joke
made my pulse race excited me

The day was not off to a good start. I was scheduled to begin work at the PD that afternoon, but I had been running behind all day. I ate lunch at home and, as I hurriedly headed back toward school, I bolted across Greenville Street against the light. Out of the corner of my eye I saw a motorcycle cop, but I didn't really think about it. I was in too big of a rush. As soon as I hit the other curb, though, I heard the cop on the corner yelling at me to come over.

It was Borja, a big, strong cop who still had the thick accent he brought with him from his native Mexico. His voice was deep and powerful; it seemed to rumble out of him. He had a reputation as a cop not to be messed with. He **took no guff** from the *vatos*, and he wasn't afraid to mix it up with the bangers. I think he stopped me because I **had the audacity to jaywalk** right in front of him.

"You know what you did?" he asked. His face was dark-skinned and you couldn't see his eyes behind the shiny, mirror sunglasses.

I squinted in the sun as I looked up. "No, what did I do?" My voice was **dripping in sarcasm**. It was the wrong way to win any sympathy.

He wrote out the ticket and handed it to me, the first one I had ever gotten. "Thanks," I said in a pained voice, and I headed off toward the school, cursing myself and him beneath my breath.

When I finished my last class that day, I headed toward the street where my dad was waiting in his brown '59 Chevy. He was smiling and happy when I got in. I had told him I was only going to be a clerk, but he didn't want to be bothered with details. His daughter,

---

took no guff would not accept rudeness

had the audacity to jaywalk was disrespectful enough to walk across the street on a red light

dripping in sarcasm rude

his second-born, was going to pursue his dream after all. All the years of trouble and clashes seemed to be gone from his mind as we drove through the streets in that big car. He had one hand on the wheel, and the other hand was wagging a finger at me. "Make sure you ask a lot of questions. Be polite to everyone you meet . . ."

I hadn't seen my dad this happy in years.

"Try to make new friends," he was saying, "because the friends you got are no good, no good at all."

I didn't answer, I just kept nodding and watching the trees roll by out the window. He looked over at me.

"Are you sure you can go dressed like this?"

"What? What's wrong with the way I'm dressed?"

I was wearing a black tank top with a shiny Pink Panther cartoon iron-on in the front, along with my first name in Old English-style lettering. Over that I had a black jacket, along with black Levi jeans and black Hush Puppy shoes. I had decided I was going to dress like I always did. I would take the job, but I wasn't going to **be somebody I wasn't,** I wouldn't do that for anybody.

My dad already had moved on to a new lecture. There was only a few blocks left before we reached the bunker-like police station on Greenville Street, and he had to make sure he **got everything in.** "Pay attention so they don't have to tell you things twice—you don't want them to think they hired a stupid girl, do you?" I just rolled my eyes and said nothing.

When I walked in, a cop at the desk directed me to personnel. As I walked up the stairs, I passed by Borja, who had given me the

....

be somebody I wasn't pretend to be a different person
got everything in told me everything he wanted to

jaywalking ticket a few hours earlier. **His eyes bugged out** when he saw me.

"What are you doing here?" he asked.

"I work here now," I said, holding up the card I was told to bring. "Today's my first day."

"Well, you should have told me you worked here," he said. "I would have **given you a break**." He laughed and walked away, and it occurred to me that he didn't look nearly as frightening when he was smiling.

I mostly filed police reports that first day. I think they didn't want me in a place where I could meet the public. The tasks were boring, but it was interesting hearing the cops talk and seeing the different reports that passed through.

If cops had to run a license plate or pull an old file or whatever, they had to come through our office. When there was a slow moment, I would thumb through the folders, which were fascinating. Some of the cops were friendly and made conversation; others were cold or even mean. They didn't like the way I looked and dressed, the way I talked. My reaction, of course, was to wear the mask and mad-dog them.

When my dad picked me up, he had nothing but questions about my first day. He had always wanted to be a cop, and I could tell that he had been watching the clock all day, waiting to hear what it was like inside the mysterious station. I told him about the people I had met, what the job was like, and what things looked like. I could tell

---

His eyes bugged out He looked shocked

given you a break let you go without a ticket

he was extremely excited.

I didn't mention the ticket.

After a few months, I was moved from Records up to Traffic. One of the things my father always pushed me to do was learn to type. My father had worked many jobs in his life, all with his hands or back, and he said everyone must have a skill that makes him different than the next person, something that he can use to get the job he wants or find work when **times are tight**. "You know how to read and write, but so do a lot of people," he said. "If you can type, that will make you the better job candidate." Typing was one of the few classes I enjoyed, which surprised me. In the tests, when a lot of the students were pecking away and searching for keys, I was going at 100 words a minute. My father's advice turned out to be a good tip. It was my typing skills that landed me a spot working in the Traffic Division, up on the second floor.

The hectic flow of work made the days pass faster, but I wondered if the new assignment was just a way to keep criminal case files out of my hands. In Traffic, I guessed, there was **less damage a gang spy could do**. The thought made me laugh every time it crossed my mind, but it also pleased me on some level that my presence was making people nervous. In the new job, I didn't have contact with nearly as many officers (almost all cops pass through the records department to check on old or open cases), so there was less opportunity for **friction**. I was assigned to the front desk, and there was plenty of work to do. Three women worked the area and,

....

times are tight he needs the money

less damage a gang spy could do not as much information about police cases that I could look at

friction problems, conflict

while they all had pleasant words when they met their new colleague, I could tell by their surprised looks and shared whispers that I was a little too outlandish for their tastes. Looking back, I can see that my devotion to the gang fashion and makeup really **shook people up**, but at the time all I saw was suspicion and resentment that I thought was aimed at me as a person.

As I worked side by side with the three women, I remembered my mother telling me that women can be far more cruel then men. For the first time, I really knew what she meant. One of the women, a slender, smiling woman nicknamed Puff, was genuine and sweet, but the other two always had sharp words and criticism for everyone. They would smile to someone's face and, as they walked away, **tear into** them with brutal insults. I suppose they thought saying these things in front of me would make me feel like part of their group, but I always wondered what they said about me when I left. Also, I sometimes felt like they were trying to make me feel foolish or unwelcome, and instead of helping me become a better employee, they found subtle ways to **set me up for failure**. I learned a lot about people and the workplace during those long afternoons, and the lessons were not always pleasant.

I was thankful that Puff was assigned to train me, and when she was away from the desk I would just work silently. The less I said the safer I was around the other two. Sometimes, I could tell, they wanted to pry into my life, but I **volunteered** nothing. I knew whatever I said would be twisted or taken the wrong way and spread throughout the station. My F-Troop friends and I had an expression

....

shook people up made people nervous
tear into make fun of
set me up for failure make me fail
volunteered told them

taken from an old World War II movie title: "Run Silent, Run Deep." That was my attitude around my coworkers.

The work itself was easy, although my coworkers complained so much you would think they were shoveling coal. All we had to do was file parking and moving violation tickets and type up courtesy notices for overdue citations. We also had to answer questions, either from people calling on the phone (which never seemed to stop ringing, from the moment we arrived in the morning until we shut off the lights on the way out) or lined up at the window. A lot of the people were rude and angry about their tickets, or confused, or just plain stupid. That part of the job was tiring. When I was working on the paperwork, though, my mind would wander, taking me on daydreams while my hands kept busy. I would think about the weekend, going to the backyard parties with my homegirls. Invariably, when my mind went on those adventures, I would be jolted back to the present by the stone-faced Sgt. Redwine, my new supervisor and an old-time cop who made no effort to hide his true feelings about me.

Things were looking up. **I got a chilly welcome from** a lot of people at the station, but I was making some money and my dad was suddenly willing to forgive **my past lapses.** He was hopeful that this job would change the downward direction he thought my life had been heading in. He and I also found some new common ground.

I had bought a car, a Chevy Malibu, at the end of the summer from Yogi's mom. It was in pretty rough shape, but I got it for just fifty dollars because Yogi's mom was buying a new one and just

....

I got a chilly welcome from I felt unwanted by
my past lapses the mistakes I had made in the past

wanted to get rid of the troublesome old car. My dad agreed to help me with the extensive repairs, and for most of my senior year, we toiled together in the garage, fixing up the car and our relationship.

I saw fatigue in his eyes on many of the days, when the back pain would get to him. He would never say anything, no complaints or requests to postpone the work, and I would always be the one to suggest we **call it a day**. We didn't talk a great deal, I suppose. My father is a man of few words, but the time together really strengthened some bridges between us. It was the first time we had spent a lot of time together since I was little. The friendship with him that defined my childhood was **being rejuvenated** there in the hot, dusty garage, while we worked to the sounds of Motown or that Western music I detested. We could agree on some Elvis and most Motown, but I couldn't stand that cowboy music. I would tease him about it and he would mimic an old-style hat dance and laugh, a sound I hadn't heard in years. I laughed, too, and thought about how quickly things can change for the better. I didn't know I was about to get a lesson that everything can go bad twice as fast.

---

call it a day stop working
being rejuvenated returning

BEFORE YOU MOVE ON...

1. **Evidence and Conclusions** Reread page 91. Give 2 examples that show Mona was conflicted about working at the police station.

2. **Problem and Solution** In what ways did Mona's relationship with her father improve?

LOOK AHEAD Read pages 99–122 to find out what slowed down Mona's progress.

~ Chapter Six ~

TWO WORLDS

It was a few weeks before graduation when I got called in to speak with a counselor. It was the same woman who had **lined me up for** the clerk job, the one who seemed to have very little time for me or people that looked like me. When I walked in, she was thumbing through a manila folder that had my name typed across its label. "You're **three credits** short of graduating," she said after I sat down. I waited for her to go on with the thought, or tell me this was a joke or a mistake. She started reading more out of the folder. "P.E. You're three credits down in physical education."

I could barely speak. My parents had ordered announcements, they had bragged to all the relatives. I had already bought a cap and gown; my mom had made me put them on and pose for pictures that she had sent out to family members who wouldn't be able to make it to the ceremony. To **come up short**, now, so late, it was a nightmare. "Why . . . why didn't you tell me before? I could have gone to summer school or **made it up**, or . . ."

....

lined me up for gotten me
three credits one class
come up short not be able to graduate
made it up earned the credits

"It's a little late for that, Ramona," she said. I hated when people used my full name; it made me feel like I was a three year old in trouble. "You should have taken care of this before now. There's nothing you can do now."

Red was flashing before my eyes and my head started to throb, the way it did right before fights. "But it's just P.E., I passed all the major subjects, isn't there a way to **get by** . . . ?"

She was shaking her head and looking at the clock over my shoulder. There were other students that needed to be hustled through. She was talking again, but I wasn't listening. I was thinking how much I wanted to punch her. How I wanted to grab her by the hair and punch her and slam her head into the desk until she passed out. She was everything I hated about the school. All rules and requirements with no feeling. They didn't care about us, the students; it was just a factory where everything had to keep moving. All they ever taught you was that you couldn't win. I got up and walked out.

The screaming seemed to last all night, even in my dreams when I finally fell into a fitful sleep. It felt like a punishment for being so **optimistic**, for being so pleased with myself and my work. Just when things were looking up, I got slapped down, just to remind me of who I was and where I belonged. My dad was **crestfallen**, shamed that his wife would have to call all the relatives and friends and tell them that his daughter—the one he had given his name—would not walk across the stage. My mother was furious and denied me the comfort of blaming **my misfortune on fate**.

....

get by make an exception
optimistic positive, hopeful
crestfallen very disappointed
my misfortune on fate the problem on bad luck

"Always you blame someone else for these things that happen to you. It's never your fault," she shouted, almost the same words I had heard her fling at Lydia and Roni. "Don't blame the school lady. Blame yourself and those damn friends!"

She was right. But I was certain that other seniors were **given notice when they foundered**. I imagined I was on a list of the junk-heap kids, the ones who were expected to fail, so no one sounded the alarms when the slide began. I thought: If that's the role I'm given, fine, then that's what I'll be.

My eighteenth birthday was weeks away, and I turned with a vengeance to the party scene. I wanted to wash away the expectations and the optimism and make myself so numb I wouldn't hear the other seniors plan their graduation festivities. I went to afternoon parties and, when there were none, started one. I relaxed, like a swimmer floating in calm water. At work I was a sleepwalker, constantly **hung over and sullen**. The day that would have been my last on campus, I drank a bottle of wine on my own and shoved my schoolbooks in a rear corner of my closet, down with the clothes I had outgrown.

I had learned my lesson.

I was done with education.

I was down on life and growing **bitter and cynical**. The days seemed to slip away from me in the months after my departure from Valley High. I was drinking a lot, too much, and became increasingly moody and distant as I traveled between the police station and the

....

given notice when they foundered warned if they did not have enough credits

hung over and sullen sad and sick from drinking too much

bitter and cynical angry and miserable

gang scene. I wasn't especially welcome in either place anymore.

Searching the files for old traffic tickets, I sometimes heard police officers muttering about me, wondering if I was a spy or making unkind comments about my background and appearance. Conversations would abruptly end when I walked in rooms. Some of the cops would make snide remarks about my friends and ask whether I was on a gang mission. Beneath the so-called jokes I could **sense a very real hostility**. I wasn't sure exactly how my presence could have been considered a threat, but I rarely offered logic or any other defense. Other officers took a more direct approach. In the hallways, they would **glower** at me or say threatening things about gangs so I could hear them, hoping, I guess, that I would get intimidated and quit. I didn't. In fact, while the comments **did sting**, after a while they were almost funny. I tried to ignore it. I tried to ignore a lot of things. At home, I was barely communicating with my parents. At work, I was an outsider with an attitude. I was so upset with my failures that I practically invited confrontations, but, somehow, I didn't cross the line that would cost me my job. In November, 1979, I even managed to land a full-time job at the station.

The new position meant wearing a uniform to work. The civilian support staff wore clothes that resembled a security guard's outfit, with light blue shirts with patches and dark blue pants. I went down to a uniform specialty store on Main Street, near the Bowers Museum. There, a kind, older man with a tape measure hanging around his neck used small pieces of chalk to mark the alterations on my new uniform. The sight of myself in a uniform in the mirror

....

sense a very real hostility tell that they really did not want me there

glower stare angrily

did sting hurt me

was **oddly unsettling**, but exciting, too. It wasn't a police officer's uniform, of course, but it still **had an official air to it**. My father was **ecstatic when I donned** the clothes for the first time. It made no difference to him what the job title was, I worked at the police station and I wore a uniform. He could almost forget the graduation disappointment when he saw me off to work in my starched, stiff new clothes.

While my father was pleased, the new post and uniform made things rocky between me and my fellow gang members. More and more often, I heard the whispers questioning my loyalty to the gang—**an odd reversal of** the rumors that swirled around me at work. A new Trooper generation was coming to the forefront of the always changing gang, and the newer Troopers were more rabid in their hatred of cops. Drugs and guns had raised the stakes in Santa Ana, and the community was up in arms over the drive-by shootings, so the police had responded with large arrest sweeps and the hiring of more officers. The increased pressure angered the gang-bangers, and my job made me a convenient target for their frustrations.

"Nah, she ain't invited." The banger in the wraparound sunglasses didn't look at me, he just put his arm across the doorway to block my entrance to the keg party. My three friends had already passed, though, but he said he didn't want "no cops in the crib."

Smiley tried to argue, but I waved her off. "I don't need this," I told her. "It looks like this is a party for little boys anyway."

I had grown tired of explaining myself to cops and bangers alike, so instead I started closing myself off more, returning insults with

....

oddly unsettling strangely uncomfortable
had an official air to it felt official
ecstatic when I donned thrilled when I put on
an odd reversal of very different from

insults. In both places, my reaction made matters worse. I didn't care. The novelty of both my worlds was long gone and my strength was **at an ebb.** Everywhere I looked, I saw hypocrisy and distrust. The world felt beyond my control, so I saw no reason to fight back. My supervisor, Redwine, added to my woes. He had been hostile to me from the start, in my opinion, but then **the bad blood really set in** after a cop reported seeing me out one night with some **"questionable persons."**

On **the night in question,** I was playing bus driver for a whole crew of friends. We were headed to a party on Seventh and Holly when I saw the spinning bright lights behind me. The El Camino was loaded down, maybe eight of us piled in. The cop walked slowly to my door, pausing to check out everybody in the back, searching out each face with his bright flashlight. I winced when the bright light hit my eyes as he leaned down and asked for my ID.

"Where you going?"

I handed over my license and registration. "A party."

"Uh-huh. You guys start the party early? Is there any alcohol in the car?"

With that question, the flashlight left the driver's license and hit my face again, waiting for my answer.

"No."

"Uh-huh. Anything else I should know about in there? Any drugs tonight?"

The cop shined his flashlight toward the back seat, where whispers and giggles greeted his questions.

....

at an ebb weakening
the bad blood really set in our problems got worse
"questionable persons" troublemakers; gang members
the night in question that night

"No. Nothing like that." I was nervous. I didn't know what anybody had in their pockets. There were two guys in the car, friends of friends, whom I barely knew. I hoped they **wouldn't make a liar out of me**. I also hoped the cop wouldn't recognize me. But it was like he **read my mind**.

"Don't I know you from somewhere, missy?"

"No, I don't think so." I hated when cops called me "missy." That was such a cop thing to say.

He was studying my license again, trying to place the name. It was the face he recognized, though, and then it hit him. "Where do you work?"

There was no sense in lying, so I told him. I heard some groans from the back seat. Were they frustrated with the cop's question or my answer? I was getting mad, but I wasn't sure why. I didn't like when **my two worlds spilled into each other**.

"Did I do something wrong? I don't think I was speeding." I asked the question through gritted teeth.

"This is an interesting crowd you're running with here. You guys in a gang?"

Red flashed in front of my eyes. I was feeling trapped and embarrassed, the same way I felt with my parents. I hated it. "Why? Just because we're a bunch of Mexicans? Is every Mexican in a gang?"

I could sense the cop's temper flare up. They hated to be challenged or questioned in any way. They hated to take the same stuff they dished out.

....

wouldn't make a liar out of me did not have drugs

read my mind knew what I was thinking

my two worlds spilled into each other my gang life and my job at the Police Department connected or mixed

"Now listen . . ." Before he could continue, his police radio squawked with a dispatcher rattling off a bunch of codes and addresses. I couldn't tell what she was talking about, but it was clear the cop no longer had time for us. He leaned in close, trying to catch my eye, but I was watching the reflection of his blue flashing lights in my windshield.

"Listen, I could be a real asshole about this," the cop said. "I could march you guys out of this car and rip it apart. I could run a warrant check on everybody you got in the back, and I bet at least one of them would go to jail tonight. Who knows, someone might have some weed, too. But instead, I'm going to let you go."

He paused, waiting for a thank you, I guess. My eyes were still locked on the blue lights. The flashes were almost hypnotic.

He handed me back my paperwork and his radio squawked again. He was pissed, but he had to go. "Okay, then, maybe I'll stop by and see your supervisor, too. Now you all have a nice evening."

When Redwine **got wind of** what happened, he summoned me to his office. He spoke with a cop's street voice, loud and gruff and condescending. It's the voice you would use to command a half-deaf and dumb dog.

The door closed behind me and he pointed at the chair in front of his desk. He paused a long moment, sitting with his fingers locked in front of him, like he was waiting for me to say something. I just locked eyes and **played the staring game**.

"Sandoval, would you please tell me why our officers are

....

got wind of heard about
played the staring game stared back at him

106

reporting to me that you, a police department employee, have been seen with . . . well, let's call them questionable people?"

"Who said that?"

"Several officers. I can have them come in here if you don't believe me. Do you think I'm lying?"

"I didn't say that."

"You haven't said much of anything."

I stared harder, like I could stare him right back off his seat and through the wall. He didn't flinch. He had been a cop too long to get put off by some mad-dogging. He lectured on for awhile and asked me questions, but I was like a wall, giving nothing back at all. Finally, he leaned back in his chair and **his demeanor seemed to soften**.

"Listen, if you have hopes of being successful, either here or anywhere, you better change your friends, I can tell you that," he said.

I didn't flinch or even breathe.

"Do you understand that? If you want to stay in this department, you have to make some decisions about your life."

It was the same worn-out lecture he gave me once a week. Usually I said nothing, just mumbled or shrugged. This time, though, I had an answer for him. "I have family members in gangs. I can't do nothing about that. Look where I live. What should I do, huh?"

He seemed startled by the reply, like he had forgotten I could talk. He **shot back**, "Then get out of there. If you want to do something with your life, then you're going to have to stay away from them."

....

his demeanor seemed to soften he seemed kinder
shot back replied

"From my family? Stay away from my family?"

"If you want to **make anything of your life**, yes," he said. "You have a questionable background, your family is questionable, your friends are questionable. No one will take you seriously until you distance yourself and create a life away from all that."

I waited for the anger to come up inside, but it didn't. It was like I was seeing around a corner for the first time, seeing the future. He was right. No matter how harsh, he was right. I had never thought about it before in that way, but to get to a different sort of future, I really would have to trade in my present and close off my past, just flat out deny it. But was anything worth that? Did I even want to change?

❖ ❖ ❖

Later, when I was alone and Redwine's words still bounced around in my head, I started to grow angry at him and myself. To deny who you are is wrong, I shouted inside my head. I was **a sellout** to even think for a moment that Redwine might be right. Everything was confusing me.

One thing that was clear to me was that Redwine and the other cops **had a double standard about judging people**. The cops were cold and unfair, willing to dismiss you because of the way you dressed or the neighborhood you were from, or even the color of your skin. But what about them and their own associates? If I were to be judged by the actions of people who look like me, why shouldn't cops be judged by the worst among their own ranks?

To grow up in the barrio is to grow up seeing cops as an

---

make anything of your life be successful and happy

a sellout betraying my family and gang

had a double standard about judging people treated people like me unfairly

occupying army. Once, when I was still in school, I had been at a Friday night party where the music was still pumping loud after midnight. The cops came and started to hustle people away, and some of the kids grumbled and were slow to leave. I remember a tall, broad cop grabbing some kid by the throat and slamming him into a chainlink fence. He started screaming at the kid, calling him a "filthy wetback" and telling him to "go back to Mexico." The kid, of course, was a local who had spent his whole life in Santa Ana.

My homegirl and I ran over and told the cop to let him go. We shouted, "You can't do that to him!"

"I can do anything I want," he said. "Now get the hell out of here."

My homegirl shouted that we would **report him**. I still remember the evil look in the cop's eye when he turned away from the frightened kid, told us his badge number, and invited us to report him. "Like anybody cares what you say," he snapped before tossing the kid to the ground.

Growing up in a gang gives you an interesting view of police and, at times, a bizarre relationship with cops. In the gangs, you learn to almost smell the newness on a rookie cop. They walk stiffly, like there might be land mines beneath the sidewalk. Their uniforms are a little too clean and pressed, their hair cut a little too short. And a rookie's badge shines like a brand new nickel. The *vatos* on the street could see the rookies coming a mile away, and they took great glee in hazing the new cops, playing mind games with them and leading them on confusing chases through the city's back alleys. Once, they got a new cop to leave his keys in the ignition and then snuck up and

....

report him tell another police officer what he did

locked his car door behind him, forcing the red-faced officer to call for backup on a pay phone while his patrol car idled nearby.

There were other stories about cops on the streets, and not all of them were funny. Sleepy and I often talked about the cops and their actions. She was one of the few people whom I trusted enough to tell about my dreams to become a cop, and she took me seriously. But she also **held me accountable for the perception of** police officers.

"So if you become a cop," she asked me one day, "does that mean you can do whatever you want, like old Long Sleeves?"

I had heard talk about some cop called "Long Sleeves" by the *vatos*, but I didn't know if he was fact or fiction. I never heard his real name, but the story was hard to avoid in the barrio's tight network of gossip. And to this day I believe it was merely gossip. The story went like this: There was a cop who, even on the hottest summer day, would never switch to the short-sleeved uniform. He needed those long blue sleeves to cover the track marks that dotted the insides of his arms, the trail of pockmarks that kept a diary of his heroin habit. On the street, the junkie cop's secret was well kept by the handful of dealers who traded **product for protection**, but the rumors still spread. Was it a myth? I don't know, but it didn't really matter. We always heard about cops who did the wrong thing, cops who did stuff as bad as any banger. The cops who took **bribes, either cash or dope**. And the cops who would beat people up, reserving their most brutal attacks for faceless, voiceless persons who wander Santa Ana's streets. The cops who stole, slipping money into their pockets the way a waitress tucks away a tip after clearing a countertop. The

....

held me accountable for the perception of wanted to know if I would act like other

product for protection drugs for police protection

bribes, either cash or dope money or drugs and then promised to give police protection

cops who drank for courage or numbness, or just because they liked to drink.

Looking back, it was clear that all these varieties of bad cops were **in the minority** at the PD, really just a handful among hundreds, but to my young eyes, every offense was proof that the cops were just like the gang members, so full of themselves that they think they're above the law. They pretended to be above everyone else, their sins somehow excused by their badge and gun. It made me sick. It also convinced me that my father was wrong: There was no true good or evil, just a **blurry, corrupted** version of both.

I knew when Sleepy asked me about Long Sleeves, she was really asking about all the bad cops. I tried to explain how confused I was about everything in my life and what role I wanted to play.

"I know if I became a cop, I'd be the kind of cop who does the right thing, someone who looks out for the barrio."

Sleepy was skeptical. Were there such cops? Her view was that cops didn't want to help you out of trouble if you were in the barrio; they wanted to keep you out of sight, down and poor, away from their world. I told Sleepy if that were true, then I wouldn't ever wear a badge.

The tall stack of folders threatened to spill out of my grip, but I managed to keep hold by leaning back a little as I dodged cops walking through the narrow, bustling hallways of the PD. The department headquarters was extremely overcrowded, **a testament to** Santa Ana's huge growth. The PD's ranks had doubled in size in a

....

in the minority just a few people
blurry, corrupted confusing
a testament to proof of

decade to try to keep pace.

I found the office number I was looking for and, instead of knocking and risking **my precarious stack**, I pushed my way in. A plain-clothes cop inside, an older man with short-cropped hair and big, black boots, looked up from his desk. His eyes ran over me, from the thick mascara down to the V-neck shirt and jeans. His expression made clear he didn't like what he saw.

"What the hell . . . Can I help you?"

He was up and coming toward me and, when I mumbled, he yelled that he couldn't hear me. He was a big man, and he talked funny like some people on TV, people from the South.

"I work here," I finally managed to say.

"You work here? Huh."

He took the files and slung them on a desk. I didn't know him, but I hated him. He was the kind of cop who thought people like me were **dirt**. My memory flashed on the cop who had shoved me when I was in school, the one who told me to "go back where I came from." So arrogant, so judgmental and so wrong. I was in the city where I grew up. They were the outsiders.

My work in Traffic took me back to that office many times in the following weeks, and I found out that the broad-shouldered veteran cop was named Billy Brown, a gruff former Marine. He shared the office with his partner and friend, a handsome, tall cop named Felix Osuna. The pair were traffic investigators—I wasn't sure exactly what that was—and on a small, scratchy radio in their office they also had twangy, old-fashioned country music playing, the type of music

....

my precarious stack dropping all of the files
dirt terrible and useless

my father listened to in his workshop. After our first meeting, I tried to lock my face into a glowering mask when I saw Brown. I knew how he felt about me, and I wanted to make it clear how I felt about him.

But it didn't work out as I expected.

When the civilian officer introduced me as a new assistant to Brown and Osuna, I could tell it didn't **sit well with** either of them. Osuna gave a short but polite welcome, while Brown just nodded and buried his nose into his paperwork. I tried to mad-dog Brown, but as the days passed, my attitude softened. They weren't as bad as I thought. Brown wasn't the hateful ogre, just a loud old-timer who **was more bark than bite**. And the young Osuna, whose name and skin tone seemed vaguely Hispanic to me, had a serene, confident air about him and, I found, an open mind. I soon learned to enjoy talking to both of them.

"Why do they always sing about trains and drinking?"

"What?!" Billy looked up from his papers with his mock bulldog expression. He tried to sound mean. "What the hell did you say?"

I pointed at the transistor radio on his desk, but I kept my eyes locked on the paperwork in front of me. "I said, 'Why do they always sing about trains and drinking?' It's either that or some dog that ran away . . ."

Osuna was trying not to laugh as Billy leaned back in his swivel chair, which gave a groan under his weight. He crushed out his cigarette and pushed the ashtray away. His pointy boots landed with a thud on his desk and he locked his fingers behind his head.

"Country music is the best goddamn music in the world, missy,

....

sit well with please

was more bark than bite acted meaner than he really was

113

and nobody who listens to that jump-jimmy-jump crap you call music should be saying otherwise," he barked.

"Okay. I was just like wondering, y'know, that's all. I mean . . . I like trains, I guess."

Billy could barely hide his own grin as he turned back to his work. "She's never heard of Johnny Cash or Roy Acuff, and she thinks she's a goddamn music critic."

"I've heard of Johnny Cash. My dad listens to that."

"Well then, missy, you got yourself a pretty smart dad."

The pair took turns making fun of me and the way I dressed. It didn't bother me, though, because as the months wore on I could tell the two genuinely liked me, actually cared about me. Insults and **bluster** were the way Billy expressed himself, the language he was most comfortable with after three decades in police stations and military barracks. I couldn't even tell if he believed some of the things he said about women and the barrios, but it was just his way of speaking. He meant no harm. Just the opposite: His **good-natured barbs were** a sign of affection. Osuna was less **ornery**, more at ease with his emotions, but he played along with his mentor and partner, following the big Southerner's fashion and providing him with **a straight man for** his long, loud stories. For the first time, I felt there was someone at the PD who actually knew me as a person, and after so many dark months my outlook was starting to brighten up a bit. Still, the banter in the cramped office did occasionally give way to more serious talks, conversations unlike any I had ever had with an adult, let alone a cop or somebody outside my barrio.

....

bluster loud, bullying talk

good-natured barbs were friendly teasing was

ornery grouchy

a straight man for someone to listen to

During lulls in the work, the three of us gradually shared **our backgrounds and glimpses of** our personal lives. Billy, I learned, was from Florida. I had always thought of that state being a string of beaches and places like Miami, but Billy said he had grown up in part of the state that was like the South, where people chew tobacco, drive pickup trucks and wear boots. It didn't sound like a place I wanted to go to, but I kept that to myself. Osuna, on the other hand, was a Californian, of mixed Latino and Native American heritage. He was only in his fourth year at the Santa Ana PD and had already made investigator. Before coming to the city, he was a street cop in Bell Gardens, where he had seen up close the death and pain caused by the intense gang scene of East Los Angeles. When he talked about those days, he watched me closely. I could tell he wanted me to **take a lesson from his accounts**, and it made me uncomfortable. They both wanted to know about my world and warn me of its risks. But I knew the risks, and for a while I resisted their efforts to pull details of my life out of me. Eventually, I told them things I never dreamed I would share with a cop, or anyone else, for that matter.

"Mona, you have to get out of that life." Osuna was leaning against his desk.

I had just told him and Billy about a friend of mine who was in the hospital and how the streets were buzzing with talks of a payback for the gang rivals who put him there.

"It's a matter of time until you **take a fall**. Every night you put yourself in the wrong place at the wrong time. Eventually, it'll **catch up to you**."

....

our backgrounds and glimpses of information about
take a lesson from his accounts learn from his stories
take a fall get hurt or killed
catch up to you affect you

The words made sense, but the warnings weren't new. I had heard it all before. So why did it sound different this time, more reasonable? Maybe because someone was **talking to me, not at me**. It was different, but I wasn't sure that it mattered.

"Listen to me, you're too smart for that life," Osuna said more than once. "I know those homeboys, I've seen their dead eyes— there's nothing there, no intelligence, no remorse. You got, I don't know, a spark or something, something they don't have. You deserve better."

Brown echoed the same message, but it was always accompanied by some long story, laced with profanities and exaggerations. Always, he wandered back to the same point: "You can't run with them bangers out there, Mona," he would say darkly. "You're too smart, too good. You're gonna end up dead or in jail or, Christ, pregnant or whatever. It's no good. Goddamn, what do you see in them anyway?"

There was a sadness in Brown's voice. I wondered if it was from the things he had seen on the streets as a cop or something else. The gruff jokes and the swear words were **a front**, a way to keep his distance. I wondered where his pain came from, but I never asked.

It became a mission of sorts for the pair to prove to me that there were ways to change my direction in life. They often corrected my grammar and tried to get me to shake the low mumble I spoke in. "People meet you and the way you speak and express yourself tells them who you are," Osuna nagged. "Speak up louder and use real words, not that street talk."

"Sheeeeit . . . Okay, *ese*, I'll try, homes." I barely got the sentence

....

talking to me, not at me discussing it with me, not just yelling at me

a front covering up his true feelings

out without laughing. Osuna wagged his finger at me and tried not to laugh himself.

Some days, though, the mood **grew heavy** in the tiny second-floor office. I had a tall stack of work waiting for me one morning and I was dreading it. I had gone out the night before, a Thursday night, and drank too much. My head was pounding with a hangover. When Billy Brown walked in with a sour expression, my day got worse.

"Say there, Mona, I was just downstairs talking to the patrol guys who were on the night shift last night. One of them asked me why he saw an employee of this office at a party where four arrests were made. What do you **make of that**?"

He was trying to play it cool and casual, reading his mail the whole time he was talking, without even looking up. I hated games. My head hurt. I only knew one of the four guys who were arrested. They had all been fighting and either had warrants out or were caught carrying dope when the cops broke up the brawl.

"Now I know it wasn't me," Brown went on, "cause I was home watching a damn John Wayne movie last night. I don't think it was Felix either . . . now who else could it have been at a banger party?"

I shrugged. "There's no law against parties." It was a weak answer, and one that invited more lecturing. I really wanted it to be lunchtime.

"There're laws against carrying guns and snorting coke, though, and that's what those people they busted were doing at that nice little legal party of yours."

"I can't help what other people do."

....

grew heavy became serious
make of that think about that

"You doing drugs, Mona? You're not looking so good these days."

My head yanked up in anger, a move I immediately regretted. "No! You know I don't do drugs."

"Yeah, well, people **assume the worst** when they see you hanging around with scumbag dope-dealers and bangers, y'know, Mona?" His voice was strained. I think he felt bad about accusing me, but it was too late for him to back down. I got up and ran out as he called after me.

"Wait, I didn't mean . . . come back, Mona."

Osuna came looking for me later. "Hey, I heard what happened. Billy wants to apologize. He didn't mean to hurt your feelings. He just **gets in people's faces**, y'know? And he's worried about you. He's sorry. Come on back and he'll tell you himself. He's just worried about those friends of yours . . ."

My jaw tightened and I searched the walls with my eyes. I really liked Osuna—no one at the PD had ever been nicer—but what the hell did he know about my friends?

Osuna sensed he was losing me. "Look, I'm not trying to badmouth them, but . . . listen, Billy and I both know a lot of cops who believe that there's a bullet out there **with their name on it**, okay? And they say that if they stay on the force too long, someday, that bullet is going to find them. It's like that with the gangs, too. You've been lucky so far, but you never know when the bullet will find you. The longer you run the street . . ."

His voice trailed off. I stood with my arms folded, blocking him and his message out. My headache was getting worse. "Okay," he

---

assume the worst think you are doing bad things

gets in people's faces likes people to know what he is thinking

with their name on it waiting for them

sighed. "Go ahead. Get going. We'll see you tomorrow."

A week later, the cross words were forgotten and the office returned to its usual banter. After lunch, Osuna walked in beaming and handed me a piece of paper. I thought it was something to be filed, notes from one of the scores of hit-and-runs he and Brown investigated each month in a city overflowing with unlicensed and uninsured drivers.

"No, it's for you. I made some calls. We're going to get you a high school degree."

I had never heard of the GED, but Osuna explained the process to me. Take a test, get a degree, that simple, he said. I wasn't so sure. School tests made me nervous, they always had, and I was worried that he and Brown would think I was stupid if I couldn't **make the grade**. I tried to **backpedal**, get out of the whole thing, but Osuna would have none of it. He had already signed me up and even brought some study materials. He even drew me a map to the site of the test, Bolsa High in nearby Garden Grove.

I felt a nervous knot in my gut, but there was no way of backing out.

I got to the school early the next Saturday. About fifteen people were there to take the exam, and the man who was giving instructions told us that if we waited afterward, we could find out **on-the-spot** whether we passed. He said the test would cover basic skills and include math, English, science and history. My palms were sweating, I was so nervous. Two and a half hours later, I turned in the test. I thought I did well, but I wasn't sure. I knew sometimes the

....

make the grade pass the test
backpedal convince Osuna I could not do it
on-the-spot right away

wrong answers sound right on multiple-choice tests.

The man who graded my test smiled at me and handed over a yellow sheet of paper. "You passed. Congratulations, Ms. Sandoval."

I was **bursting with pride**.

"This is from the school? Did they make a mistake before?"

"No, this is different, Mom. I took a test . . . but it **counts like** a high school diploma."

I wanted to take the paper away from her. She was bending the sides back, the way you would read a newspaper. She had no idea how much that piece of paper meant to me.

"Well, this is good," she said in an uninspired voice. "But you should have gotten the real one last year."

I should have known better. She could still taste the humiliation she swallowed when I left Valley High, and no sheet of paper was going to change that.

"Yeah, whatever. Thanks a lot, Mom."

"Don't speak to me with a voice like that . . ."

I was off to my room. No matter what she thought, Osuna and Brown will know what this really means. I couldn't wait to show my two friends. If I thought at all about using that word, how remarkably strange and unlikely it was that I would use it to describe my bosses, it wasn't for long. I was too excited.

One afternoon, not long after, Osuna and Brown rose and grabbed their jackets. Brown looked at me and asked me about my lunch plans.

....

bursting with pride so excited and proud of myself

counts like is the same as

"Huh?"

"Lunch, you know, when people eat every day. It comes between breakfast and dinner . . ."

"What Billy is asking, Mona, is would you like to join us for lunch? Our treat. **In honor of** your degree."

"Yeah, you're a homegirl and **a scholar** now, so you can have lunch with us."

The two couldn't have known what that day meant to me. Walking with them through the hallways, down for the first time into the cavernous police garage and then out onto Ross Street. Sitting in the hulking white car's rear seat, I listened to the police radio squawk and watched the streets pass by like I had never seen the neighborhood before that moment. I soaked in the moment and giggled with delight, covering my mouth to stay quiet as we turned up Broadway and drove past the Spanish signs that marked the downtown shopping district.

Billy turned in his seat, looping his fingers in the **security grill** that separated the suspects from the cops up front. "Hey, you'll like this place we're going. But, uh, we don't want to be embarrassed. Y'all from the barrio do know how to use a fork, right?"

I didn't miss a beat. "Yeah. We're good with knives, too." We all roared with laughter. I felt at ease with them and with myself. It was a really good feeling.

I felt energized by the new twists my life had taken. Putting my high school failure behind me and **erasing the label of** "dropout" made me look at my future with a new optimism. At work, I started

---

In honor of To celebrate
a scholar an educated person
security grill material, chains
erasing the label of no longer being a

asking more questions and paying closer attention to the answers. A year in the PD had taught me a lot about the **tide of paperwork that records** every reported crime and arrest, but for the first time I was taking a step back to better understand the process. Osuna was a patient teacher, which helped greatly, but the real difference was my attitude. I wasn't smarter than before, obviously, just more confident and, for the first time, genuinely interested.

I wanted to celebrate my triumph.

I had been so focused on work and studying, I hadn't seen many of my friends for a month. They were going to a "Dress to Kill" party a few weeks after my GED test, and I told them **to count me in**. I couldn't know it then, but it would become a night that would forever change my life.

---

tide of paperwork that records amount of paperwork that must be filled out after

to count me in I would go

BEFORE YOU MOVE ON...

1. **Cause and Effect** Reread pages 101–102. Mona found out she would not graduate. How did this news affect her?

2. **Comparisons** Reread pages 115–119. How were Brown and Osuna different from other people in Mona's life?

LOOK AHEAD Read pages 123–139 to see who Mona met that changed her life forever.

~ Chapter Seven ~

RUNNING AWAY WITH ME

It was Saturday night and Smiley called to see if I was still going to the house party, Negra was sick, so Smiley needed a ride. I told her to come over and we would go in my car. I was in the party mood. The party was pulsing with music and laughter when we arrived at the door. The house was on Van Ness and Parton, but you could hear it from a few blocks away, and the line to get in stretched through the yard. We paid **the cover charge** and squeezed past a group of drunk *vatos* to the living room. Everybody was shoulder to shoulder; the place was packed. The heavy smell of weed and cigarettes filled the house. I had on a long tan skirt, a matching summer blouse and heels that were high for me. During the slow dances, you could hear the DJ, but when the fast dances were on, the funk music was too loud to hear anything. A lamp with a crooked shade threw fractured shadows everywhere. Styrofoam cups, some still half full of beer, were everywhere. I was splitting a bottle of Boone's Farm wine with Tiny, but my spirits were so high, I felt tipsy before I had a sip.

....

the cover charge money to get into the party

The living room had been cleared to make room for the dancing. As usual, all the boys were on one wall and the girls were clumped near the opposite wall, **scanning the prospects**. I always liked the "Dress to Kill" parties. Everyone took the time to look their best, and it gave us a chance to dress up. The only part I didn't like was the heat. The close quarters and summer temperatures had prompted many of the *vatos* to take off their jackets. I watched one homeboy, a dark-skinned guy with angular features, carefully fold his Pendleton shirt over his arm. He was sure to **delicately observe the crease** from pocket to bottom hem before draping it over his forearm. I had to chuckle at his neatness, and then again when he walked up to Tiny and some other girls and asked one of them to dance. I wasn't close enough to hear what they said, but the body language was clear: The girl had said no, flat out. The *vato* bowed his head and took a sidestep to the right, then asked Tiny if she would dance. Again, the answer was no. The homeboy was cool about the whole thing, keeping a pained smile on his face, but I felt bad for him as he made the long walk back across the room to his hooting buddies.

I walked over and talked to Tiny. "Damn, that was cold. That guy just wanted to dance, and you just **blew him off**?"

Tiny's eyes were on a tall homeboy across the room, a guy bulging with muscles. "Smiley and I have a bet on who will get the first dance with that other guy over there. That's the only reason."

I still felt bad for the disappointed *vato*. I didn't know his name, but he was really cute, and I thought it was cold to make him feel dumb in front of his homeboys. A little later he walked toward me

....

scanning the prospects looking for people they wanted to dance with

delicately observe the crease fold the shirt very carefully

blew him off told him no

and I made eye contact with him. We were each sending the signals people use to **encourage a connection**. It's funny how people do that. His eyes were asking if he could approach and my eyes were inviting him. He was even cuter up close.

"Would you like to dance?"

"Sure," I answered. It was a slow song, and he was a good dancer. He smiled at me. I had liked him at first because he was a sad puppy being teased. Now, with his arms around me, I wondered what it would be like to kiss him.

"My name's Frank."

"I'm Mona."

"What's your last name?"

"Sandoval."

After the dance, he asked me if I wanted to step outside, and I said yes. The night air felt great after sweating inside, and the breeze on the back of my neck sent a chill through me. Frank took my hand and led me out the door.

We talked for a while about the party and the neighborhood, about school and even cars. He was good with words, which surprised me. Most of the homeboys are sullen or awkward with words. They just talk with cuss words and dirty looks. Others try to **talk with their hands, until you set them straight**. It was rare to find a *vato* that wouldn't spend the whole night groping you or talking about his reputation and who he knew. I guess that's what they thought the *hinas* liked.

There was no silence in Frank, I could tell right away. He was a

---

encourage a connection let someone know you would like to talk

talk with their hands, until you set them straight kiss and touch, until you stop them

hinas girls (in Spanish)

talker and someone, I guessed, who liked to lead and be the center of attention.

His voice was low and rumbled out in the *vato* mutter, almost sing-song but with the heavy he-man rasp. While he expressed himself well, every sentence seemed to begin with a cuss word and end in "homes" or "*ese*" or "man," but I didn't notice any of that then. His voice was the rhythm of my neighborhood and generation, the **dialect of youth and the streets**. I found myself looking too long at his smile. His skin was dark tan, which made his almond eyes twinkle.

Frank pounded down half a beer in one gulp and said that he was one of the Ruiz brothers. He waited a moment and then asked if I had heard of him before. I almost laughed at his ego, but I held it in. "No, I haven't," I told him.

He seemed really disappointed. He went on to name his brothers and all their exploits, their barrio and gang. Some of the names started to sound vaguely familiar. "Yeah, I think some of your brothers kick back with my cousins."

"Who's that?"

"The Elizaldes. Jesse and Eddie and the rest."

He recognized the name right away, I could tell by his face. "Huh. Yeah, they know me. Surprised you don't. Are you sure you never heard my name?"

This time I laughed. We talked some more about our families, and he made me giggle with his jokes. Frank and I leaned against one of the parked cars in the yard and stared at the sky. Then, out

....

dialect of youth and the streets language of kids and gangs

of nowhere, he said, "I should tell you, I'm a daddy. I got a baby girl, born last month, y'know?"

I pulled away and folded my arms. I should have known things were going too good. "What about the mother? You guys still together? I don't want no problems . . ."

"Nah, we **broke up**. We broke up a long time ago. Really. I still, y'know, care about the kid and all."

He leaned over and pulled me back toward him. "I just wanted to tell you. Really. Just give me a chance."

"Yeah, okay. I just don't want to be caught in the middle. I don't want to be used," I said. In my head, I was telling myself to ditch the whole thing, walk away while it was easy. Ex-girlfriends with kids were the worst kind of trouble, a lot more trouble than any guy was worth. Still, most guys wouldn't be so **up-front** about it. And I really liked him, he seemed different than the other guys. Maybe he was worth some trouble. We talked some more and kissed a few times. I wondered if he could smell my perfume. I wondered if he thought I was pretty.

The front yard was full of kids, including one *vato* passed out in the grass, spread-eagle and soaked in beer. His buddies sat around him, bellowing at some joke or maybe the sad sight of their drunk friend. Frank and I chuckled but we were getting bored with the scene.

"Do you have a car?"

"Yeah, over there . . . the El Camino."

"Nice car. C'mon, let's go cruising."

---

broke up ended our relationship
up-front honest

I told him I had a homegirl with me so I couldn't leave. He said we could take a cruise and be back before the party broke up so I could give my friend a ride home, so I agreed. Frank asked if he could drive and I handed him the keys. I got in the passenger side and he smiled at me. "I won't bite," he said, tugging at me. I grinned and slid across the big seat to be as close as I could. We turned up the radio and drove through the city, talking about our favorite songs and our friends.

He asked where I lived and I told him Golden West.

"Golden West? I met some of your homeboys. They like to party and get high a lot. Man, they get some good stuff, y'know?"

Golden West had the reputation of getting the best PCP on the streets, and it helped them keep **a neutral stance** with the other local gangs. The rumor was that the 18th Street gang in Los Angeles was **funneling the whack down** to Golden West, but I didn't know if it was true. I didn't much care, either.

Frank was still talking about the Golden West *vatos*. "Me and my homies hit them up once and they didn't say anything. They're just a bunch of punks."

"I just live there, I don't claim Golden West. I don't get high, either. I hang out with the homies from the park. But, y'know, don't talk badly about Golden West in front of me or my sister, okay? She kicks with them, and so if you got something to say, say it to those guys face to face."

I think he was surprised by the strength of my words. A lot of girls talked tough to one another, but not to the *vatos*. I always said

....

a neutral stance peace
funneling the whack down selling drugs

what I thought no matter who was listening.

Frank told me about his homeboys, how close they were, how they were going to make a name for their barrio. He had been jumped into Southside Varrio Artesia, a branch of F-Troop. Their turf was a handful of blocks, south of Edinger and Greenville and down to Fairview and Warner, a good two miles from the Trooper hub. F-Troop's stronghold was considered Salvador Park, which was near Santa Ana High School and the city's busy Civic Center Plaza. When I told people I kicked back with the "girls in the park," everyone knew that meant I was a Trooper Girl.

F-Troop was so big by then, spread throughout the city, that a lot of the newer homeboys felt **lost in its ranks.** They wanted something of their own, something where they could be a star within their own set. By the late 1970s, a lot of **splinter** gangs were forming. Frank **fit into that mold.**

"Nobody seen a barrio like ours . . . y'know? We are tight, *ese,* tight."

We parked in a dim parking lot at Centennial Park, over on Fairview and Edinger. The trees bustled as the wind blew through them. The night had gotten pretty chilly. Frank's arms around me felt nice. We kissed for a while and I felt like I was floating.

We talked some more and he spoke dreamily about the future, all his big plans for making money and building a life. He was learning to weld, he said, and there was good money in it. It was rare to hear a homeboy talk about the future, especially one that didn't involve crime or kicking back. I grew so tired of hearing them talk

....

lost in its ranks like they were not a part of things

splinter separate

fit into that mold was one of the people who wanted to be known and joined a separate gang

about fighting for the barrio and getting high. Frank was different. I couldn't take my eyes off him as he spoke.

It was getting late, close to 2 A.M., and I told him I should head back to the party to find my friends. The streets were empty and I watched the houses we drove by, wondering about the lives that went on inside them. Santa Ana seems so peaceful without the sunshine, so quiet and at ease with itself. On the way, he asked for my phone number, and I told him. He wrote it down on the white side of the foil wrapper in his pack of cigarettes. We both laughed when I asked him how many other girls' phone numbers he had jotted down on scraps at home. I suddenly remembered Frank's words about his baby and ex-girlfriend and my smile vanished. What was I getting into?

I got back to the party, and saw Tiny with the *vato* she had been eyeing earlier. I leaned out of the car and called her over. She said Smiley left early with some other homegirls and a guy from the Classics Car Club. Tiny was excited herself about **hooking up with** the homeboy she had been **stalking** all night. She ran off into the night and said she'd call me the next day. I was happy my homegirls had met some cute homeboys, and it thrilled me to think that we had each found somebody on the same night. Maybe it was magic. I slid back over next to Frank and laughed and smiled the whole way to his darkened house. We shared a long, passionate kiss and said good night. My earlier worries were no longer on my mind. As I watched him go through the front door, I told myself I had met the man of my dreams.

Smiley came over the next day with a huge hickey on her neck.

....

hooking up with meeting
stalking following

She grabbed me by the arm and yanked me toward my room, bursting with news from the night before. She wanted to tell me every detail. My sister, Sandy, listened in, interrupting with questions about the guy's car and what he did. I shushed her so Smiley could talk. The new guy was named Flaco and he had a *"**firme** ride*," Smiley gushed, and he was going to pick her up again tonight for a **cruise** down Main Street. He didn't claim a gang, but he told Smiley he kicked back with the guys from the park. My sister and I nodded approvingly. Then it was my turn. Talking about boys seemed to be our main topic of discussion in those days, and I always wondered what guys shared with one another. When it was my turn, they both made sour faces when I mentioned Frank.

"What? Girl, you crazy? Don't you know who that is? You don't want to mess around with him," Smiley said. "Tell her, Sandy."

My sister said Frank was the father of a kid with Sad Girl, an Anaheim homegirl who was the stepsister of Flaca, one of my sister's homegirls. The name of the mother was news to me, and I wondered why I hadn't asked Frank who she was the night before. Maybe I didn't want to know. Sad Girl was a friend of both Sandy and Smiley, and a local homegirl with a reputation for being wild and jealous. I tried to picture her together with Frank. Then I wondered what their baby looked like.

"That dog Frank, already out **scamming** for girls a month after his kid is born," Sandy said. "It's not the first time. He used to go out on her all the time, and she never knew. He's **bad news**."

"He said they broke up," I protested weakly.

....

*"**firme** ride"* great car
cruise ride
scamming looking
bad news not a good guy

"No way," Sandy said, "that's **just a line**. I can check around, but I would have heard if they had split up. You didn't tell that *vato* to call you, did you?"

I shrugged. "I gave him my number, but when he calls I'll just tell him I can't go out with him. I didn't know about Sad Girl."

The two tried to continue the conversation but I cut them off. "I'll deal with it." I wanted to change the subject. Everything that seemed so right the night before seemed painful now. There was no doubt about it now, I had to **steer clear of** this guy. I didn't want to come between a mother and father. I didn't want to cross Sad Girl.

The call came the next day.

"Hey, it's Frank."

"Frank who?"

"Aw . . . like you could forget me."

The brashness didn't seem cute anymore. "Oh, I know, the Frank that has a month-old baby and goes out with Sad Girl."

I had been practicing the conversation in my head, my anger building each time. I had planned for the words to come out casually, but instead they came out sharp and accusatory.

"Girl . . ." I thought he might hang up, just retreat from my anger. Instead, he tried to **negotiate**. "Listen, me and my old lady, y'know, we're over. It's history now. She knows that. We're not together."

"Yeah, well . . . look, we had fun, you seem nice and all, but I think that should be it. I'm just not ready . . ."

....

just a line what he is telling you so you will be with him
steer clear of stay away from
negotiate explain; make peace

"Okay, okay . . . but hey, I can still call you, right? We can be friends, right?"

"Yeah, sure. That's cool." I hung up a few minutes later and cursed myself for giving in. I liked him and I was letting him stay too close.

The next few weeks we would talk on the phone and see each other at parties. He made **frequent advances**, but I pushed them off. It was flattering for me, but I knew I was **flirting with danger**. Frank knew I liked him and, like all the boys, he wanted to push and charm his way as far as he could. It was like a game, and the fact that I played it at all let him know that, on some level, I was interested. Around his homeboys he would swagger and show off to impress me, but during our frequent late-night phone calls he would tell me quietly that I was the one for him, the only girl that could make him happy. I found myself falling for him, despite my friends' warnings that he **was a playboy and a two-timing smooth talker**.

Frank kept insisting I go out with him, and I finally gave in. We went to a dance club in Anaheim, which I hoped was far enough out of the barrio to escape the eyes and whispers of our friends. Halfway through the night, we were kissing again and I was cursing my own weakness. Later that night, I felt foolish for a different reason.

We were talking about the future and Frank was outlining his plans. One sentence started with, "When I turn eighteen . . ." I stopped him and asked him how old he was. Somehow, it had never come up before. He said he was sixteen, and I felt my face turn hot and red, more from embarrassment than anger. I had assumed that

....

frequent advances many attempts to kiss me
flirting with danger starting trouble
was a playboy and a two-timing smooth talker dated a lot of girls and lied to them all

Frank was eighteen or even nineteen, like me. But sixteen? Not only was I seeing a guy with a kid and another girl, but he was a damn child himself—at least that's how my friends would describe him. I imagined what was already being said about me around the neighborhood. I wanted to hide.

Frank, as usual, talked me out of my worries. He seemed to be so confident about the future, so sure of himself and me, that the anxieties melted away. I could feel **everything speeding up**, and I wasn't unhappy about it. But I had to be cautious. I didn't need a war with Sad Girl, the type of confrontation that tends to quickly **get ugly**. Finally, one night, I asked my sister, Sandy, to call Sad Girl and **feel her out**. I wanted to know exactly what was between them.

My sister came back with the worst news possible, the news I was expecting: She says they're still together. She said they're gonna get married "'cause they got that kid." She also wanted to know why I asked.

I confronted Frank, and he limply denied it all. He wasn't looking me in the eye, and I told him he was a liar. He stammered a protest and my fury grew. How could I do this to myself?

"Look, we're through. Don't call me, okay? Go take care of your old lady and your kid."

I stormed off, and he didn't even try to chase me.

A few weeks later, I saw Sad Girl at a party. We sized each other up and, after I had a few drinks, I stepped close to her. I could feel the eyes on us. There were very few secrets in our neighborhood.

She cut me off when I introduced myself. "I know who you are."

....

everything speeding up our relationship getting serious very quickly

get ugly get violent

feel her out find out what she thought about Frank

I started to tell her that whatever she thought Frank and I had going, it was over. She interrupted again. "I know. He told me and your sister told me. I don't trust him, but . . . everybody says you **walked off** when you heard he was with me, so I got no problem with you. Frank lies. He's real good at that."

Sad Girl looked a lot older than thirteen. I was glad she was being cool with me. Her voice had an edge to it, enough to tell me she didn't like me or what had happened. But Frank was the one she blamed, not me.

"Are you guys still together?"

She glanced around at the party crowd, and for a second I thought she was looking for Frank. "No, he's no good for me, so I told him just to . . . No, we're not together."

I didn't say anything. What could I say?

It was a week later that Frank and I started dating again.

Frank and I **went out on and off** for the months that followed, breaking up when he would go back to Sad Girl and, once, when he dropped both of us to date another girl. Sad Girl and I became bitter foes as Frank **played us off one another**. It was always Frank that would call me or track me down at the Trooper parties. I never stepped in to take him away from her and the baby. I even tried to see other guys, but Frank would have none of that. He hit up anyone that showed interest in me. I remember once I went on a date with one of his friends. The next day, the homeboy called me up and said there would be no second date.

"Frank asked me what I was doing with his old lady, so, y'know,

....

walked off stopped dating him
went out on and off dated sometimes
played us off one another used us both

out of respect for him, we got to forget it, Mona," he said sheepishly. "I can't go out with his old lady, man. He still cares about you. You belong to him."

Before I could tell him that I didn't belong to anyone but myself, the voice was gone, replaced by a dial tone.

My feelings for Frank were hard to deny, but I tried to do just that. It wasn't just the mind games with Sad Girl and the stress of the rocky romance, it was the lifestyle that Frank represented to me. I was growing tired of the gangs again, the whole party scene and the fights that seemed to break out every weekend, the constant jockeying for position among everyone. The blur of booze and fast living gave me a place to hide after my failure at Valley High, but now I was feeling strong enough to **face life full-on**. I liked my friends, but it was all so tiring, such a dead end. Osuna seemed to sense I was at a turning point, and, with subtle hints or even full-blown lectures, he was hammering away at me to **make the final break**.

"So, Mona," Osuna asked one afternoon, "who's the guy?"

"Huh?" My head jerked up. How did he know?

Osuna smiled broadly. "I thought so. Now I know for sure."

I blushed and shook my head. "No, there's nobody . . . he's just, I mean . . . well, you wouldn't . . ."

His smile faded. His voice took on the **edge of an interrogator**. "He's not a banger, is he? What's his name?"

I started lying. "No, he's not a banger. He's just some guy, but I

....

face life full-on fully commit myself to having a better life

make the final break leave the gang forever

edge of an interrogator tone of someone questioning me

don't think he even likes me that much."

"Make sure it isn't one of those bangers, Mona. You've come a long way, and your whole future is ahead of you. Don't let some lousy banger **take you down**."

I shot him a hard look. "I can take care of myself."

I didn't like that Osuna was bad-mouthing Frank. Sure, Frank was a *vato* and he and his buddies lived **on the edge**, but still, Osuna had no right. If he insulted my boyfriend, he insulted me. Later, when I saw Frank, it was as if he knew that my coworkers were asking about him.

"So why don't you quit that job?" The question came out of nowhere as we watched a drive-in movie.

"Why should I?"

"Damn pigs. Why would you want to work with the *jura*? You think they don't talk behind your back?"

"They're nice to me. I work hard, and I need the money. How else could I pay for the gas to drive you around all the time?"

His eyes narrowed, and I **braced for** an argument. Money was a sore spot for Frank. He was out of work at the time and hated it. It was a **cheap shot on my part**, and I expected him to scream at me. But instead of lashing out, his face softened and he pulled me close to him.

"I just think you'd be happy working somewhere else, y'know . . . I hate cops, all the guys do. I don't like you doing stuff for them."

"I'll think about it." It was a lie. I had no intention of giving up my job.

---

take you down ruin your life
on the edge dangerously
braced for prepared myself for
cheap shot on my part mean thing to say

A battle had started between Osuna and Frank even though they had never met or even heard each other's names. Each **lobbied me hard** to turn my back on the world of the other. Osuna preached about the future and Frank **harped on my roots**. The cop warned me about dangers around me and my handsome *vato* whispered that he would always keep me safe in his arms.

"What they say to you and what they really think ain't the same, Mona," Frank would say. "Don't trust them."

Osuna and Frank were saying the same thing.

I dismissed Frank's warnings, He didn't know Brown and Osuna, he didn't see the way they treated me, the way they helped me. He couldn't be right.

One afternoon, though, Frank's **admonishment seemed to ring true**. There was a lull in the work, and Brown and Osuna were chatting about their plans for the future. With sweeping hand gestures, Billy was laying out his plans for impending retirement, the lazy days fishing and traveling, seeing the country and returning to Florida. Beneath his enthusiasm, though, I sensed some sadness. He had been a cop, and before that an MP in the Marines for so long, I think he feared his days would be empty without the badge. Billy changed the subject by nodding at me. "What about you kid, what do you want to be when you grow up?"

"I don't know . . . maybe a cop. My dad always wanted me to do that."

The two looked at each other and then at me to see if I was joking. Billy mumbled a one-liner about the career's lousy hours and

....

lobbied me hard tried to convince me

harped on my roots said I belonged with the people in the barrio

admonishment seemed to ring true warning about how others felt about me seemed true

Osuna studied my face for clues to my sincerity. Finally he spoke: "If you really mean that, Mona, then you have a lot of hard work ahead of you."

The words sounded **diplomatic**, but they were flat and hollow to my ears. I had seen the **incredulous** look they had given each other, a shared glance that said far more than Osuna's words. As friendly and as open as they had been with me all those months, I was still an outsider in their world, someone who couldn't even be considered for a badge. There was nothing mean in it, it was just the way things were and I had to get used to it. I was from a different world, their shared look told me, and while I could visit their world, have nice lunches and pretend to belong, at the end of the day I was still an outsider. Frank was wrong about many things, but even he was smart enough to see what I had been ignoring.

I was silent for the rest of the day and, for a week or so, I was cold to both Osuna and Billy. When they asked me what was wrong, I told them I wasn't feeling well and they let it go at that. Things between Frank and me, meanwhile, were going well. He was spending less time with his buddies. Things felt right when I was with him, kissing him and talking about the future. He said he wanted to stay with me forever and he talked in that dreamy voice about the job he would get, the money he'd make to take care of me. I closed my eyes and I could see it all happening.

---

diplomatic kind and careful
incredulous surprised

BEFORE YOU MOVE ON...

1. **Argument** Reread pages 137–138. Frank wanted Mona to leave the station. What reasons did he give to support this argument?

2. **Paraphrase** Reread page 139. Mona said she was "an outsider in their world." What did she mean?

LOOK AHEAD Read pages 140–155 to find out what drastic decision Mona made.

~ Chapter Eight ~

El Oso

It's funny how your mind works sometimes. For so long, I had felt like one of those people in the circus who walk on the high wire, barely keeping my balance while I walked the line between two worlds. It was confusing deciding where I belonged, who I could trust, and who I really was inside. Osuna and Brown seemed to care for me, but I **bristled** when they said things I found insulting about my barrio and friends. What did they really think about me? And Frank seemed to be someone I could spend my future with, but then there were so many problems surrounding him, how could I be sure? I wanted things to be clear. Somehow, with all these things crowding my head, I decided to **make a statement about myself**, something that would prove to Frank and all the others that only I was going to decide my future and my allegiances.

I stayed up late with my sketchbook until the image was just right. I **ducked out of** work early the next day and went to a place a friend had told me about, a small cinderblock building on the east

----

bristled was offended; did not like it

make a statement about myself do something to show who I was

ducked out of left

140

side of town. The tattoo parlor was the size of a small garage and samples of colorful patterns and characters covered the walls like the wallpaper in a kindergarten class. A white biker guy ran the place, and he was well known for his talents. I showed him my sketch.

"Nice," he said approvingly. "We can do this."

Thirty grueling minutes later, I let out a gasp as he dabbed my stinging flesh with cotton and a burning disinfectant. The **ink and alcohol** looked slick on my skin and the vibrant colors shone through like bright coral beneath water. The image: A thick heart, red and dripping blood from the spot where it was pierced by a flaming dagger. Across the wound, a hovering scroll declared my devotion with two words: Frank Ruiz. The pain and permanence suddenly had my heart beating fast. Did I do the right thing?

The next day, at work, I tried to hide the bandage behind file folders as I walked through the halls, which were decked out with plastic Christmas decorations. The holiday season meant a lot more drunks on the road, so the Traffic Division was swamped with work, chasing after **DUI offenders** and the inevitable hit-and-runs that go with them. Brown and Osuna were **out in the field** for much of the morning, so I practiced working with one hand, tucking the wrist with the bright white gauze down in my lap. Every half-hour, with my back to the closed door, I'd peel back the wrapping to peek at the tattoo. I scratched at the lines and colors, still amazed that they were bonded to me. I couldn't wait to show Frank that afternoon.

When Osuna walked in, I nearly fell out of my seat.

"Hey, why **so jumpy**?"

....

ink and alcohol tattoo
DUI offenders drunk drivers
out in the field working on the streets
so jumpy are you so nervous

"You startled me." The words had an edge I didn't intend, so I smiled. "I mean, it's been so quiet in here . . ."

"Remember what we were talking about the other day? Were you serious, Mona? You know, when you asked about being a cop?"

"No, I was just, y'know, making a joke." A bad joke, I thought to myself.

He noticed the bandage, which I was trying to hide with my other hand.

"What happened there?"

"It's just a burn. I was ironing and the table sort of slipped and I got burned. It's not that bad." The explanation sounded **rehearsed and hollow**, like the lines in a bad school play. If Osuna noticed, it didn't show.

"Ah. Well, just in case you were serious, I circled some classes that would help." He tossed a booklet on the desk in front of me. It was a **directory of courses** at Rancho Santiago Community College. I had already started attending classes at the campus, which was near Santa Ana High, but Frank was **giving me a lot of grief over it**. He didn't want anything making me think about a career.

"So, if I took these classes, I could become a cop?"

"It would be a place to start. It takes a lot more than that. You have to go through an academy, too, but it would help you figure out if it's something you want to pursue."

I didn't say anything and Osuna leaned over. "I just want you to know that if this is something you want to do, Billy and I will do whatever we can to help. It wouldn't be easy for you, but nothing

....

rehearsed and hollow practiced and untrue
directory of courses list of classes
giving me a lot of grief over it not happy about it

worthwhile is ever easy."

If Osuna thought I could do it, I had to try. I had been wrong: What I had thought was **contempt for** my dream of being a cop might have just been surprise. Osuna left for the day not long after that, and I worked alone for the rest of the afternoon. I turned off the radio and sat quietly, lost in thought. I peeked at the tattoo again and again. The tape holding the bandage was starting to sag and lose its strength, so I took the wrapping off and studied my wrist in different poses. I stretched out my arm and flattened my fingers, the way you would examine a new ring. When I put my hand down on the desk, I noticed the red heart was the same color as the small ink circles Osuna had made in the college course booklet. "Introduction to Criminology" caught my eye, and I started to read the class description. My mind suddenly flashed to me raising my hand to answer a question and all the eyes in the room turning to see the screaming tattoo on my arm.

I sagged in my seat. How could I get out of this? I knew already that I couldn't, the same way I knew I wouldn't be able to hide my tattoo from my coworkers for much longer. And what would Frank say about classes to become a cop? I felt afraid and foolish, surrounded by accusing eyes and disappointment.

The tattoo began to **throb in warm pulses**, and I felt a headache coming on. I rubbed my temples with my fingers and watched the clock. The same thought bounced around in my mind: Which life do I belong to?

Later that night, I met up with Frank and showed him my new

....

contempt for disapproval of
throb in warm pulses hurt

tattoo. He loved it, especially because it bore his name. "No doubt now," he told me. "No doubt. Every guy will know who you belong to now." His enthusiasm raised my spirits only a bit. I could feel the forces in my life **squaring off**, and I knew things were going to change soon. I knew it would be messy.

"What the hell were you thinking?" Brown's voice thundered through the office. He threw his pen across his desk and slammed shut a folder he had been looking at. "Goddammit, girl, what the hell were you thinking?"

I just shrugged. There was no answer to give, no defense. I stood there and waited for it to be over. I rubbed at the tattoo to hide it from their eyes, but Osuna surprised me when he grabbed my wrist and held the offending mark up to his face. The ink flames seemed to glow under the office's fluorescent lights.

"Frank Ruiz. Just great. I thought you weren't seeing him anymore." A week earlier, I had slipped and mentioned Frank's name. Osuna immediately checked him out. I had to tell him that Frank and I were split up just to calm him down.

"Well, we got back together . . . but look, he's not as bad as you think. He works hard, y'know, and he loves me."

"Unbelievable," Brown was still shouting. I wasn't sure he had heard anything Osuna and I were saying. "It's unbelievable. You talk about changing your life, and now you go out of your way to make yourself look like a no-good, goddamn gangbanger!"

Osuna nodded solemnly. His quiet words were somehow more

---

squaring off fighting each other

frightening than Brown's ranting. "He's right. No matter where you go or what you do from now on, people will see that and that's what they'll judge you by. What does that tell people about you?"

My voice was thin and weak. "Look, I . . . I still want to go to the college and work here. I'm not even in the gang anymore, really, and Frank is not what you think."

"I hope not, Mona," Osuna said. "For your sake."

A few nights later I found myself in another confrontation. I tried to **spill the news** casually, hoping I could convince Frank that returning to school was no big deal, just something to fill my time. The **ploy** didn't work. He was livid. He saw college as another rival for my attention, another ambition of mine that jeopardized his view of our future together. And, I suspected, like a lot of the homeboys, he was insecure when it came to education.

"Maybe you're mad because you think this makes me smarter than you. But it doesn't. I just want to . . ."

"Is THAT what you think?!" His voice was thundering and he charged toward me. "Is that what you think?!"

His eyes grew dark and he seemed to swell up with anger. He was spitting his words out and backing me up. I had never seen this side of him.

"You ain't smarter than me . . . just 'cause you sign up for a class or work with the *jura*? That makes you smart? All that shows is you don't know who you are or where you're from! They're laughing at you behind your back and you're too stupid to notice!"

His hands flew above his head in rage and for a split second

....

spill the news tell him
ploy trick

I thought he was going to hit me. The moment was frozen as we locked eyes. I didn't **answer his charges**. I just turned and walked off. Frank's anger was a **wake-up call**, a frightening glimpse of his **volatile nature**. I remembered what Osuna had said about Frank, and I recalled Sgt. Redwine's words about putting distance between myself and everything that had to do with the gang if I ever wanted to make something of myself. Would I have to guard my heart against falling further in love with Frank? The tattoo seemed to mock me and my thoughts, telling me my future was already decided, written out in letters that couldn't be erased. Frank Ruiz. Was he a danger to my dreams of building a better future? And that fury in his voice: For the first time, as his hand reared back, it occurred to me that he might even be a danger to me.

Christmas Day came and went, and I didn't hear from Frank. He was still simmering about my decision to enroll in classes for the spring semester and was waiting for me to change my mind and come back to him. I was resolved, though, that I was going to follow Osuna's plan. I felt I had deeply disappointed him by getting the tattoo, and I wasn't going to let him down again. The holiday had an edge to it in my family household. My parents were upset by my tattoo, but their anger was vague and half-hearted. There had been so many disappointments for them that I think they were somewhat numb to this latest **transgression**.

My sister, Roni, saw I was glum and invited me to go out for the night with her and some friends. We hadn't been close in years and in

....

answer his charges say anything
wake-up call warning
volatile nature violent personality
transgression mistake

high school we had grown increasingly cold toward one another. Our friends were different cliques and often didn't see eye to eye, and the rivalry drew us apart. She was into a scene she knew I **frowned on**. For years, she thought I was judgmental and I thought she was too wild, too close to the edge. After I left Valley High, though, some of the tension melted.

She and her friends were going to a New Year's Day party to celebrate the arrival of 1980, a new decade and, I hoped, a new start. I agreed to go and, packed in with a carload of her friends, we headed off to 17th Street gang territory, a strip of four or five city blocks that seemed like **foreign land** to me even though it was only a few miles from my home. Roni was in love with a new boy, a 17th Street homeboy named Tony, and she wanted us to meet.

When Roni introduced Tony, my first thought was that he was the skinniest *vato* I had ever seen. His waist seemed too narrow for his body, and his baggy pants, which looked brand new, increased the effect by ballooning out and down to his shoes. Roni cackled when she saw the khaki trousers with their perfect crease. "Where'd you get those? Are those Art's pants you're wearing?" I knew Art was Tony's older brother, the huge homeboy everyone called Oso, the bear. Roni's teasing made **Tony's face screw into a scowl** as the *vatos* around him laughed.

"No, these are mine," Tony answered in a *vato's* street-sly mutter. "What you saying that for, huh? Art's pants are over there on Art."

He nodded toward a hulking figure at the edge of the yard drinking from a beer can and talking to some girls. He looked like

....

frowned on did not approve of
foreign land a strange new place
Tony's face screw into a scowl Tony look angry

147

Tony, the same expressive eyes and a similar jawline, but he was towering and broad. On the drive over, Roni had told me how close the two brothers were and how much Tony admired his **senior sibling**. I could see at least one reason why: Oso seemed **larger than life**.

A dozen people or so were gathered around the front of the house on Euclid. We began to circulate through the crowd, which was growing as the night crept on. Roni wanted me to meet as many people as possible, so she could introduce me as her sister. I was **in enemy turf**, so to speak, so she wanted everyone to know my connection to her to **diffuse** any trouble. The Troopers were on pretty good terms with 17th Street, and I was past my fighting days by then, but it was best to establish me as no threat to any of the 17th Streeters at the party.

I knew I was probably safe anyway, just as long as I stuck with Roni, who had a far-reaching, fearsome reputation in the barrio.

Everyone was hanging out drinking and talking. I was watching their long shadows move across the yard's short grass when my sister tugged at my arm and told me she wanted me to meet one more person.

"Mona, this is Art."

"Hi."

"Hi. So you're the nice sister, right? At least nicer than Roni, right?"

I smiled and nodded. "Oh yeah, you got that right. She's the bitchy one."

....

senior sibling older brother
larger than life strong, powerful
in enemy turf in another gang's neighborhood
diffuse stop, prevent

We all laughed as Roni shot Art a bird. She clapped him on the back affectionately and sipped some wine. "Y'know, Mona, Art is the guy who introduced me to Tony, so I guess I gotta be nice to him."

The two brothers were talking then, laughing loud and long about a mutual friend, a two-timing *vato* who found himself **snagged** by both his girlfriends when they ran into each other at a carnival. The story was funny, but it made me think of Frank. I wondered where he was and what he was doing. Like everyone else, I didn't see the blacked-out Toyota coasting toward the house.

With the headlights out and its low speed, only the muffled crunch of wheels on old asphalt might have announced the car's presence. The deep pops, two or three in a row, didn't catch my attention either. The shots would have sounded just like the rest of the neighborhood's distant celebratory gunfire if it weren't for the yell. The yell, a defiant shout in a young man's voice, is what made my head turn toward the street and the Toyota rolling from the shadows into the bright circle cast by an overhead street light.

"Fifth Street! Fifth Street!"

I saw the boy's mouth moving, forming the words again and again. Then I saw the gun and the flash. A shotgun, he's got a shotgun, my mind shouted at me. Paboom, paboom. The world **had turned into a stop-action**, like someone had turned on a strobe light. I dove for the ground, my arms and legs moving like I was in water. On the way down, I distinctly felt a sharp breeze tug my hair back away from my shoulder just as a searing slash of pain made me gasp and grab at the side of my neck.

....

snagged caught

had turned into a stop-action seemed to move slowly

149

When I hit the cold softness of the grass I heard someone behind me groan loudly and fall backward into a flower bed. My attention shifted to a pair of shoes not far from my face: I realized the girl that had been standing next to me was still standing, frozen and shrieking in fear. I grabbed at her knees and yanked her to the ground. I heard a shot hit the house with a dull thud, and I knew we had to get out of the yard and **get to cover**. The girl was still screaming and shaking her head, so I grabbed her wrist hard and told her to follow me.

As we crawled toward the house, I had only one thought: Where's Roni?

The Toyota was speeding off now, its tires screeching as they tried to find the road after the driver slammed down on the accelerator. How many guns did they have? It seemed to me the shooting went on forever. Could all of that have been just one gun? I looked toward the street and for a moment I saw the face of the shooter, still hanging out the passenger side window. He was laughing.

Tony and another homeboy chased after the Toyota, emptying their handguns at the fading red lights **with no effect**. It was too late; they were gone. The music was still playing, as if nothing had changed. The girl next to me was sobbing lightly, like a lost child. From both directions, I could see neighbors walking or jogging toward the commotion. My God, there were so many shots . . .

I spun around looking for Roni and began shouting her name, grabbing frantically at people to ask where she was. After **an eternity**, someone pointed toward the flower garden. "Over there,

....

get to cover hide somewhere
with no effect but failing to hit the car
an eternity what seemed like forever

she's over there."

I turned and was sure I could feel my heart skip a beat when I finally saw my little sister.

The yard seemed suddenly crowded. People were running around and shouting, some in anger, others in fear, and I wondered if anyone had thought to call for an ambulance yet. "It's Art, it's Art," Roni kept saying over and over. She was kneeling in the flower garden's black soil and the *vato* they called Oso was laid out in front of her. His striped shirt was soaked in blood from his chest to his waistline. His hands were twitching, and his eyes were closed.

"God, oh God . . . no, God," Roni was sobbing and looking for Tony as I scrambled over to feel for Art's pulse. It was faint and uneven, and I could see the crimson stain on his shirt was growing. He had **taken the shot full** in the chest. It suddenly occurred to me as my mind began to sort out everything that had happened: Oso was the shadowy form I had seen out of the corner of my eye during the attack, the person who groaned and fell. I had heard him die. A cold sweat made me shiver in the night air. Someone brought towels to put behind Oso's head. We packed some around the wound in his chest, trying to **stem** the flow of blood, but the cloth quickly turned red and seemed to do little. Oso's eyes opened and he was trying to speak then, but only gurgling noises escaped his mouth. So much blood . . .

"Somebody call a damn ambulance!" Roni was hoarse from screaming. "Where's Tony? Tony!"

Suddenly he was there, panting hard and still gripping his

....

taken the shot full been hit by the bullet right
stem stop

handgun. I saw the intense wave of pain and shock in his eyes when he realized his brother was shot. The emotion was too much, and I had to turn away. Tony leaned down, close to his brother, his sobs mixing with Roni's.

"Everything's going to be all right, Art, I swear," Tony whispered to his fallen sibling. "**Hang in there**, *ese*. It's gonna be okay. Hang in there."

The sirens were getting closer, drowning out the dance music that seemed somehow obscene against the tragedy unfolding. Help was on the way, but I wondered if it mattered. Art seemed to be turning grey, fading like the last image on a film screen. My neck was sore and—No! Suddenly I felt a wave of nausea as my still-confused mind latched onto another realization. My hand flew to my neck where heat and pain confirmed my suspicion. The slash of heat I felt was the shot that killed Oso. It **grazed me** as I fell to the ground. **I was inches from death, if that much**. My knees got weak.

The crowd was parting to make way for an old woman from down the street. She wore traditional Mexican clothes, a simple dress and shawl, and seemed bent over by her years of life. She leaned over Oso and began praying, pausing to drip holy water on his forehead and using her finger to make it in the sign of the cross. Who was she? It was so quiet, all I could hear were the wailing sirens—where was that ambulance?—and the old woman's quiet prayers. Roni was running to the street where Tony had found his parents. I didn't want to see Art's mother when she found her bleeding son, but I couldn't move. I was transfixed by the old woman's face, so calm in

---

Hang in there Do not give up

grazed me flew past me, barely touching my skin

was inches from death, if that much had nearly been killed

the face of all this chaos. They cut his shirt off and I saw the bullet hole. His chest was still moving up and down, I realized, so he was still alive, still had a chance. Someone tapped on my shoulder. I turned to see a tall, young cop. He started asking me questions about what I saw. There was little I could tell him. "Two guys, in a dark, small car. They drove by and shot into the crowd. We were just trying to enjoy the New Year." He wrote it all down, along with my name, and moved on to the next person. Tony and Roni ran past and shouted for me to meet them at the hospital. I went with another homegirl, and when we got there I saw Oso's parents clinging to each other and weeping. They were waiting patiently for someone to tell them their son was going to be okay. I was still watching when a doctor came out to them, and I could tell by his sagging shoulders that **the news was not good**. I was too far away to hear the surgeon's words, but the cry that came out of Oso's mother **will stay with me for the rest of my life**. It was the sound of someone's heart being torn away. The homegirl next to me began crying, but I had no tears. Only anger and hate for the cowards who did this, and anger and hate for the stupid **war that pushed them into it**. Oso was gone. For a moment, I saw myself in his place, still and lifeless on a hospital gurney with the shotgun slug in my head instead of his heart. I wanted to cry but couldn't, I wanted to run out of there but my feet weren't moving. I felt myself turn and quickly aim for the exit, almost running into Roni and Tony as they were walking in. I walked like a robot toward them, feeling the blood pound in my chest and my head. They didn't know yet. "Tony, I'm sorry. They

....

the news was not good Oso had died

will stay with me for the rest of my life is something that I will never forget

war that pushed them into it gang fights that made them do it

153

just told your mom. He died." Roni buried her face into Tony's chest. The *vato* stood there in shock. I felt so helpless watching my sister grieve. This was something I couldn't fix or make better, something a big sister couldn't solve. I remembered when we were little kids and I would come to the rescue. It seemed like a million years ago.

I didn't attend the funeral that day but Roni told me Oso looked different in the coffin. His face seemed smaller and rounder, fake somehow, and for a moment I had a child's fantasy that maybe that wasn't really him on the white satin pillow, maybe he wasn't really dead. But I knew he was gone. Even though we had only just met, I felt a huge sense of loss and grief. I had seen him alive and then I saw him die. I saw him take a shotgun blast that could have just as easily killed me. Maybe even should have killed me. I glanced over at Roni and Tony. They seemed to have aged overnight. Sitting together, their faces were stone like. They seemed to have no tears left. The days following Oso's death were tough, and not just because of the tragic loss. **Reprisals were already underway**, and the death of the popular *vato* was sure to mean more **mayhem** in the weeks to come.

"*Ese*, they're going down," one angry *vato* pledged as the mourners filed out of McDougal's funeral home. "Those guys are gonna pay, *ese*."

The threat echoed in my head as Roni told me how Tony's homeboys promised a payback for Oso's death. The words were still in my head hours later as I stared at the ceiling above my bed. "They're going down." I felt tears start rolling down my face. I couldn't tell if they were from anger or sadness and I wasn't sure

....

Reprisals were already underway People were already planning revenge

mayhem violence and murder

who they were for.

What were the things I saw in the gangs that once made me defend them, fight for them? I couldn't remember any of them, only vague and hollow words about honor and loyalty—how ridiculous the words sounded now. Was some neighborhood's name more valuable than Art Carmona's life? Eighteen and dead instead of eighteen with a future. I was angry at myself, too. Others I knew had died, but the lessons had never **sunk in**. Why? I knew the answer: This time I had felt the sting of the bullet myself. Death had touched me on its way to claim Oso, and that had changed me. My father was right, Osuna and Brown were right, and the voice in my head was right. The gangs offered nothing but pain and loss, and I wanted no more of it. I wanted to go to school and pursue a career, even if it cost me Frank. I promised myself that the gangs would no longer be my life. It was time to follow my dreams.

I got down on my knees and prayed for the first time since I was a child. I asked God to show me a way to change my life, to **become a peacemaker**. I felt a sense of calm wash over me, and in some weird way I felt like my life with the gangs was over. But, I had no idea that my newfound resolve would make no difference at all. My **trials** were just beginning.

....

sunk in meant anything to me
become a peacemaker help gang violence end
trials problems

BEFORE YOU MOVE ON...

1. **Conclusions** Why did Mona get a tattoo that proved her loyalty to Frank?

2. **Simile** Reread page 140. How was Mona like a circus performer on a high wire?

LOOK AHEAD Read pages 156–188 to see why Mona's father became furious with her again.

~ Chapter Nine ~

SMILE NOW, CRY LATER

"Another hangover, Mona?"

I looked up from the paperwork and tried to force a smile, but gave up when I saw the two greasy slices of pepperoni pizza and half-eaten crusts on Billy Brown's desk. The heavy smell hit me and I had to swallow hard.

"Hey, you okay, kid?"

"Yeah . . . y'know, too much partying, I guess." It was a lie. I had been in bed by 10 P.M. the night before, and the waves of nausea rolling through my stomach had nothing to do with wine.

"Hah! Well, you better **lighten up on that party schedule**," Brown said as he began munching on a slice. "Osuna will kick your butt if you don't **pull down** some good grades in school."

"Yeah. I'll take it easy."

The sickness had come every morning for a week. A bad meal, I thought at first, or maybe the flu, I thought on the third day as I gagged and bowed over the toilet at home. By the fourth day, I was

....

lighten up on that party schedule stop partying so much
pull down get

shaking with fear and crying as I hunched over in the bathroom and tried to stay quiet. Please God, I thought, please don't let it be . . .

I went to my doctor. I prayed the night before that he would tell me **my fears were unfounded**. I wanted him to say anything, to tell me I was sick or needed an operation, that I was dying even— anything except the thing I suspected. I remember waiting for the results, sitting up on one of those clinic beds with the rolls of paper for bedsheets and that hateful hospital smell. I stared at my dangling feet and felt my stomach, searching for some difference, some clue. Maybe my appendix needs to be removed, or maybe it's one of those ulcer things I had heard about once. The doctor walked in fast, like a man late for a bus, and he never looked at me as he thumbed through the pages on his clipboard and hummed.

"Well, Ms . . ." He stopped and scanned the medical form on the clipboard, "uh, Sandoval, yes. Well, Ms. Sandoval, you're pregnant. Now, we'll need some more information. What's the name of your husband?"

He pulled a pen from his white lab coat's pocket and waited. My head was swimming. Nerves made my knees quiver against the side of the examining table and I felt a hot fear in my gut. How, how could I be so stupid? What would I do? My mom's face appeared in my mind, and I thought I was going to be sick.

"Husband's name?" He said it slow and loud, like I was stupid.

"I'm not married."

The nurse who had appeared a moment earlier looked up as if I had whispered a dirty word. The doctor **clicked his tongue** against

---

my fears were unfounded everything was fine
clicked his tongue made disapproving sounds

his teeth and shook his head. "All these unwed mothers, what is it these days? Are you just going to get on welfare now?"

"What? I . . . no, I mean, I don't think . . ."

"Right, right. You don't have any plans for the future, right? Or a way to take care of this child? We see far too much of this, believe me. Now, what . . ."

I cut him off. "I have a job, and I go to college." I was furious. I had come looking for help and he was calling me garbage, some kind of street trash. "This is just . . . just something I didn't plan."

He asked me what type of birth control I had been using. I looked away, my **indignation stamped out** by shame. My shoulders sagged and my voice was limp with embarrassment when I finally answered. "I wasn't using any."

The doctor and nurse exchanged another look and shook their heads. I wanted to cry or hit them or run away. Instead, I sat there, waiting, while he wrote some more notes. He began talking again, but I didn't hear him. I was staring at my stomach and wondering how it would look in a few months. I left feeling humiliated and stupid. I wasn't some sixteen-year-old who didn't know better. I was twenty-one. There was no excuse for my lapse in judgment. Frank and I should have been more careful. When did it happen? I told myself I deserved the doctor's scorn, and that I had better get used to people **looking down their noses at me**.

On the way home I imagined running red lights, **ending everything** in a flash with the shatter of glass and metal. People would say nice things about me, remember me the way I am now,

....

indignation stamped out anger replaced

looking down their noses at me believing they were better than me

ending everything crashing the car and killing myself

158

not as . . . as what? I wasn't sure. I wanted to keep driving, hit the freeway and escape, drive off to a place where no one would shake their heads and call me a failure.

When my grades started sliding, I started spending more and more time with Frank. I promised myself I would go back next semester. How could I concentrate on school with everything falling apart in my life? Whenever I thought of breaking the news to my father, tears would roll down my cheeks. I had already disappointed him in so many ways. This would kill him. In our neighborhood, with its traditional ways, my shame would be shared by my parents. They would take the blame in the eyes of their judgmental neighbors, who would whisper that the Sandovals failed as parents. But it was truly my mistake, and mine alone. I was not a child anymore. How could I have been so stupid? I replayed the moment in my mind again and again, imagining all the ways I could have avoided this terrible situation. I was weak and I was foolish. **Love makes us blind**, sometimes, and you never see the mistakes until they have been made.

There was no relief to be found at work. Billy was getting suspicious. The old detective's attention was hard to avoid in the **tight quarters** of the small office. I tried to disguise my trips to the bathroom as errands to other parts of the building, but my face betrayed me. Anyone who looked at me could see I was hurting.

I was sitting at my desk one afternoon **poring over** some paperwork when I paused to rest my eyes. My stomach felt tight. It

....

Love makes us blind Love makes us do stupid things
tight quarters crowded space
poring over working on

had been a full day since I had a meal I could keep down. All I felt like doing was lying down. When I opened my eyes again, Billy was staring right at me. It was just the two of us that day, and it was hard to escape his stern eyes. I jumped when he asked me if I was depressed about something.

"No, I'm just tired. I was up late." That answer wasn't good enough, I guess.

"I think that's bullshit, Mona."

He walked toward me and leaned over my desk, planting his big hand on top of the folders spread out in front of me. He leaned in close, searching my eyes with that pitbull expression on his face. I thought he was going to yell, but the words came out low and quiet.

"Are you pregnant?"

I had learned to expect Billy to **be blunt**, but he still caught me off guard. I tried to answer but nothing came out.

"You are, aren't you? I know you're pregnant." His voice was building as he spun and began pacing. "Damn, you stupid girl, you are, aren't you? I knew it."

I wanted to lie, but I couldn't. "Yeah, I guess I am."

"You guess? You don't know for sure?"

"No, I know. I am. The doctor says so."

He began rubbing his forehead like he had a migraine. He started to yell at me some more, I think, but he stopped, biting his tongue. I could tell he wanted to scold me the way the doctor had, the way I knew my parents would when I finally told them, but he held it all in. He just rolled his eyes and took a deep breath. Then he

....

be blunt ask me things directly

asked softly what I was planning to do.

I told him I wouldn't get an abortion, that I planned to keep the child. He closed the office door, and we talked some more. I could tell he was disappointed and frustrated, and it made me feel even more ashamed. At the same time, it felt good to **share my burden**.

"If there's anything you need, money or anything, you let me know," Billy said, standing with his hands on his hips. "Anything."

"Okay. Thanks." My eyes were watering up. Now that I heard someone else talking about it, it was starting to sink in and feel real.

An hour later, Osuna came in the office. Billy told him I was pregnant, cushioning it the way you tell someone a friend is dead. I sat there like a child, silent, in the corner while the adults talked about me. I wondered if there would ever be another day in my life when I didn't feel humiliated.

Osuna took the news hard, too. He had **invested a lot of hope in me**, and now I could read in his eyes how let down he was by the news. He stared at the wall for a few moments, and I wondered what he was thinking about. The hurt in his eyes made me feel like I had stabbed him.

"You know you screwed up your whole life?" he asked me. "Is Frank more important to you than your future?"

His words hurt, and I said nothing. I was sure I deserved them.

After a long silence, Osuna walked over to open the door and Billy shot me another look. "What about that boyfriend of yours, what does he think about all this?" I shook my head. "I don't know. But I guess I'll have to find that out pretty soon."

....

share my burden talk to him about my problems
invested a lot of hope in me had dreams for me

I found out two days later. It was a Friday night, a full three weeks after I had found out I was pregnant. Frank and I had made plans to go out with his friends to see a movie. We hadn't seen each other in days, partly because Frank was running with his buddies a lot more, but mostly because I was **postponing the confrontation**. I didn't know what Frank would do when I told him he was going to be a father again.

Three carloads of homeboys made the trip west to an old drive-in theater on Highway 39 in Stanton. The homeboys never went to regular theaters, only drive-ins where no one would notice or care if they brought in a case of beer and a few joints to get loaded on during the movie. The guys that didn't have any cash could get in for free, too, by cramming themselves into the car trunk until we were inside, where they would pile out like clowns in baggy pants. The drive-in also gave the guys a **venue** where they could make out with their girlfriends, talk and laugh as loud as they wanted or listen to tunes if the movie was no good.

I don't remember what the film was that night. I think it might have been an action movie, but I couldn't say for sure. Even though I stared straight ahead the whole time, I really didn't see anything that played out on the huge bright screen. Instead I was **rehearsing in my head** what I would say when Frank and I were alone later.

After the movie, we took everyone home, and I told Frank I had to talk to him. I drove us to a park and turned the engine off in a spot beneath the trees. It was a cool and clear night, and the breeze

....

postponing the confrontation delaying telling him
venue place
rehearsing in my head planning

felt nice as it passed through the car. Frank was pretty drunk by then, but he was in a good mood from the night's partying. He was swaying his shoulders and head and singing along to the Miracles song on the tape deck. I turned the engine off and looked down at my hands on the steering wheel.

"Frank, I'm pregnant," I said flatly. My eyes were still on my knuckles when he stopped singing. I braced myself for anything. He would deny it was his, I thought suddenly, or maybe he would say nothing, slam the car door and walk home.

I looked over after a few heartbeats, and our eyes met. He didn't look mad or scared, or even surprised, just sort of sad in a tired way. "Well, we'll get married then," he said. "I got a job and all. I'm making good cash at the machine shop. We'll just . . . get married."

It was hardly a romantic **proposal**, but I was surprised at how much I felt for him when he said those words. I had planned to **go it on my own**, but there, in the night alone with him, I knew I would not turn him down. I loved him, and now we would be together forever. We would make it if we just stuck together, I thought. We talked quietly for a long time, making plans and holding hands. We kissed, and he told me everything would be all right, that he was ready to settle down and start a family.

"I screwed up before with Sad Girl, but you know I've grown up since then. I wasn't a good old man for her, and I wasn't around for her when she was pregnant, you know? And you're the right girl for me, Mona, the only girl. This time, I'll make it work."

I still had my doubts that he was ready to give up his playboy

....

proposal way to ask me to marry him
go it on my own raise the child alone

ways, but it felt good to have someone to share the weight I had been carrying. He smiled at me, but it was a nervous smile. He liked to act like he had everything under control, all the *vatos* do, but I knew he was intimidated by the responsibility he had just agreed to take on. I didn't let myself wonder whether he would walk away from that promise. That would be bad luck, I thought. Instead, I kissed my new fiancé, the father of my unborn child.

"Hey, we're gonna be a great couple, Mona, right? You and me, forever. You'll see."

The Miracles were singing the same songs for the third time that night when I started the engine and flipped on the headlights. As I turned the car toward home, Frank reached down and turned up the volume before staring out his window. His head was turned away, but his hand reached out to hold mine as the song filled my ears. It was just my imagination, once again, running away with me . . .

The next day, Frank called me. We talked like teenagers, saying little that actually meant anything, but happy to stay on the line through the silence just to feel **some connection**. After awhile I started to tell him I was going to go. He stopped me, though, so he could repeat some of the promises from the night before.

"Y'know, I just want to say, y'know, I meant what I said, about being with you and everything. You know I'll be there for you, right?"

The words were a relief: Frank hadn't changed his mind **when the sobering morning arrived**. Still, his reassurances sounded halting, as if he was trying to convince himself as much as me.

....

some connection like we were together

when the sobering morning arrived about marrying me after he had time to think about it

Maybe I was being too harsh. After all, he was taking the hard choice. And no matter what, I told myself, it was better to have him with his doubts than to have no one.

"You and me, Mona, you and me. Hey, uh, did you talk to your dad yet? Do your parents know about us and the . . . y'know, the baby."

"Not yet. Soon, though. I don't know what they're going to do." An image of Lydia flashed in my head, her face blazing red from my mother's slapping. "I don't know how to tell them."

We spoke a little longer after that, whispering gentle words. He made a joke about wanting a boy because he never knew how to handle girls. Tears filled my eyes: My God, I'm going to have a baby. It **hit me like that every few hours**. Most of the time I thought of my pregnancy as a situation or a condition, only in terms of actually being pregnant. But Frank's words, the first he had actually said about the baby on the way, reminded me that in a matter of months he would be holding my child and our future in his arms. It was an overwhelming feeling.

"Hey, what's wrong? I was jus' joking. I don't care if it's a girl."

"No, it's okay. Hey, I have to go Frank. I love you. I'll talk to you soon."

My Dad and I had started growing closer when I took the job at the police station. Relations between us were far better than they had been when I was running the streets with the Troopers. Still, a coldness would creep in his voice when he spoke of Frank. He

....

hit me like that every few hours suddenly felt real

had made it quite clear that he didn't approve of a young man who had a reputation in the neighborhood as a gangbanger and who had abandoned the girl who had had his child. Frank's shame **rubbed off on me**, as my father put it, and Raymond Sandoval had made his views quite clear to my boyfriend. He dismissed Frank as a *cabrón*—a rare profanity for my father—and a worthless *pachuco* who could do nothing but drag me down. As Frank and I grew closer, my father's lectures became more common than conversation.

"Always he has a beer in his hand," my father would say. "He's a bum, nothing more, and you're a fool if you let him mess up your life."

I had brought Frank home a few times, and my Dad would only give a gruff nod and head out to his workshop, refusing to acknowledge the young *vato* he considered to be a street punk. If my Dad would not accept him even as a guest, how would he react to him joining the family? He would be **devastated**, I knew, and he would despise me for letting it happen.

The house on Golden West seemed much smaller to me as I walked through its doors and halls with my secret. On the day I finally **confessed**, with my belly already starting to swell and threatening to reveal me, I walked like a sleepwalker up the driveway and past the spot where the grand old tree once stood. My parents were in the kitchen and I listened to them talk before I walked in, noting the way their voices sounded. They talked about **mundane** things—some tools my Dad was selling, Mom's plans for a weekend family get-together—and I wished it could all stay that way, simple

---

rubbed off on me was also my shame
devastated terribly disappointed
confessed admitted I was pregnant
mundane ordinary, normal

and calm. Standing there, I tried to imagine how they would react. Roni had told them she was pregnant just a few months earlier, but my parents had approved of her boyfriend and, because of Roni's wild years, had steeled themselves against any shocking news she might bring them. They more or less **shrugged the matter off**, happy, I suppose, that she was alive and settling down after surviving the drug and gangbanger scene. It was far different from the reaction Lydia had gotten years earlier. My mother's rage that night, and my father's resigned grief, were all I could think about as I approached the kitchen. They were so angry when I dropped out of school, when I got the tattoo, and now this, the final blow. I was expected to be mature and plan a career, the strong, second-born who was going to carry the family's pride.

I walked in and just said the words, my voice **detached and monotone** like a robot.

"I'm pregnant. Frank and I are getting married. I'm sorry."

My mom began scolding me. "Well, I knew it, I just knew all along, I was wondering when you were going to tell us!" She didn't really sound all that mad, but I wasn't looking at her anyway. My eyes were on my father's face, waiting for him to speak or even look at me. Finally the words rumbled out of his throat in a spiteful growl.

"You have ruined your life," he said, raising his eyes and staring a hole through me. "You are **giving your life over to trash**. Now you are trash. The police department, you think they will **look twice at** someone married to that *pachuco*? He has other women, too, and their children! You are a fool . . ."

....

shrugged the matter off did not let it bother them
detached and monotone unemotional
giving your life over to trash with a man who is worthless
look twice at hire

I started to speak, but he would not have it.

"I don't want to hear anything you say! There's nothing left for you to say to me. My daughters have left me with nothing to be proud of. Nothing!"

I thought he was going to strike me. Instead he walked away, stopping every few steps to turn and hurl more words at me. His open hand shook in front of him, like a desperate man **calling to the heavens**.

"I don't want to even look at you now! You are not my daughter. I don't know who you are."

My lip was trembling when he slammed the door behind him. He left the house and drove away, his dusty old car groaning under the sudden acceleration. I stood there for a long time, just staring at the space where he had been, replaying his words. Trash. Fool. Nothing. My relationship with him would never be the same again, I was sure of that. Tears filled my eyes as my heart grew cold. My father was gone. I was dead in his eyes.

My mom tried to comfort me. I think she saw how hurt I was, and she **reached out to me** despite all the harsh words that had passed between us through the years. I felt like a child again, afraid in the night and listening to my mother's voice.

"He's just mad, Mona. He doesn't mean it. He'll get over it after a while. He's just disappointed because already your other sisters let him down, and because you're older. He thought of you as the last chance, and . . ."

Her voice **trailed off**. I knew my father would not get over it. He

....

calling to the heavens asking God for help

reached out to me tried to make me feel better

trailed off got quiet

168

meant exactly what he said, as he always did.

I packed up my things and left, sure that I would never return to live in the house I grew up in.

I moved in, as planned, with Frank's family. It was a nightmare. The aged house was small and crowded, and the tensions were high, mostly because **of my presence**. Frank's mother, a short, **quick-tempered** woman with a shrill voice, hated me and did not try to hide it. She favored Frank's ex-girlfriend and saw me as some sort of intruding tramp, trying to steal her son away from the mother of his first child. More than once I overheard her muttering insults through the house's thin, yellowing walls. At first, the comments made me simmer and bite my tongue, but soon they seemed almost comical. Did she really think I had **engineered** my pregnancy to swipe Frank and, as she often said, take his money? I wasn't sure what wealth she believed Frank possessed, but I saw none of it. Frank knew how uneasy I felt and he tried to play the peacemaker, but I knew that any relief would only come if his mother and I settled our differences one-on-one. It was not a confrontation I was looking forward to.

The Santa Ana winds were blowing as I hit the mid-months of my pregnancy in July 1980. The dry, strong desert wind made the streets dusty and unbearably hot, and the close quarters at the Ruiz house made matters worse. To avoid his mother's insults, many days I would stay in Frank's room while he went to work, pinned there by the heat, the clumsy burden of pregnancy and my own growing despair. I wondered if I was ever going to be happy again. Frank was still dead-set against me pursuing either school or work, an opinion

....

of my presence I was living there
quick-tempered angry, impatient
engineered planned

he said had nothing to do with my pregnancy.

"Listen, the only women who work are married to men who can't **provide for them**," he would say. "School is a waste of money, money we don't got. You stay home and take care of my kids, keep the house clean and cook meals, and that's the way it is."

His mother, always wearing her housedress, would beam proudly at her son as he said these things. She had raised him and she was pleased with his training. I wanted more. I had no desire to live my life as Frank's maid, but my strength was low in those months. It was a debate that could wait, so most days I just kept my mouth shut. My frustrations and depression were made worse by the situation with my own family. In the weeks following the **painful split** with my father, I avoided his house and his gaze as much as possible. I feared what he might say or do. Finally, in my eighth month, I went home. My belly was huge, challenging my father to accept my pregnancy and daring him to deny me. The weather was far cooler and Thanksgiving was around the corner. In my mind, I pictured my father forgiving me and inviting me home for the holidays, away from Frank's mother and her unwelcoming house.

He was on the porch when I walked up to him, hands on my hips, **feigning confidence**. My voice was trembling, though, like a bashful child.

"Dad, I want to talk to you."

No response. His eyes never met mine. He folded up the Spanish newspaper he was reading and pulled off his glasses.

"Please, just listen, give me a minute."

....

provide for them make enough money to support them
painful split argument
feigning confidence pretending to be confident

He got up and walked into the house. I caught up to him inside and blocked his path as he tried to leave the living room. "You have to at least look at me!"

He only brushed past with a sour look on his face.

"This is not fair," I pleaded after him. "How come you don't treat my sisters this way? Will you ever forgive me?"

But he was gone, out to the back porch, the screen door rattling closed behind him. He would not give me the answers I already knew.

A month later, on December 19, 1980, I married Frank Ruiz. We were dressed as if we were going to the grocery store. No big wedding, no flowers or even a white dress. Nothing fancy, no romance or family, no photos and smiles for **the big day**. Frank was sweet. He had offered to dress up or invite friends, but I said no. It was like I was punishing myself.

I wore some old painter's pants and a billowing cotton maternity blouse. My groom stood next to me in a plain white T-shirt tucked into a pair of baggy khakis with a sharp crease. It was over in minutes. As we walked out of the Orange County Courthouse, across the vast concrete courtyard, I shielded my eyes from the sun so I could see the Santa Ana police station on the east side of the Civic Center. In my mind I named each of the offices behind the windows within sight. One of them, I knew, was the Traffic Division. Billy Brown and Osuna could see me if they looked out their window right then, I thought. They could see me on my wedding day. It had been eight months since I had seen them or anyone from the PD, eight months that had brought me into a whole new life. I pretended the

---

the big day our wedding

old me was sitting in the office, looking out across the courtyard to the very spot where I was standing. What would that old Mona think about me?

A week later, my beautiful boy, Frank Ruiz Jr., was born after one hour of the most pain I had ever felt in my life. His face made me forget all my shame and pain, at least **for a time**.

I took my newborn son to see my father. My strength was returning—it had been almost two weeks since Frankie Jr. was born with his head of black hair in ringlets and soft dark skin that made his wide brown eyes so bright. My father could not refuse me, I was sure. He could not deny his grandson.

"Dad . . ." I stood there, bouncing my cooing son in my arms. There was no need for words. **My presence was a question**, and I was waiting for an answer. Raymond Sandoval studied me the way he might inspect one of the broken machines in his grimy workshop, some old gadget that had failed in an unknown way. His eyes, surrounded by wrinkles and his coarse, heavy brow, briefly turned toward my baby. But there was no change in his expression, no softening of his stare.

He just walked away, again, refusing to hold or even acknowledge the child named after a man he despised. I watched my father stride away, his back bent more than ever by his old injuries and the advancing years. He had turned his back on **two generations**, now, I thought.

I took my son home and hugged him for hours, burying my

....

for a time for a little while

My presence was a question Just being there was like asking for forgiveness

two generations both my son and me

sadness in the softness of his cheeks and the warmth of his little laugh. No matter what, I whispered to Frankie Jr., I have you and you have me.

Frank had finally saved up enough money for us to move into our own apartment. I had **badgered** him for weeks, insisting he come straight home from work and not drop forty or fifty dollars after hours with his drinking buddies at the strip joints **dotting the seedy stretches** of Harbor Boulevard. "You have a family now," I said as I changed Frankie Jr.'s diaper. "We need a place of our own. There's no room here for us to raise a little boy."

Frank groaned but **kept up his end of the deal**, especially when I warned that I would have to work if he didn't bring home more money than he spent. The new apartment thrilled me. It was small but we had our own place, and for a while I began to think that my new life was not as bad as I had feared. Frankie Jr. was growing fast, and I could lose myself for hours in the minor miracles of a small child learning his way through a big, mysterious world. Everything was looking up until Frank began celebrating our modest successes.

He began to stay out late and come home falling-down drunk or high on something. I let it slide at first, but that only encouraged him to push further, to play the big spender with his damn buddies. His paycheck continued to shrink. When he started bringing the friends home, I thought at first that it might be a better alternative—beer is cheaper by the six-pack than it is in a lounge, after all, and I could keep an eye on him. But sitting around the house meant more opportunities to do drugs, and, almost overnight, our apartment

....

badgered bothered
dotting the seedy stretches that were all over the bad parts
kept up his end of the deal did what I asked

became a kick-back house for Southside and Frank's burly coworkers. A lot of his friends lived out of cheap motels and were eager to take up Frank's slurred offer of a free place to crash for the night. All the **shady characters** that Frank's mother would never allow him to bring over were thrilled to hear that their homie had his pad now. Frank and I began to argue almost every night, but he would thump his chest and say that as long as he paid the bills, he could do what he wanted.

"But you're not paying the bills, Frank." I threw a handful of white envelopes on the cracked dining room table. "Phone bill, power bill, car payment. You drank all the money, Frank, so how are we going to pay for these?"

"Damn, don't you ever shut up?"

"I'll shut up when you grow up."

A bitterness entered our words and we began to say things we had never said before. I was edgy and tired, feeling unappreciated and increasingly worried that Frankie Jr. would have to go without because of his father's **excesses**. On some level I was jealous, too. I didn't want to drink myself into a stupor or sample Frank's drugs, but I resented the fact that I never had a night off or to myself. The party was always raging at our house, but I was never invited. Our venomous arguments worried me. I knew that Frank and I could not take back the things we said to one another, no one could. Pressure was building, and neither of us wanted to blink.

"You listen," Frank told me one night, his voice low and hard. "You best respect me, woman. You don't want to make me mad.

....

shady characters untrustworthy people; troublemakers
excesses drinking and drug use

You hear me?"

Everything was escalating. I should have known what was next, I should have seen it coming and found a way to do something, found some way to stop it. Instead, I was blindsided. In many ways, it was the beginning of the end.

It was late. Friday night had turned into Saturday morning, hours earlier, but the party in my living room showed no signs of **slowing down**. I was in the bedroom, eyes wide open in the darkness, wondering when I would get some sleep. Frankie Jr. was in his crib near me, dozing lightly despite the pounding music and loud laughter from the living room. Frankie Jr. had been sick for a few days and irritable, and I wanted him to get some rest. He tossed and turned and his eyes fluttered open a few times. What he needed was some peace and quiet and a good sound sleep, but that didn't look likely. Four or five of Frank's buddies were out there, little boys in adult bodies with adult appetites. The voices would quiet down every once in awhile, after Frank shushed them, I suppose, but a few minutes later the volume would swell again. The jokes and songs and shouting matches were punctuated by the sound of empty beer cans rattling into the kitchen sink and the "snick-snick" of lighters igniting yet another cigarette or one more joint. The dope was likely soaked in PCP, one of Frank's favorite treats, which meant the party crew would **be fueled well into the dawn**.

I bolted upright in my bed when I heard something crash to the floor in the living room, a clatter immediately followed by bellows

....

slowing down ending

be fueled well into the dawn have the energy to party until morning

of hearty laughter. Jolted awake, Frankie Jr. began to cry. I threw the covers off and stormed into the living room, where Frank was leaning over a broken lamp.

"Damn it, Frank, that's enough! Your son is sick and needs sleep, and so do I!" I was groggy and angry. My words came out loud and high-pitched, and the party **abruptly ground to a halt**.

Frank was wide-eyed, surprised by my voice. He squatted there with a silly expression on his face. Shards of the lamp were spread out in front of him. The room smelled of stale beer and smoke. Fast-food wrappers, chips and beer cans littered the floor. The TV was on and the radio blaring. I was furious.

"Did you hear me? Get them OUT!" I threw a finger toward his friends, who were giggling and bent over laughing at my anger.

Frank turned toward his buddies, and I could see his face tighten and his eyes narrow. He hated to be laughed at.

"*Ese*, **you whipped or what**?" A chorus of laughter greeted the mumbled comment from one of Frank's buddies, whose face was down while he rubbed his short-cropped hair with his hand like he was shining a bowling ball. Like a class clown, he didn't want to look anyone in the eye while he stirred up trouble.

"What?" Frank was standing now. The four homeboys on the couch were still laughing, but Frank was dead serious. "What did you say?"

I was watching the *vatos* clumped up together on my couch, waiting for their response, so I never saw **the backhand coming**. The slap caught me right under the chin and I flew backward,

....

abruptly ground to a halt suddenly stopped
you whipped or what does your wife control you
the backhand coming Frank's hand coming at me

tumbling into a table, knocking over a second lamp. I saw stars and had a hard time pulling myself upright.

"That will teach you how to talk to me!" Frank was towering over me.

His friends were silent then, although I saw two of them were smiling, enjoying the show. I could hear Frankie Jr. crying louder.

"Your kid needs you," Frank barked. "Get in there."

I did what he told me. The party didn't last much longer after that. Frank threw his friends out, upset that they had **questioned his manhood**. When I heard the last of them leave, I held my breath waiting for the door to open and his silhouette to appear. But he spent the rest of the night in the living room, drinking and smoking, and sometime in the early morning he slipped out of the house without me even hearing it.

He hit me. I just couldn't believe it. He really had hit me. He had shaken and lightly shoved me before, but I never thought he would strike me. It was as hard for me **to stomach** as the bullies in my old neighborhood who punched girls or kids smaller than them. I couldn't comprehend it.

It was because of his friends, I decided as I listened to Frankie Jr. wheeze in his sleep. My jaw ached, but not as much as the back of my neck, where I had slammed down into the table with the lamp. All because of his buddies. They **goaded** him. He was high and drunk and they pushed him to the edge, and I hadn't helped with my screaming. It wouldn't happen again. It was a one-time thing, it had to be.

....

questioned his manhood suggested that he was not strong and in control

to stomach to accept

goaded encouraged

I dozed off, sleeping on my stomach so my neck wouldn't hurt. Frank betrayed me when he hit me, and that couldn't be taken back. He won't do it again, the voice in my head promised me in reasoning tones, but you can never, ever, trust him again.

Frank was on his best behavior. He still drank and smoked weed, but he was in early most nights and his **demeanor suggested** he was laying off harder drugs. He was extra attentive to Frankie Jr. and, for a while, saved up more money than usual, giving me his uncashed paycheck and good behavior as **a peace offering**.

He turned to me one night as we sat in the living room, which was lit only by the flickering blue glow of our battered old television. "About, you know, when I hit you the other night. Well, you know, my father hit my mother all the time." His eyes were downcast. It was the first time we had spoken about the incident a week earlier. "I just wanna tell you, I don't want to be like that. I got all crazy. I don't know, I just lost it. But when I saw my dad doing that, I always said I wouldn't be like that when I grew up and beat on my old lady."

He turned toward me and, in the dim light, his sad eyes made him look like a lost little boy. "I just want you to know, I won't do it again. I'm not like that."

I leaned over and kissed him and thanked him. We didn't speak for a long while after that. We just sat close together, lost in our thoughts. I was impressed that he had opened up. Frank, like most of the *vatos*, usually had a hard time expressing himself or dealing with his own emotions. When I first fell in love with Frank, it was

---

demeanor suggested behavior made me think that
a peace offering an apology for hitting me

his tender, heartfelt words that drew me to him, the confidence that allowed him to drop the tough guy act and open up. In the years since, I had all but forgotten that side of him.

Frank's words made me hopeful. Maybe the backhand was an isolated incident, just as he said. Maybe that night was a fluke, and, if it drew us closer, maybe it was even worth the pain and that awful **flash of betrayal**. That was my hope. I could not have been more wrong. The violence that night was a passage, it turned out, the first **stone in an avalanche of heartache**.

It began with the Sherms, the PCP-soaked joints that one of Frank's new buddies seemed to live on. Frank had smoked them before, many times actually, but they became a daily ritual with the influence of his new party companion. The PCP was in a liquid form and kept in a small bottle like the perfumes my mother would give my sisters and me when we were little. Frank would roll up a joint and dip it in the bottle. The results were terrifying. The steady diet of PCP turned Frank into a raging, incoherent monster. The drug attacks the brain and nervous system, I'm told, and the symptoms are as bizarre as they are frightening: Users **hallucinate wildly**, and much of the world comes to them in jagged, jerky images accompanied by distorted echoes. The sounds they hear seem deafening in their hypersensitive state, meaning a normal speaking voice can send them into a mad fit of rage. Their joints stiffen and they walk like robots. Scariest of all, the parts of their brain that register pain are somehow disconnected and their strength is almost superhuman. Someone tweaking on PCP can be shot, stabbed, and

....

flash of betrayal moment when I realized he would hurt me

stone in an avalanche of heartache attack in a long life of being hurt

hallucinate wildly see things that do not exist

dying without ever slowing down. In their fury, they can break their own bones and rip muscles with their exertions and never show a hint of pain.

Stoked by the drug, Frank began to hit me all the time. Even when he was off the drug, the beatings still came. I suppose he just got used to doing it and, once that had happened, he saw no reason to stop. Frank had despised his father for being a wife-beater, but like so many people, he seemed doomed to **follow in his parent's footsteps**. I fought back when I could, but mostly I just tried to protect myself and keep Frankie Jr. out of danger. The PCP made Frank **like a runaway train**.

Frank was coming down off a two-day drug binge one Sunday morning when I confronted him about his using. All our money was being used to feed his drug appetite, and I was worried I'd have no money to buy groceries. I approached him gingerly, not wanting to get another beating. Bruises already lined my arms from a tussle with him a few nights earlier. "Frank, give me your wallet."

"Huh . . . Whah?" He was hunched over and muttering. The room smelled like beer and pot, but the overriding odor was an ether-like smell, a pungent, sickening scent that accompanied burning Sherms.

"Wallet. I said give me your wallet. I need money to buy food for your son."

His hands were over his ears and he mumbled something about "too loud." I lowered my voice. Noise often triggered the PCP rages, I had found out the hard way. "Frank, please," I whispered, "I need

....

Stoked High, Affected
follow in his parent's footsteps behave like his parents
like a runaway train lose all control

180

your wallet, okay?"

His head began to rock back and forth, and I stepped back.

"Frank?"

Like a top, he jumped from the couch and began spinning in a ragged loop around the living room, his arms straight like a windmill as he crashed into me, the couch, the wall, and tabletops. A growl was coming through his clenched teeth, and I dove for cover in the kitchen. His eyes were shut tightly, but he came after me. With a quick move, I closed the kitchen door on him, but his fingers dug into the wood and he ripped the door clean off its hinges and threw it toward me. I threw a coffee cup at him, but it bounced off his chest with no effect. Only when I started screaming did he back off. The shrill sound made him grab at his ears in agony, and he turned and ran out of the house with no shirt or shoes on. I didn't see him again until the next day, when he walked in wearing a new shirt. He looked around the house as if he had never been there before. He walked to the refrigerator, popped open a Budweiser and nodded to the bent, empty hinges in the kitchen doorway. "What the hell happened to this place?"

When the beatings became an almost weekly part of my life, I began **seeking refuge** at my parents' home. It was an old instinct, I suppose, to run home when I was hurt or feeling lost. But I quickly **abandoned that habit**. The reception I got at home was not a welcoming one. My bruises and bloody lips earned me no sympathy in my childhood home. Instead, they were **held up as evidence** of all my mistakes.

....

seeking refuge looking for peace and safety
abandoned that habit stopped going there
held up as evidence proof

When I was a teen, it was always my mother who attacked me with insults and cold criticisms, but now she was not alone. "Did you listen to me, eh?" My father was pointing to my black eye as if it was a list of my failures. His silence toward me had finally ended, but only to lash out at his sorry excuse for a daughter. "Huh? Did you listen to an old man who knows better? This is what you asked for, so this is what you get. He is no different from what he was before, he is the same man. It is only now that you can see what we knew then."

I started to respond, but his two hands flattened out in a swiping motion in front of him, like an umpire ruling somebody safe. The conversation was over. He was right and he had been right all along, I knew, but I didn't need another reminder of that. I knew now that I had **closed my eyes to** Frank's addictions and his tendency for violence. I had been around those traits for years, many of my friends showed them, and I had accepted them as part of life in the gang scene. I thought when I was married, though, that Frank would grow up. Instead, he just grew cold.

I tried to convince my parents, and myself, that I would be able to get things straightened out. Even in the 1980s, divorce was **taboo** in our community, which clung to Catholicism and had a vicious gossip network to enforce its tenants with threats of humiliation. When you married, it was assumed you would die with that person, just as the oath said. I was prepared to **follow up on** that promise. I just hoped I wouldn't be dying as a young woman.

A pattern was forming between Frank and me. Frank would party and spend money until I said something, but my comment

....

closed my eyes to accepted; stopped thinking about
taboo disapproved of
follow up on keep, complete

would always start a fight. The topic was usually the drugs or his friends or our budget. The fight would build, either over minutes or days, and eventually **boil over**. Frank would then either hit or shove me or—if he happened to be sober or feeling less violent—he would just bolt, leaving Frankie Jr. and me alone for a day or more. He would return, sober and **contrite**, and we would make amends, pledge to find a better way to treat each other and, after a week or month, start the cycle over again. Because I could recognize this pattern, I blamed myself for not putting an end to it. In some ways, I told myself, I deserved the beatings because I should have been smart enough to avoid them. Frank often cited my poor housekeeping skills as the reason he got mad enough to hit me, so I committed myself to doing a better job, something that would prevent the flare-ups, I hoped. If I tried harder, he wouldn't get mad, and everything would be different, giving us a chance to build a better life, I believed.

I had elaborate dinners ready for him when he came home from work, and the kitchen floor was shiny clean from scrubbing. Frankie Jr. was always dressed nicely and I began to pay more attention to myself, trying to look more attractive for Frank. I hung some new curtains I had bought at a discount store and I dusted most every day. When he was home, I jumped like a scared rabbit to get him a beer or change the TV channel, eager to keep him happy and home. Surely, I told myself, he must be pleased.

Nothing changed. If anything, Frank began to stay out more. The dinners would grow cold waiting for him as he and his buddies went off into the night without explanation or notice. Then I began

....

boil over it would get violent
contrite feeling bad about what he did

hearing the stories from my sisters and friends: Frank was with his old Southside buddies when a store burglary went down on Fairview Street, or he was seen in the bar parking lot where some *vatos* held up a businessman. I was skeptical at first, but then I noticed Frank's paycheck was no longer reduced by the amount I knew he regularly spent on drugs. I tried to ask innocent-sounding questions about his activities, but he always seemed to be in a drug rage or stupor. I began to **let the house slide**, along with my own appearance—why bother? As the second year of our marriage began, some new stories came to me through **the grapevine**: Frank's party friends were no longer just men. "He's got some girlfriends," a sometime friend told me with a little too much delight one day. "And prostitutes, too. I just thought, you should know."

I got a part-time job. If Frank was going to do as he pleased, so was I. We needed money for rent and to buy Frankie Jr.'s clothes and food, so I took an evening shift at a local factory. The work was dreadful. No matter how unpleasant the job got, it was better than asking **for loans or handouts**. I had done that a few times already, and I was nearly sick with shame, especially because I had no idea when I would be able to pay back the money.

Frank was furious when he heard about the job.

"No, no, no! You go back over there and tell them you quit, that your husband pays the bills, so you don't need no job."

Frank was screaming, and the baby was crying in the next room. I was trying to get dinner ready, and I was exhausted from my new schedule. But I tried to stay calm.

....

let the house slide stop taking care of the house
the grapevine friends and other people
for loans or handouts people to give me money

"I understand how you feel, but it's just for a little while so we can save up some money. No one has to know. I didn't tell anybody."

"No! Do you understand that word, huh?" He was **rummaging through** a pair of his work pants looking for some misplaced cash. There was no beer in the refrigerator. "Where is that money? Listen, you don't think I'm man enough to provide for my family?"

He was throwing clothes everywhere, and I had just cleaned. Frankie Jr. was still bawling and the food in the oven smelled like it was burning. I was losing my temper. I could feel my control slipping.

"This isn't about you, Frank. I'm sure you could provide for your family if you didn't have to support so many damn drug dealers, bartenders and whores, too."

I immediately regretted it, but before I could take back what I had said, Frank was on me. His fist landed right under my chin and I landed on the dining room table. He pinned me there with a hand on my throat and punched me twice in the left eye with two quick, hard jabs.

"There!" he shouted into my face. "Now you call that place and tell them you can't come to work because you fell down and hurt yourself."

I scratched him hard, nearly **drawing blood**, and took a swing, but he was already gone, leaving me lying there in the broken dinner dishes. My eye was throbbing with blood and the coming bruise.

He didn't come home that night. The next day, I inspected the deep purple and black ring around my eye, which I decided was too large to hide behind sunglasses. I called my new boss and told her I

....

rummaging through searching the pockets of
drawing blood making him bleed

was sick. She didn't sound very sympathetic. The way she said, "We'll see you tomorrow" made it clear that I had no sick days left. I knew I had lost the job. It would be a week or more before the bruise was gone. I wouldn't be able to stand the whispers of the other workers, their snide remarks or, even worse, their pitiful nods.

Frank had **gotten his way** again. He wanted control over every part of my life. The idea that I could work and make money threatened him. He hated to think **his grip did not extend to** every part of my existence. It was a lesson I learned very well one afternoon when Frank tried to **snuff out** the parts of my past that intimidated him.

I came home that day and smelled something burning. I put Frankie Jr. down, told him to wait near the front door, and I raced around the apartment expecting to find an abandoned cigarette or joint smoldering in the cushions of a chair. Instead, I found a pile of blackened papers jutting out of a small tin wastebasket in the bathroom. At first, I couldn't tell what they were. Then with a jolt of shock, I recognized the black ink lines on one of the charred sheets. It was the drawing I had done the night before I was jumped into F-Troop. All the pages were my old sketches, some **dating back to** sixth and seventh grades. I had saved the ones that meant the most to me, the drawings of my sisters and friends, the ones that pleased me or reminded me of a time and place. Most were from those early days in F-Troop, when the scratch of a pen on paper in the middle of the night helped me sort out my jumble of thoughts and feelings.

An empty can of lighter fluid was on the counter near the trash

....

gotten his way won; gotten what he wanted
his grip did not extend to he did not control
snuff out erase; get rid of
dating back to from the

186

can. I sifted through the pile, hoping to save some of the sketches. The drawings that weren't burned black were soaked beyond recognition by the water Frank had poured on the fire. There was nothing left.

I cried and cried. Later, I asked him why he had done it. In a haughty tone, he told me he knew those pictures were about my old boyfriends, "all those *putos* you used to sleep with," and he didn't want them in his house. "Why do you need that crap anyway, huh? Unless you're still seeing some of those guys."

It was too ridiculous to argue. Some of the sketches in the stack were by friends and other Troopers, unique gifts that Frank jealously assumed were some kind of love letters. Some were even sent to me by friends who were doing time in prison. They used their art to write **diaries of their ordeal**, the jailhouse postmarks on the ornately decorated envelopes **attesting to their authenticity**. Many of the other drawings were from friends who were dead or gone. They were treasures to me, like photos of places you can never visit again. I wondered if Frank was telling me the real reason he destroyed the drawings. I remembered a time several months earlier when we were going through a closet and came across a different set of my old sketches. He held one up to the light with a puzzled look on his face.

"What is this?" The drawing was a syringe turning into a snake, while in the background a row of young girls filed past a coffin. There were other designs surrounding the image, most of them whatever was floating through my head the night I drew the picture.

....

diaries of their ordeal about their experiences in jail
attesting to their authenticity proving they had come from prison

"What does this mean?"

I shrugged and took the sketch from his hands, flattening out a rolled corner. "It doesn't really mean anything. They're just how I felt then, the way the world looked to me. . . . They don't mean nothing."

He didn't like the answer, I could tell, but I didn't know why at the time. But **sorting through charred** pages months later, it made sense. It was part of my life that was closed to him, **hard to decipher**. He despised that. It made him feel his hold on me could never be complete. So he destroyed them and destroyed a part of me with them. It hurt more than any beating he had ever given me.

....

sorting through charred looking at the burned
hard to decipher a part he could not understand

BEFORE YOU MOVE ON...

1. **Author's Point of View** Reread pages 158–159. Mona was pregnant. What did she think about her situation? How do you know?

2. **Inference** Reread pages 186–188. Why did Frank burn Mona's pictures?

LOOK AHEAD Did anyone protect Mona from Frank? Read pages 189–217 to find out.

~ Chapter Ten ~

CORNERED

Domestic life had become a dangerous high-wire act for me. Even when it seemed that we were getting along well enough, I was always on my guard in my own home, afraid that I would slip up and send Frank into one of his rages.

At first I had thought it was the drugs, but then I realized they only **magnified what was already there**. Frank hit me because that was the only way, the easiest way, to handle difficult situations. It was a tactic he had learned at home, I discovered. Once Frank smacked me at a Ruiz family gathering. We were away from everyone, but his brothers and their wives knew what had happened, as did Frank's mother and aunts and uncles. **None of them blinked.** I was amazed. I guess they saw marriage as a private affair between two people. Mad one minute and then kissing and making up the next just like any other couple or so they thought.

Relations with my mother-in-law had improved somewhat, mostly because she began to realize that I was a fixture in Frank's

....

Domestic life Living with Frank
magnified what was already there made things worse
None of them blinked. No one seemed to care.

life. I think she was quietly happy with me as a mother, and I saw flashes that she felt sympathy for my suffering at Frank's hands. She would still lash out at me, **dredging up** the name of Frank's ex or insulting my housekeeping, but she was usually civil.

Once, while I was at her house, she began telling me about her life. She was washing dishes and staring out the window in front of her, oblivious to the water splashing her housecoat. She talked about her husband coming home with another woman, daring his wife to protest. She told me about how she struggled to raise her six kids as best she could on her own. She had left her husband because of the abuse, I was surprised to learn, and started over without him. I admired her bravery and hard work, but I was amazed that Frank had not learned from it. She nodded to my bruises and clucked her tongue. "There's no excuse," she said, and I nodded, surprised she was criticizing her beloved son. She wasn't.

"There's no excuse at all," she repeated as she turned off the faucet. "You're an idiot not to leave him. You deserve whatever you get."

Frank and I were spending more time apart, even when we were in the same small apartment. I didn't mind the distance. I was content to spend my time with Frankie Jr., and Frank was always satisfied with his booze, drugs, and the television. No matter what I did, though, it seemed impossible to **dodge** Frank's periodic explosions of violence. There didn't need to be any real reason, I had learned. **I had become a punching bag to relieve** whatever pressures he felt from an unfair world. I no longer assumed that I

....

dredging up mentioning

dodge avoid, escape

I had become a punching bag to relieve Beating me was Frank's way of releasing

was to blame for the beatings, nor did I cling to the hope that things would change. By my third year of marriage, all I hoped for was survival.

"I'm going to kill you! I'm gonna KIILLLL you!"

Frank was rushing toward me, grabbing at my hair and arms as I ran into the bedroom. He had been drinking since morning, and I had been nagging him throughout the day to fix the car, which was dead outside. I was very good at **pushing his buttons**, knowing how to **infuriate or belittle him**. The two of us were **locked in a hurtful dance** by then, and I was just as good at abusing him as he was at hurting me. His anger this time had a different tint to it, and I worried as he banged on the bedroom door that he might actually follow through on his threat. As the door bent from his attack, I called 911.

Frank smacked me hard when he made it into the bedroom, but he paused when he heard the fists pounding at the front door.

Frank, who was on probation from **a grand theft sentence**, was coherent enough to stop his raving when the police car pulled up. He didn't want to end up in the county lock-up again. The cops walked in like tough guys, their hands on their billy clubs, but, when they saw that Frank was calm and unarmed, they became uninterested.

"So what's the problem?" the older one asked.

"My husband threatened my life, that's the problem. He beats the crap out of me, too, and that's a problem."

A third cop jogged in, saw there was no fight to join, and sagged

....

pushing his buttons knowing what bothered him
infuriate or belittle him make him angry or feel ashamed
locked in a hurtful dance constantly fighting
a grand theft sentence stealing a car

into a corner, looking bored.

The older one, a sergeant, sighed and rolled his eyes like I was **putting them out**, like they had better things to do. I tried to tell them what Frank had done, how he hit me and bloodied my face, how he threatened me. The sergeant smirked, while the other two younger cops made faces at one another.

"Listen, he's threatened me," I said, holding Frankie Jr. against my hip, "and I want you to do something about it. He already beat on me once. Isn't that against the law?"

I could see my neighbors milling around the yard, craning their necks to glimpse into our house. The cop who looked bored waved at them like a moron.

"Now listen, lady, I haven't seen this guy break any laws, and he says he didn't and you say he did . . ." He was talking slow, as if he thought I was having trouble understanding what he was saying. I knew damn well what he was saying.

"So, it's okay to assault somebody or kill somebody if there's no cops around? Or is it just okay as long as you marry them first?"

His face hardened and he put his hands on his hips.

"If you don't want to be here, then you leave when we walk out," he snapped. The other cops were already walking out the front door, and now Frank was the one smirking.

"Why should I leave?" I was getting madder. "I didn't do anything! He's the one breaking the law. Look, he assaulted me. Take him to jail, I'll **press charges**. If you have a piece of paper, I'll sign it."

....

putting them out bothering them; wasting their time
press charges report the crime

"Listen, for the last time, there is no crime here. So your husband had a few drinks and got mad because you burned dinner or said the wrong thing, whatever. So he hit you. Get over it. He's sorry, you're sorry. Everybody's sorry. Okay?"

"That's bull." I wanted to kick in his chubby red face and his yellow teeth. He was saying I **was a designated victim because my name was written on a marriage certificate**.

"As a matter of fact," the cop continued, pointing at Frank's arm, "with these scratches here, I could take you in for assault."

My jaw dropped. I couldn't believe what I was hearing. The cop asked Frank if he wanted to press charges. The two of them were trying to hide their grins. The boys' club, sharing a good laugh over some stupid woman. I thought I was going to be sick.

"No, no, I think I'll let it go. You know how emotional women are," Frank said with a **conspiratorial** wink to his new pal. I wondered how friendly the scene would be if the stranger standing in our trashed living room knew of Frank's true feelings about the police, the way he and his friends liked to fantasize about standing over a dead cop.

The sergeant, satisfied with himself, muttered some number codes into his walkie-talkie and turned to go. "Next time," he said over his shoulder, "just do what he says and everything will be fine."

The door wasn't completely closed when Frank shot me a look and shook his head. He smiled. "You're really going to get it now."

I ran past him and outside. As Frank waved to the departing cops, a neighbor said she'd give me a ride to my parents' house.

....

was a designated victim because my name was written on a marriage certificate deserved the abuse because I was Frank's wife

conspiratorial friendly

Under my breath, I cursed a world where men always win and the law doesn't protect everyone.

Frankie Jr. was walking and starting to talk, and no matter how bad things got, I could always find joy in my time with him. He was my strong little man, the one who would grow and do the right things. It was hard to imagine a time when he wasn't part of my life. Being his mother was my greatest joy. So the news that I was pregnant with a second child **left me with mixed feelings**.

The thought of another child, a sibling for Frankie Jr., made my heart jump with excitement. But, looking around at my life, I wondered if it was unfair and cruel to bring another youngster into a home **being torn apart by** drugs and violence and always teetering on the edge of poverty. Abortion was not an option, though, so I knew no matter what, a new baby was on the way.

My sister Roni was happy for me when I told her the news. "Well, Mona, look at it this way: Maybe he won't hit you if you're pregnant."

Three months later, Frank proved my sister wrong.

He stumbled into the living room about 4 A.M. Lying in bed, I could follow his progress through the dark house by the sounds of him bumping into furniture. He must be wasted, I thought, as I heard him grunt and fall to the floor near the couch. When he walked into the bedroom, I feigned sleep, hoping he would retreat to the living room to sleep off his party. The smell of beer surrounded him and I could also detect the vinegary smell of the speed or PCP he had probably used all night to keep his body awake under the alcohol

....

left me with mixed feelings made me feel happy and sad
being torn apart by filled with

onslaught. There was another smell, too, one I didn't recognize.

The light from the bathroom went on and, through half-closed eyes, I could see him swaying a few feet away. He walked over, leaned down to inspect me and, satisfied I was asleep, walked toward the light. His head lolled back and forth when he paused there and his fingers were busy trying to get something off his shirt collar, a smudge of some kind. Lipstick? I immediately recognized the mystery smell: It was perfume, the cheap and clinging kind the hookers wear.

I knew I should keep quiet. He was tanked, obviously, and at his most dangerous. I just couldn't keep quiet.

"What's her name?"

He **flinched** at the sound of my voice, and I could see him sway in the darkness. "Is it a girlfriend, Frank? Or did you have to pay for it?"

"Damn you." It came out slow and slurred. He was really loaded.

I wanted him gone. He moved toward the bed, and I could see his eyes were wide and unfocused. I was getting scared.

"Just get out, Frank. Go back to your whores. Go to a friend's house, I don't care, just . . ."

He threw me on the bed. He started to move toward me, but his feet got tangled up in the sheets on the floor. Stiffly, he tried to balance himself, but instead he began to tumble toward me like a falling tree. Somehow, some way, I managed to bring my legs up just then. My feet caught him right under the rib cage as he fell and, with a hard push, I **sent him reeling head first** into the nightstand.

....

flinched moved

sent him reeling head first pushed him hard

I had to get away. I grabbed Frankie Jr., who had managed somehow to sleep through the noise. Frank was still wrestling with the bed covers and the furniture and didn't see me when I ducked through one of our large bedroom windows facing our cluttered back porch. I knew I couldn't jump the fence with Frankie **in tow**, so I needed a hiding place. I stepped past a broken bicycle, a tarp covering some rusting tools and other assorted junk, and pushed open an old trunk. As I climbed in, I could hear my husband rampaging through the house, searching for me. Frankie Jr. was still sleeping, unbelievably, and I remember hoping that there were no spiders in the musty trunk as I climbed inside with him.

The muted sounds of Frank crashing through the house seemed to **die down** after ten minutes or so, but I was too terrified to move. It was hot and tight in the trunk, which was cracked open about an inch, and one of the hinges bit into my shoulder as I ran my free hand over my belly, searching for any hint of danger to my unborn child. Most of the kicks were to my side and back, but more than one caught me full in the stomach. I prayed that the child was okay.

An hour must have passed and I felt Frankie Jr. starting to stir in my arms. I didn't want him to wake up inside the trunk. If he cried out in fear we might be found. So I slowly pushed open the trunk's lid. The sun was starting to come up. I **unfolded myself**, careful not to wake Frankie Jr. or make too much noise. Hot pain flared across the small of my back and I wobbled as the circulation returned to my legs. A breeze was sending a flutter through the ripped curtain hanging in the still-open bedroom window. I walked closer and

....

in tow in my arms
die down stop
unfolded myself stood up

saw that the room was trashed, the furniture upended, broken or shattered. I didn't even care anymore. Everything Frank and I owned seemed to **bear scars** from our violent marriage. I edged closer to the window and saw that my closet door was open and my clothes were strewn across the room and **in tatters**. He had cut huge gashes in most everything I owned. I shifted positions again and saw Frank, passed out in a pile of my ruined clothes, his mouth open. He still had a pair of scissors in one hand.

I would have cried if I had any tears left. Why was I being punished with this life? Then I noticed Frankie Jr.'s crib. It was collapsed, all jagged edges and **splintered supports**. What if Frankie Jr. had been in there? What if I couldn't have grabbed him on the way out? My stomach began to hurt from where Frank kicked me the night before. Two of my babies. He could have killed two of my babies. I was mesmerized by the sight of the crumpled crib. That's when I snapped.

I laid Frankie Jr. down on the couch and walked to the kitchen to find a knife.

I wrapped my fingers around the handle of the steak knife. My hands were steady and I knew exactly what I was going to do. I was going to free myself and protect my children.

I walked through the house with the knife held out in front of me, pointing straight ahead like it was guiding my path. I stood over Frank and studied him like an insect. I couldn't find the face that I fell in love with, the face of the proud young man. He was breathing in deep gasps and his eyelids weren't closed all the way, revealing the

....

bear scars be ruined
in tatters ripped to pieces
splintered supports broken wood

whites of the eyes rolled back in his head.

He looked like he was dead already. I would have to kill him with **the first blow** or he might wrestle me down and take the knife away, or use the scissors he had his fingers looped through. I would kill him and then I would cut him up and throw him in the dumpster like a bag of garbage. He would be dead and gone and everything would be better. In my head, I could see all of it . . .

Just then, a long, high-pitched wail **shook me to my senses**. Like a sleepwalker, I looked around in a daze and realized that Frankie Jr. was **screaming his head off**. He had been quiet and still all night, through all the noise and danger, until that moment. I shushed and calmed him down. My husband, sleeping off his drug binge, never stirred. I stared long and hard at the knife in my hand. What was I thinking? I was really going to do it. I never could have **gotten away with it**, I knew. My children would have been raised by strangers with their mother in prison. Nothing was worth that and, thanks to my son's well-timed crying, I had a chance to realize that. I put the knife away and fed Frankie Jr. before gathering up the few clothes that were still intact. I took the car and the money in Frank's wallet and left.

On the streets that led to my mother's house, I stared at everyone that passed, amazed to see that normal people living normal lives still existed.

Frankie Jr. was asleep again. I noticed a deep bruise across my arm and wondered when it got there. I would have to go to the doctor as soon as possible, I told myself, to see if anything had

....

the first blow one stab of the knife
shook me to my senses made me stop
screaming his head off screaming loudly
gotten away with it killed him without getting caught

happened to the baby. At every red light, I stared into my own eyes in my rear-view mirror. I was really going to do it, wasn't I? I was going to kill him.

My unborn baby was unhurt by Frank's vicious kicks, the doctor told me. The remorse Frankie felt about that night had won me some measure of peace. We still argued and he used his hands to settle fights, but the incidents were fewer and less severe. Our relationship had cooled and the chill kept us far apart, even when we were in the same room. As the months rolled by, I was excited about my second child's upcoming birth, but I was still **shuffling through life** in a depressed **funk**. I had been steadily letting my appearance go—after all, why bother?—and I was really feeling low.

It was a blistering hot day when our car lurched to a stop, the engine **giving out** under the heat and its own age, I turned the key again and again, but the engine was silent except for a strangled whirling sound. "No, please, just get me home." I pounded the steering wheel and tried again. Nothing worked. Frankie Jr. was miserable from the heat, just like me. I pulled myself up and out of the car seat and slammed the door with all my strength, almost losing my balance in the process. Standing next to the car, I watched the hazy waves of heat surrounding an abandoned washing machine that someone had dumped into the concrete flood channel beneath the bridge. The channel was barren, dry as a desert, the white of its walls broken only by bright graffiti and sturdy weeds pushing through its seams. I imagined my car down there, joining the other

....

shuffling through life living my life
funk mood
giving out stopping

useless litter, and I wished dearly I had the strength to push it over the edge.

Cars were whizzing by and even the breeze they made felt hot. I wasn't sure what to do next. I wasn't going to leave Frankie, of course, but I also didn't think I could carry him the five long blocks to the gas station. When I saw the **black-and-white** appear around the curve approaching the bridge, I figured my problem was solved. I'll get the cop to give my car a push. I waved my arms and reached through the car window to flick on the hazard lights.

My heart sank, though, when I saw the tall, familiar figure rise out of the parked patrol car. Better to walk twenty miles in the sun than face this shameful confrontation. It was Billy Brown. I knew it was him even before I could see his face, just by the way he carried himself and by those damn cowboy boots. I suddenly wanted to join that old washing machine and my dead car down in the desert dumping ground.

"Goddamn." He stopped near the rear of the car and inspected the scene with a **dumbfounded** look. He had not realized it was me, I could tell, until he had gotten a few feet away.

"Hello, Mr. Brown." The words sounded silly, too formal and awkward. I folded my arms self-consciously. I couldn't imagine a worse time **for a reunion**. Frankie was still whining, and Billy Brown bent over to look in at my son, the first time he had ever seen him. Billy himself looked exactly the same, as if not a day had passed since I had walked out of his office.

"What's wrong with your car? Did it die on ya?"

....

black-and-white police car
dumbfounded very surprised and shocked
for a reunion to see him again

"Yeah, it just died. It might be the alternator or something, I'm not sure. It's an old car."

He wiped his brow and shaded his eyes. "Hot one today. Old cars and old cops don't do so good when it gets this hot."

He stepped closer and I began to run my fingers through my hair, trying to pull it back out of my face.

"How are you, Mona?"

"Good. Y'know."

"Yeah, right."

"No, really. Frank's got a new job, and we're making good money, living in a nice place. A new place." Lies, bad lies. The new place was Frank's family home, back with his angry mother. We had been **evicted from** our apartment a week earlier. I felt Billy could read all of that in my eyes. I really wanted to be gone.

"Hey, uh, can you give my car a push up to that gas station?" I pointed up the block.

"Sure. What kind of work is he doing these days? Frank, I mean."
Translation: Is he dealing?

"Oh, he's doing some welding stuff, and I'm thinking of going back to school, too, like you and Felix always wanted. After I have the baby, I'm going to do that and then . . ."

My voice trailed off, **giving up on the flimsy fiction I was trying to sell.** Billy was staring at me hard, and I suddenly remembered the bruises on my arms. I moved to cover them, but the effort was obvious and stilted. I felt my face and neck grow even hotter.

....

evicted from forced to leave

Translation: Is he dealing? Billy was really asking if Frank was selling drugs.

giving up on the flimsy fiction I was trying to sell I did not want to tell any more lies

"Aw, Christ, Mona, when are you going to get rid of that bum? He hits you a lot? Hey, one of these days he might hit **junior over here**, and then what? Or has that happened already?"

"Nobody hits my kid." My voice was sharp and louder than I intended. I had to escape. This was bad for both of us. I was too far gone. "Look, uh, I have to get him home. It's hot, and he needs to eat. Can you give me that push?"

I watched his stern face in the rear-view mirror as we slowly coasted down the bridge to the gas station. He had turned on his flashing lights to warn other drivers, and I felt like I was being chased in a slow-motion police pursuit. When we arrived, I got out of the car quickly and went to his car window, hoping I could say goodbye and get him on his way without a lecture.

"You need a quarter for a phone call?" His eyes and whole expression had softened.

"No, I'm good." The squawk of his police radio was **an oddly nostalgic sound**. I wondered how life was across town at the station, which seemed like a distant world.

"Okay, Mona."

"Hey, thanks again. Tell Osuna I said hi."

"I will."

Frankie Jr. had quit crying and was asking for a soda. I told him to wave bye-bye to the nice policeman, which he did. Billy waved back as he steered onto the street, but the frown never left his face.

A week later I worked up the courage to call the Traffic Division at the PD. The meeting with Billy had **gnawed at** me. I knew he

....

junior over here your child
an oddly nostalgic sound a sound I missed hearing
gnawed at bothered

would tell Osuna a horror story about me, about how bad things had gotten. I couldn't **leave it like that**. I talked to a cautiously cheerful Osuna on the phone and tried to explain how Billy had caught me on a bad day and how he was wrong about Frank. Osuna was warm, but I sensed he doubted my story. There was something else in his voice, a question he wasn't asking. When he suggested dropping by to visit and meet Frankie Jr., I **stammered a halfhearted invitation**. I hung up and wondered what the hell I had been thinking.

A few days later, I spent half the morning staring in a mirror, making sure my face and hair were just right. I had scheduled the visit for a time when I knew Frank and his mom wouldn't be home, but that plan fell apart when Frank called in sick. He had a bad hangover, he said, but I suspected he was also curious about my plans for the day. When I realized there was no way to talk him into leaving, I told him about the unlikely visitors.

"No. Call those cops and tell them you changed your mind, you don't want them around."

"I can't. They're not in the office. Besides, if I did that they might get suspicious and come back with a warrant or your parole officer or something."

Frank chewed on that for a moment and yawned deeply. I knew he had drugs stashed in the house and maybe some other things he didn't want discovered. He ran a hand through his uncombed hair and across his unshaven stubble. He was pretty hung over, I could tell, and not really up for an argument.

"Talk to them outside, I don't want no *jura* in my house."

....

leave it like that let things end that way

stammered a halfhearted invitation invited them to the house, though I was not sure it was a good idea

I waited at the window for an hour, turning every minute or
so to check the clock. I was wearing my best dress pants, and I had
my long hair styled. Frankie Jr., who was working over a coloring
book, was scrubbed clean and wearing a striped shirt that my mother
had bought for him. I was genuinely excited to see my old mentors,
especially the always encouraging Osuna. Deep down, I hoped they
would be able to help me somehow.

The car that pulled into the driveway was **unmarked**, but no
one who saw it would doubt for a moment that it was a police car.
Before the veteran cops could close their car doors, I was outside and
walking down the driveway to greet them, Frankie Jr. at my side.

Osuna smiled warmly and walked toward me, while Billy Brown
grunted a hello. I could tell right away that the southerner **was
present under protest**. He scanned the house and street like a
soldier suspecting an ambush.

I introduced them both to Frankie Jr. before I awkwardly blurted
out that we couldn't go inside the house.

"Why?" Billy stared at the windows as he asked the question.

"My mother-in-law is scrubbing the floors, so, you know, we
can't go in." Maybe this was all a bad idea, I started thinking. Osuna
made some small talk about Frankie Jr. and the neighborhood, and
Billy just leaned back on the long, white hood of the car. He was
trying to look relaxed, but his face was tense and antsy. I wondered
what was on his mind. Finally, the burly cop could contain himself
no more. He stubbed his cigarette out beneath his shoe and walked
toward me, cutting in front of Osuna and startling me a bit.

....

unmarked not painted like a police car
was present under protest did not want to be here

"Mona, roll up your sleeves."

I paused, stunned. I searched Osuna's eyes for an explanation. Now I knew the question Osuna had wanted to ask me on the phone. I also knew the true purpose of this visit. "Mona, are you using?" Osuna asked. "You look bad, and Billy and I are worried. Are you **on the needle**?"

I pulled the half-rolled sleeves of my blouse up past my bicep and stuck my arms out, palms up. They thought I was a damn junkie. I wanted to be mad, but all I felt was a wave of deep sadness. "I told you I would never use, I'd never do that," I said. My voice sounded small and distant, even to me.

Billy had his thick fingers loosely around my wrists, but let go when he didn't see any needle marks, and my arms sagged down to my sides. Osuna had a pained look on his face. He was searching for the right thing to say, as always.

"Mona, we were just worried." I didn't answer, I just stood there. I felt **drained**. "We know the guys your husband hangs out with, and Billy was worried—when he saw you, he said you looked . . . bad."

The three of us stood there in silence.

"Kid, do you need any money or anything?" Billy felt bad; I could hear it in his voice.

"No, thanks." Frankie Jr. was playing at my feet and I watched him, admiring his comfort with the world around him and the ease of his laugh. "I gotta go."

The two cops said goodbye. I took Frankie Jr. by the hand and we watched the car roll down the street and disappear around a corner.

....

on the needle using drugs
drained exhausted

The first time I saw the commercial, I was feeding little Frankie, who was sitting in a highchair in the living room at my parents' house. I missed the first part of the commercial, but I heard enough to **start some wheels spinning in my mind**. There was a shelter for battered women, the woman in the commercial said, a place where you can go with your kids in an emergency. I jotted down the number, but a few days went by before I pulled the crumpled notebook page out of my purse and actually picked up the telephone. Even then, I panicked when the voice on the other end answered. I hung up quickly, like a scared little kid making prank calls.

Finally, I made up my mind I would call, just to get information. I wrote out four or five questions so I would be less nervous. I practiced in my head what I was going to say. I even had fake names ready for Frank and me. Punching in the seven numbers, I wondered what I was doing: Did I really think I would ever leave Frank? I was startled when someone actually answered, like I wasn't expecting it. The woman gave me a lot of information about the shelter. It was at a secret location to protect the women. "When you want protection here, get to a safe place, a phone booth somewhere or a friend's house, and call us from there."

The whole thing was free, although I would have to **be interviewed and agree to their terms**. She said they would even help me **get on my feet**, apply for different types of assistance and find a place to live. I chuckled nervously and told the woman it sounded like a pretty good deal.

....

start some wheels spinning in my mind make me think hard about my life

be interviewed and agree to their terms answer questions and accept their rules

get on my feet begin a new life

"It is, and maybe you should think about doing it soon. A lot of women wait too long. See, the thing is, once you decide to walk away, you have to make sure you do it while you can still walk. That's what I tell everybody."

I thanked her and promised I would keep the number close at hand. What she said made sense, but I kept thinking about Frankie and my unborn child. I wanted them to have a father, even if he was an imperfect one. Running away seemed greedy. It would make my life better, but how would it affect them? Frankie might even hate me for leaving his Daddy behind. I couldn't bear to even think about that.

I started calling the shelter almost weekly after that, sometimes speaking to the same counselor, or **introducing my woes** to the other women who answered the hotline. Sometimes I would ask the same questions over and over again. It was nice to talk to someone who was on my side, even if she was a stranger. I didn't see a lot of **allies** around me in those days.

Each time, the counselors would try to talk me into coming in, **making the leap**. I put them off with excuses or empty promises, but little by little, I think now, my courage was building with each conversation.

"Okay, so you're not ready. But get some things together for when you do decide to leave this guy, all right? Money will help. Have a bag ready and your son's things. It can't hurt, right?"

Those words were ringing in my ears a few days later when Frank grabbed me by the elbows and shook me hard for pestering him about money. He pushed me off, and I bashed my knee against

....

introducing my woes explaining my problems
allies friends, helpers
making the leap leaving Frank forever

the kitchen cabinets. I didn't shout or fight back. I just stared at him.

"What? You trying to scare me, bitch?" He shadowboxed and sneered. "Anytime. I'll kill you."

After he left, I started feeling around my stomach, trying to make sure I was okay, trying to make sure my unborn child was okay. If I needed a wake-up call, the doctor gave me one when he shook his head while reading my medical chart. "Mona, you're **in pretty rough shape**."

He was right, and I could feel it. Tending to a small boy and a full-grown addict had really taken a toll on me. I never ate right or slept enough, and the financial and emotional stress circling my life had made me a jangle of nerves. I was always **fighting some flu virus and the antibiotics** I had been prescribed were no longer working. Bruises ran up and down my body.

"Mona, does your husband beat you?"

"No. I just . . . no, don't worry about it."

"This baby, that's what you have to worry about now."

"Is there something wrong with my baby?"

"Not yet, but this lifestyle of yours is going to **put the fetus in jeopardy**, quite frankly, not to mention you. You need to take better care of yourself. If not, well, you may not go full-term with this child. This will be a far more difficult pregnancy than your first."

That night, while Frank was sleeping, I started folding up clothes and stuffing them into a backpack, along with a toothbrush and some toiletries. I crammed thirty dollars into the bag, too, the beginning of **an escape fund**. I used an old gym bag for some of Frankie's

....

in pretty rough shape not very healthy
fighting some flu virus and the antibiotics sick and the medicine
put the fetus in jeopardy hurt the baby
an escape fund the money I would use to run away

clothes. I stashed both bags behind some cleaning chemicals beneath the bathroom sink, a spot I knew Frank never went. The decision had been made. I knew I was going to either die at Frank's hands or kill him. I would not lose my new baby for him, nor would I risk my children growing up with a mother in a graveyard or in prison. No matter what, I was leaving. It was a scary prospect. Homeboys like Frank didn't like for their women to ditch them, and I would have to go fast and far to elude him. The only question was when and how. It was a decision I never had to make. My husband decided for me.

The Ruiz family is huge and troubled, with many of its members dealing with hard lives and hard issues, but one thing I always admired about the family was its large and frequent gatherings— weddings, holiday celebrations and parties. They were **a tight clan** where everyone knew all their cousins—a good way to go through life. One of these gatherings was the site of a **true turning point** in my relationship with Frank.

The barbecue was at the home of one of Frank's aunts. She lived in Stanton, a city straddling the borderline between Orange and Los Angeles counties.

I didn't want to go, but I saw no way out of it. I was dreading Frank's performance. His older brothers would be there, along with his cousins and uncles, and I knew from experience that he would try to outdrink them.

We got on the 22 Freeway and headed west toward Stanton. Frankie Jr. was playing in the back with a toy truck. A covered salad

....

a tight clan a close family
true turning point big change

sat on the seat between Frank and me. Frank had been drinking lightly since he woke up and he had also already wandered up the avenue while I got Frankie dressed, which meant he had most likely sampled and stocked up on some drugs. We stopped to get a twelve-pack of Budweiser for the party, and he **dipped into it for** two beers during the twenty-minute drive. He was on his third when we pulled into the driveway of the house.

Everyone was drinking beer and the air was thick from the barbecue smoke. Frankie Jr. was delighted to have some playmates, and he ran off with the youngsters already kicking around a kick ball. The party, as usual, was broken into age and gender groups. The old uncles were parked next to the coolers of beer and talking about sports or bragging about their old adventures. The people in their twenties and thirties were near the food and sitting in the sun. Women of all ages were in the kitchen, sharing cooking chores and the latest gossip. The kids were everywhere, running back and forth in their games.

Frank looked wobbly by mid-morning. He had been on a tear, alternately exploding in laughter and angry rantings. He was making a fool of himself, challenging cousins to fistfights and arguing over imagined **slights**. He was horribly insecure. Some of his cousins had managed to **improve their lot in life** and, more than that, Frank always felt inferior to his elder brothers.

He turned to me and ordered me to get some food for Frankie.

"I already did, Frank."

"Get him some food, that's why we're here, right?" He was

....

dipped into it for drank

slights insults

improve their lot in life live better lives than Frank

yelling and his shirt and pants were soaked down the front, wet from some errant beer, I guessed.

"He ate. Frankie had a hot dog and some of my burger. Now stop shouting."

He shuffled off, shooting me a finger. I decided to avoid him as much as I could. As the afternoon arrived, a cool wind took the bite out of the heat, and I sipped a glass of lemonade, enjoying the **rare luxury** of a pleasant day. Then I heard Frank's voice. It took my eyes a moment to adjust to the bright sun, so at first he was just a shadow standing in front of me.

"Gimme the car keys," he said, thrusting his palm toward my squinting eyes.

"Where are you going?"

"I'm leaving. Gimme the keys."

I stood up and put my cool glass of lemonade down on the nearby table, hoping Frank wouldn't **make a scene**.

"No. You're too drunk to drive. You can't even walk straight."

His hand was on my wrist, squeezing. "Bullshit. Gimme the keys. Me and my homie are going for a ride."

I knew I might not see him or the car for hours if he took off on some drug run or for a trip through the strip joints on nearby Beach Boulevard.

"No." The grip got tighter on my arm. His fingers were digging into the tattoo that bore his name.

"Who do you think you are? Huh? Trying to humiliate me in front of my family? I'll beat your ass right here."

....

rare luxury comfort
make a scene start a big fight

I **wrenched** my arm away, and he lost his balance, but not his grip. We got in a scuffle right there, with his family nearby. I could hear someone whispering but mostly everybody was ignoring us. No one stepped forward to help, either. I'd hoped someone would but those that would weren't there.

I wriggled away from him and picked up Frankie Jr., who was standing next to both of us and crying for us to stop fighting. I nearly dropped him to the asphalt when his father spun me around by the shoulder and swung his other hand toward me like an ax. The flat of his palm landed on my head with a smack, and his fingers clenched to grab a fistful of hair.

I shoved him, as hard as I could, and he lost his **footing** and stumbled backward. He was barely able to stand anyway. He must have had a dozen beers by then, along with whatever drugs **were on the day's menu**. I turned and headed off toward the car at a quick trot, whispering to Frankie Jr. that everything was going to be all right, not to be afraid. All around me his relatives were staring and growing angry by the embarrassing scene they were forced to watch. I could hear Frank coming up behind me, and I tried to walk faster. I felt for the car keys in my pocket.

He was so drunk he was having a hard time catching up to me, and he got tangled up with a laughing friend or cousin who stepped forward to mock both of us. "*Ese*, what's up with your woman?" Frank barked back and lunged toward the skinny *vato*, who I didn't recognize. I was thankful for the distraction: The car was only a few more yards, and Frankie Jr. was getting heavy.

....

wrenched pulled
footing balance
were on the day's menu he had taken

I fumbled with the keys, trying to get my fingers on the one for the car, and then calm my hand down enough to push it into the lock. I shot a look toward Frank in time to see him **toss aside the laughing interloper**. He was hunched over as he walked, muttering and red-faced. I threw open the car door and all but tossed Frankie Jr. into the passenger seat. We had to get away: I could not remember a time when Frank was so angry.

He was on top of me then, grabbing at my hair and cursing me in a guttural voice. I managed to give him one final shove, hitting him with my arm and the car door at once. "Leave . . . me . . . ALONE!" I shouted. He flailed his arms as he tripped backwards.

I slammed the car door shut and pawed at the lock. Calm down, Mona, calm down, I told myself as I clawed at the ignition with the key. I yelped when Frank suddenly filled the windshield. He had leaped onto the hood on all fours, his knee crashing down hard enough to dent the car. He was pounding on the curved glass like a madman, apparently oblivious to the crowd that was all around us, **gape-mouthed**. He was really out of control this time, like a rabid dog. I couldn't let him get to me. If he did, I had no doubt that I would be making a trip to the hospital, if **not the morgue**.

"Let me in, bitch, open that door!"

His fists came down again on the glass, and a spider web of cracks was spreading out from the point of impact. Finally, somehow, I got the key turned in the ignition and the engine turned over, rumbling loudly with my foot heavy on the accelerator. The noise made Frank pause, his fists held over his head. He stared down at me,

----

toss aside the laughing interloper move away from the man who had laughed at him

gape-mouthed shocked

not the morgue he did not kill me

his face distorted by the cracked glass between us, but the message in his eyes was clear: Don't do it, bitch, don't even think it.

I jerked the car in reverse and stomped on the gas, and then, after rocketing backward ten yards, I slammed on the brakes, jerking to a screeching stop. Frank went flying off the hood, doing a somersault before his body flopped to the pavement. All his weight seemed to come down on his shoulder and head, and I could see his face was tightened with rage and pain. He cradled his right arm and rolled directly in front of the car, trying unsuccessfully to find his feet. I didn't think twice about what I did next. He was on one knee a few yards in front of the El Camino, so I stood on the gas pedal and rocketed toward him. I saw his eyes widen like saucers as the car lurched at him, but he threw himself aside, again landing hard on the ground. I put my arm back over the seat, turned my head in his direction and slapped the car into reverse to take another run at him. If one of us was going to die, it was going to be him, I silently pledged to myself and my son. He rolled out of the way easily this time, but as I surged past him I could see the look of shock and disbelief in his eyes.

All around us, the party had grown dead silent as a few people looked toward the **bizarre duel** that must have seemed like some latter-day bullfight. The smell of burnt tire rubber had replaced the woodsy smell of the barbecue pits, and I couldn't hear any more music. Some of the male faces around me had unmistakably **belligerent expressions** and others were shouting toward me. Frank might not be the only Ruiz looking to kick my ass for daring

....

bizarre duel strange fight
belligerent expressions angry looks

to humiliate a man in front of his **kin**. It was time to go, and my mind suddenly flashed on my two packed bags at home. My escape fund was only up to one hundred dollars, but it would have to do. **Independence day had arrived**, whether I was ready or not.

I changed gears one more time and tore out of the lot, kicking up dust and skidding out onto the street. In the rearview mirror I didn't see anyone following me, but I knew they would be soon. I barely stopped for red lights as I jetted toward the freeway and, hopefully, freedom. I reached over and fastened Frankie Jr.'s seat belt. My little man was stone quiet, understanding, I think, that something serious was going on. I hoped that somehow he hadn't seen the hate etched in his father's face, but I knew that he must have. I wondered how life seemed to this little boy who had already seen so many bad things.

"Sit tight, Frankie, we're going for a ride. But first we have to make a stop by the house."

Once I got some distance between us and the party, the terror started to hit me. My hands were shaking so much it was hard to drive straight. I kept checking the rear-view mirror. I had to get home, I thought, but then I dismissed the idea. Frank would be there, waiting, maybe with his cousins. Or maybe the cops would be sitting at my step, waiting to take me to jail for assault. Everyone at the party would side with Frank, I knew. They would say whatever he wanted, whatever it took to teach his rebellious wife a lesson. I felt like I was **having a breakdown**. I didn't know what to do, so I just drove around. I headed to Santa Ana without even noticing until I

---

kin family
Independence day had arrived I was leaving
having a breakdown becoming crazy

got there. I cruised through my neighborhood—should I go home for help? Or run to my cousins for protection? I even drove by my own block to see if I could see any cops or one of the cars that belonged to Frank's family members. Fear washed over me and I barely looked before stepping on the gas and speeding off.

Frankie was asleep, and **my head was spinning**. I didn't have much money, I was eight months' pregnant and had no place to turn. I drove around all night, looping through Anaheim and Fullerton and Garden Grove before winding up back in Santa Ana. It was dawn when I found myself back at my street. I had driven in aimless circles all night. I needed food for Frankie and clothes and money. I didn't see any sign of Frank, so I decided to **make a break for** the house.

I raced through the rooms, grabbing photographs, clothes, and anything else I thought I would need. Towels, toys, my address book, the phone number for the shelter. I had **stationed** Frankie Jr. at the front window and told him to yell if anyone drove up, but I still kept running to the window to scan the street myself. I imagined that any minute Frank and his band of spiteful *vatos* would burst in and beat me to a pulp. Frankie, oblivious to my panic, was cheerfully playing in the pile of items I had tossed on the bed.

The car's tires were squealing again as I pulled away from our apartment complex, my eyes pasted to the rear-view mirror where I was sure I would see a pack of low-riders appear at any second. I raced through the city, swerving down side streets and trying to put as much distance between us and the apartment as I could. It seemed like there was a police car on every corner. Did Frank call the cops

....

my head was spinning I was panicking
make a break for quickly run inside
stationed placed

on me? My heart sank as I imagined the phone call, Frank telling the cops that his desperate and crazy wife had hit him with the car and run off with his son. His relatives would **be lined up to serve as witnesses**. I eased off the accelerator and tried to **gather my thoughts**. I pulled into a gas station and fumbled through my purse for the phone number to the shelter. I needed a place to go.

....

be lined up to serve as witnesses tell the police what they saw
gather my thoughts think about what to do next

BEFORE YOU MOVE ON...

1. **Conclusions** Why did the police and Frank's mother not yell at Frank for beating Mona?

2. **Problem and Solution** Mona hoped that Osuna and Billy would help her so she invited them over. Did the visit solve her problem?

LOOK AHEAD Was Mona able to escape Frank? Read pages 218–235 to find out.

~ Chapter Eleven ~

SEEKING SHLETER

The woman on the phone said she was afraid that I was being followed. The shelter location is **a secret site**, she said, and we can't take the security risk that your husband is stalking you right now. This was the last thing I wanted to hear. After a sleepless night, I was **weary and paranoid** and I just wanted to be somewhere safe. Instead, I was in a phone booth, jerking my head around every few seconds to see if Frank was about to grab me. The woman suggested I go to a police station, but I told her I couldn't. She didn't ask for an explanation, thankfully.

"You're in Santa Ana?"

"Yeah, at a phone booth."

"Okay, drive to the next city and find a safe spot to call us from a phone booth there. Watch behind you to make sure you're not being followed. Then we'll give you directions to get here."

"Okay."

After a fifteen-minute drive of pure panic, I found a phone at a

....

a secret site not known by anybody
weary and paranoid tired and frightened

Garden Grove gas station and I called again. The woman gave me directions to a place in Fullerton and, with relief, I hung the phone up and raced back to the car. Fullerton isn't far, but it took me hours to get to the shelter. I didn't know the city very well and I got lost, but I was too afraid to stop and ask for directions. I couldn't think straight. I kept **pulling over, trying to collect myself** and reassure Frankie. When I finally reached the shelter, I was **a wreck**.

I pushed a button on a speaker at the front door, and someone came to let me in. The place was not what I expected. Instead of looking like a clinic or something, it was an old, huge house, with six or more bedrooms. One room was an office, and nearby was a living room where a group of women and their kids was watching TV. The woman in charge asked me a bunch of questions and filled out some forms. She was kind, and she told me not to be afraid.

"We're not here to judge you or make you do anything you don't want to do," she said. "We just want to help you and give you a safe place to be right now."

The first thing we did was get cleaned up. The cold water on my face felt good, and the fresh, warm towels made me feel safe, as strange as that sounds. They gave me some food, and I realized for the first time that I was starving. The warm food helped calm me, as did the words of the counselor. I started to tell her what happened the day before.

"I'm afraid the police might be looking for me. My husband might have told them that I attacked him. But **it was just self-defense**, I swear."

....

pulling over, trying to collect myself stopping the car, trying to calm down

a wreck exhausted

it was just self-defense I just did it to protect myself

"It's okay, calm down. I believe you. We have an attorney who will talk to you about all these things. Just your being here will help show that you were in fear for your life, the life of your son and your unborn child. So don't worry about that stuff now."

That night, with Frankie in a twin bed next to mine, I got my first sound sleep in weeks.

The next morning, another woman gave me some forms to fill out to apply for welfare. I didn't like the idea, but she told me there was no reason to be ashamed. She said I had been **paying my dues** for years and that this was a temporary way for the government to help me during a difficult time. I signed my name, but I still didn't like it. A few days later, I liked it even less. The line at the welfare office was like a **motley collection** of Santa Ana's sad and shameless. One older woman, her grey hair unwashed and pinned up, was muttering to herself, and not far away from her a man leaning on a cane looked like he might collapse at any minute. Others seemed less needy and more greedy. A guy in his thirties, wearing a gold chain and sporting sunglasses, was reading the classifieds and swaying to music coming though his earphones. Does he need this money? I felt bad judging anyone, though. I wondered how I looked, whether people lumped me in with the **scammers or the genuinely needy**. I didn't like either label, and I thought about bolting out the door. But I needed the money for the son I had and the child to come. We had next to nothing.

More than an hour later, I walked up to the window and was shuttled off to the desk of a case worker.

....

paying my dues working hard

motley collection mixed group

scammers or the genuinely needy people who did not need welfare or the people who really did

"Why do you keep having children if you don't plan on working?"

I felt the shame and rage building in me, clumping like a red-hot rock in my gut. It was the same lesson I had been **force-fed** in school, at the clinic, and even at the PD: You are less than a person. You will lead a quiet life of modest expectations, and you will stay in your neighborhood. If you stray, if you expect more than that, you will be shamed and shot down.

"I have worked, and I'm looking for a job now. I had my son and got pregnant while I was with my husband. Now I'm on my own, and I just need some temporary help."

"Right," the woman sniffed sarcastically. She thought I was trash. She was arrogant enough to think she knew my whole life by looking at my skin color and a government form. She hated her job, I could tell, and I was glad.

The government money helped, but I swore I would be rid of it as soon as I could.

My next stop was the Orange County Courthouse, the site of my wedding day. This time, I was back to file for separation and a **restraining order against Frank**, documents the shelter staff had told me would **arm me with the law to** fight off Frank when he came back to haunt me. I knew he would be back. I just wasn't sure how long it would take.

I showed the separation papers and the court order to my mother to prove to her that I was serious about leaving Frank, and she nodded silently. She was on my side now, and she let me move back

....

force-fed taught
restraining order against Frank court document preventing Frank from coming near us
arm me with the law to make the police help me

into my old room.

My father said nothing. I wondered if I was **sinking lower in his view**, a pregnant woman with one child and no husband. But my mother whispered that he was glad to have me under his roof again and away from Frank. "He's happy you are safe now. That is all that matters to him," she told me.

Frank began drifting by the house, looking to negotiate his way back into my life. He looked bad. "Hey, I'm a mess without you," he confessed with a thin smile. "I need you back, so what do you think? I'll say I'm sorry."

"No, Frank. It's over for good. Saying you're sorry doesn't help me a lot. My mind's made up."

His mournful eyes tugged at my heart. The two of us had so much history, it was hard to let go. Even the bad times bond you to someone, and when they're gone, it's scary. I relented a few times in the final emotional weeks of my pregnancy, even letting him stay some nights. I even **softened my stance** and started discussing reconciliation. I cursed myself each time.

The hardest thing to explain to people about an abusive marriage is **the ebb and flow of the hatred it breeds**. In some ways, the bad times, the worst valleys, make the good times and reconciliations seem stronger, more meaningful. Like any roller coaster ride, it's hard to get off in the middle. Again and again, I told myself that my life would be better without Frank. But when my newborn son, Vincent, arrived in April 1983, I could not shake the thought that

....

sinking lower in his view even more shameful to him now

softened my stance changed my mind about leaving him

the ebb and flow of the hatred it breeds that things are not always bad a household with two boys needs a father. I let the madness creep back into my life, again, and it felt like the right thing to do. Frank and I had certainly seen our share of pain and tragedy during our marriage, but as I watched him cradle our newborn, I felt a powerful bond to my husband, a desperate desire to make things work out between us. Marriages, like people, are neither completely good nor bad, just somewhere in between.

One of the first nights home from the hospital, I watched Frank stand in the dim light above his two sleeping sons. "This is what it's all about, y'know?" We sat together and watched the two boys sleep, their chests rising and falling with a sweet gentleness. Frank **vowed to change his ways**, and I smiled and encouraged him. I had heard the pledges before, so I could not pretend to be convinced, but I hoped that each promise was pushing us that much closer to a better life. What else could I do?

Frank showed he was good to his word in the following weeks, cutting back on his drugs and quitting his drinking altogether. He slimmed up without the daily six-pack, his face thinning out to better show his strong jaw and expressive eyes. He was on his best behavior for the baptism and the family parties that followed, which helped **clear some of the air** between us and my parents. My father was still distant, but at least he occasionally spoke and, finally, began to acknowledge his grandsons. Watching Raymond Sandoval pretend to box with giggling Frankie Jr. or caressing Vincent's cheek almost brought tears of relief to my eyes.

I could live with my father hating me as long as my boys had a

....

vowed to change his ways promised to be different
clear some of the air improve the relationship

place in his heart and a chance **for a living family history**. I was so tired after Vincent's birth. My health wasn't very good. I was often sick, and I didn't eat right. But, in other ways, things were turning around for the better. My mother even got my father to agree to let Frank and me move into the small house in front of their home, giving us a chance to escape his mother and her increasingly crowded house. I was thrilled. Maybe my father's agreement meant he was softening his stance against me. Even if he wasn't, the move meant I'd have a chance to wear down his defenses. How could he ignore me if I was there every day? And maybe living next to my parents would have a calming influence on Frank, I thought, a presence that would help him **see through on his pledge**.

It was strange for both of us to be living in my old neighborhood, on my old street. I had gone through so much since leaving, picked up so many scars and secrets, I wasn't sure how I felt about being back so close to my roots. Even stranger was being there with Frank. It was like my past meeting my present. Our arrival back in the aged barrios of central Santa Ana after living in apartments in the city's south and west sides put us closer, of course, to the gang scene. Few of the faces roaming the street were familiar, though. Several new generations had joined the street games, and the gangs that I had known had all splintered and split apart—none more so than F-Troop. The new scene made me antsy because **the sparring factions** made everything more unpredictable. My anxieties were greeted by a rough week. Three of Frank's old homeboys died, one right after the other, and my husband was desperately upset. Two

....

for a living family history to learn about their family
see through on his pledge keep his promise
the sparring factions it was not always clear who your enemies were, which

were taken down in separate shootouts, and the third overdosed on smack. The funeral home spaced out the services, stretching the black mood more than two weeks. I could tell that Frank saw his own face when he looked down into the casket. The thick black sunglasses he wore as he grasped hands with glowering *veteranos* at the cemetery did not hide the fear in his face.

At the third and final service, he clenched his fist next to his chin and whispered to an old friend, "It's bad, all three of 'em, y'know, *ese*? I used to party and all with them."

"Sucks, homes." The old *vato* had a thick mustache that formed a downward horseshoe around his scarred chin. Tattoos peaked from under his shirt collar and below his black jacket sleeves.

"I mean, damn. What if all of us are gonna die? It's like a curse."

"Man, homes. Everybody's got to die."

Being back in the neighborhood reunited Frank with a lot of his Southside homies as well as the homies from Golden West, and the trio of deaths seemed to make him **thirsty for their company**. Or maybe that was just an excuse, a way to party. I began to find PCP bottles around the house and once I walked in to find Frank and a buddy snorting lines of coke off a *TV Guide* with both our sons sitting a few feet away. I was livid and told him so. Oddly, he surrendered, **moping off** with his buddy to some new haunt down the street. There was always a party within walking distance in the neighborhood.

Frank had lost some of his fire. We still argued, but he rarely raised a hand toward me and he dodged a fight whenever he could.

....

thirsty for their company desperate to see them
moping off leaving

I thought he might be **mellowing with age**, but then I saw the other signs.

I don't know how I could have missed the hints for so long. And how long had it been? Frank had hardly eaten for three days or, for that matter, barely budged from our worn old couch. He just laid there, watching TV. I thought at first he had the flu, or was just hungover or too high on weed. Then I noticed the trips to the bathroom every hour. For ten or twenty minutes, sometimes. Then, one afternoon, I heard more than one voice in the bathroom. Frank was in there with a friend, and I could not deny what I had known for weeks.

The boys were with my mother one Saturday afternoon when I walked up behind him.

"You're **shooting up**, aren't you?"

He didn't answer, so I knew I was right.

I pushed the issue. "You are, aren't you? All the other stuff you do, all the beer you drink, just isn't enough. Now you got to do this, too."

He surprised me by laughing. "Mona, you think you know everything, don't you? Come here."

He walked to the bathroom and motioned for me to follow. He took the heavy porcelain lid off the toilet and pulled out a small plastic case that had been sitting in the water. He unzipped his **junkie kit** and showed me the syringe inside, along with matchbooks and a spoon. He laughed, and even that came out slurred. I could tell he was flying right then.

....

mellowing with age calming down as he got older
shooting up using serious drugs
junkie kit bag of drug supplies

"Yeah, Mona, you're so smart 'cause you noticed I been shooting up? Big news, eh? Except I been doing it since we met, little by little. The whole time, five years. It ain't no big thing, I can handle it just like all those *veteranos* you used to hang with."

I felt like the wind had been knocked out of me. Worse, I felt stupid. All those days when Frank had been too sick to move, all those stomachaches and intense hangovers. The frequent vomiting and the way no room was ever warm enough to prevent his chills. He had always been so open and bold about his other drug **vices**. It had never occurred to me there might be one I didn't know about.

I searched back through my memories to when I was young and in love with Frank, when his strength and earnest words attracted me to him. It had all been bullshit. Even then he was an addict and a liar. I had been thinking that ours was a good love that had soured because of bad times and weakness, but after Frank's smug confession about the smack, I began to suspect it had always been **a sham**. Part of my love for Frank had died the day he first hit me, and another piece peeled away when he began to sleep with other women. Now, with this, I wasn't sure what was left. The grinning man holding the needle was a stranger to me.

Frank sensed that he had made a mistake.

Since his confession, I had become a different person around him, withdrawn and silent. Part of it was his deceit, but on another level, I was simply disgusted by the thought of sharing my house with the needle, even though I had apparently done just that for years.

....

vices habits
a sham a lie

Junkies had terrified me when I was younger. I had met a *veterano* once, when I was maybe sixteen, who had been on heroin for the better part of a decade. He was a friend of one of my cousins, I remember, but no one really trusted him. He was too far gone, too wrapped up in the junk. His eyes were flat and slow-moving, and his skin was drained of much of its color. I had no idea how old he was. It was hard to tell, and I was too afraid to talk to him. The skin from his wrist to his elbow was thin and mottled, and, in some spots, almost **transparent**. The effect was disgusting, with his arms hanging at his sides like a pair of diseased fish. In my imagination, I always thought of him as a vampire, not really alive and always feeding. When I looked at Frank, I saw that old junkie in his future, and I wasn't sure I could handle that.

Instead of trying to mend fences with me, Frank lost himself in his habits. Or perhaps his confession had **liberated him**.

Either way, he spent more and more time shooting up, snorting, smoking, drinking and partying with the old familiar friends from around the neighborhood. He started to talk like a banger again, slipping into the old street mutter and tuning back into the gang scene.

Meanwhile, things were deteriorating at home. Frank's **extended bender** did not escape the notice of his employers, who started seeing far less of Frank, or the attention of our nearby landlord: my mother. Our money started going to pay for Frank's new favorite concoction, mixing coke and heroin, called a speedball. My mother

---

transparent see-through, invisible
liberated him freed him to do whatever he wanted
extended bender excessive partying

despised drug use, and she had no intention of tolerating it from a stranger who had been forced on her by a courthouse marriage. She **had us served with eviction papers**, just yards from where I had grown up. I stared at the documents in a state of shock. My mother had managed to surprise even me. By this time my third child was born and once again we had no home. We stayed with his sister for a while and lived in her garage. Frank was working again, but not steadily. I began looking for work knowing that soon he may be fired from his job as he was before. His craving for his drug habit became more obvious when his excuses for not getting paid became more frequent than before.

Things improved when I got a job at the city library. My sister, Maryann, was a longtime, trusted employee at the city's main library, and she **put in a good word for me that landed me** the job. The new job was pretty easy: I filed books and, if a patron had a question, I would try to help locate a book or use the card catalog to find a specific title. I liked the work. I had always loved books and, in the quiet solitude of the back shelves, I would pause and thumb through the hardcover volumes that offered so much knowledge about a vast world I had never really seen. The pay was not much, but it was enough, especially since I was now supporting Frank and the kids. It was good, too, because I grew closer to my sister. Maryann had started working at the library right out of high school, and had been there a decade. My sisters and I used to joke that she had been there so long she was like a piece of the building's furniture. I think we all envied her ability to keep a good job, along with a steady marriage

....

had us served with eviction papers gave us legal papers forcing us to leave

put in a good word for me that landed me said good things about me that helped me get

that made her happy.

Maryann and I had not been close since we were kids, but working in the same building with her, taking breaks and lunches together, we started to talk and share with each other. It was really nice, and it helped me through a difficult time. We talked about our marriages and our problems, but one subject we never discussed was the violence I faced at home. She knew about it, obviously, but she also sensed it was a source of embarrassment for me. Right or wrong, I blamed myself for a lot of what happened between Frank and me, and I was ashamed that our marriage had gone so **awry**. Maryann was always encouraging, and told me to make myself happy and everything else would take care of itself. She also was supportive when **an old aspiration resurfaced**.

The library was in the Civic Center and formed an uneven triangle with the PD and the courthouse on the other tips. It even shared a parking lot with the police station. Every day I worked, I would look across the courtyard to the squat, bunker-like police station and tell myself that it was where the future lived. The library job was fine for now, but I knew where I really wanted to be. Sometimes, at lunch, I would linger near the hot dog vending carts that set up shop outside the PD, hoping **for a chance encounter with** my old friends.

Frank was home very little, so when we split up again it was not the loud, abrupt collapse it had been in the past. It was an erosion. He left, and I told him to not come back. This was the end of our marriage. He seemed to agree. I returned home to Golden West

....

awry wrong

an old aspiration resurfaced I began thinking about an old dream of mine

for a chance encounter with to see

with the pledge that Frank would not be **part of the picture**, and I knew another eviction would be coming from my mother if that deal was broken.

As the months went by, Frank visited the house only occasionally and never stayed. Maybe the message was sinking in, or maybe he was just too distracted by his busy party schedule. The stories came back to me from friends and relatives that my husband was out of control, slamming drugs and running with a wild band of *vatos*. He still came by every once in awhile, sulking or shouting, depending on his mood. The threats and break-ins had stopped, thankfully. My feelings for Frank quickly dissolved from love to pure hatred. Mostly for all the lies and broken promises of our marriage. I now felt relief and could finally enjoy my life without him.

I relished the time spent with my kids after work each night, and I was feeling a lot better about our lives. I began trying to save money for my own place and to prepare for my new life. Three mouths would be a lot to feed, I knew, and I kept looking for a better-paying job.

I had turned my back on God when I first fell in with the gangs. The world was unfair and God made it that way, I had reasoned, so His word meant nothing to me. My mother wanted me to go to the church, though, to speak with a priest about my collapsed marriage. I was reluctant, but I went because I felt compelled to meet my mother's wishes after she had **opened her home to me**. I expected the church people to tell me to return to my husband, but I was **floored** when

---

part of the picture living with me
opened her home to me let me live in her house
floored very shocked

they actually suggested divorce.

"I thought Catholics weren't allowed to get a divorce."

"Nowhere in the Bible does it say you have to live with a dangerous drug addict and put your kids in danger," the priest told me. "You've done all you can to save this marriage. Now just save yourself and your children."

That **sealed it for me**. I filed for divorce. Frank was livid. It was almost funny. He suddenly was religious and in fear of flouting God. Through the screen door, I asked him what he thought God's view was on beating his wife, ripping people off and using drugs.

He stomped off, cursing me and promising that I would regret my words. Things started happening after that: small burglaries where my things disappeared and **vandalism** that left my windows broken. I didn't even care. I was feeling stronger every day. My only regret was not leaving him sooner. He came by now and then to see the kids. He was distant, aware that things would never be the way they used to be between us. At least I hoped that's what the faraway look in his eyes meant.

Every few days, I would wander over to the job board at the PD, the spot where they post notices about new positions. My eyes would scan the job descriptions, even the ones I couldn't hope to qualify for, just for a taste of the world I missed so much. Then, after I had been at the library for a year, I read a job posting that made my heart beat fast. It was for a parking control officer, which I knew meant meter maid. Hardly the most exciting job, but the salary was nearly double

----

sealed it for me helped me make my decision
vandalism attacks on the house

my paycheck at the library. The notice also said Spanish speakers **were eligible for** bonus pay. I was thrilled. Could I actually qualify? I knew exactly what to do next.

A day later, tugging nervously at my favorite outfit, I marched up to the information desk at the PD and asked to speak with Billy Brown or Detective Osuna. Brown was gone, the woman said after checking with a coworker. He retired. "And we don't have a Detective Osuna either." My heart sank. I hadn't even considered the possibility that they were both gone. "But we do have a sergeant named Osuna," she continued. "Sgt. Felix Osuna. Could that be him?"

I beamed and nodded. I told her my name, she made a quick call and the next thing I knew I was walking through the familiar hallways toward the watch commander's small office.

Osuna smiled warmly when he saw me and gave me a long hug. "Mona, you look great. It's so good to see you."

And I felt great. Compared to the last time I had seen him, I felt like I was on top of the world. "It's good to see you, too. So you're a sergeant now?"

He nodded. "I'm on Watch Commander (WC) duty right now. Which means I sit in here and shuffle papers all day and listen to the radio calls." At his desk, a bank of small black and white screens showed camera images of the holding cells in the basement while a large speaker crackled with police radio traffic.

We chatted for twenty minutes or so. He told me about Billy's retirement and his move back to Florida, and we laughed as he

....

were eligible for could earn

described the big southerner trying to get used to **civilian life**. I told him about my job, and he asked me about my kids, so I described each.

"Wow, three kids? Mona, you've got your hands full."

"I do. I know. But it's okay. I can handle it."

"What about Frank?" He asked the question slowly, and I could tell he was unsure if he should ask at all. He looked relieved when I told him I was on my own for good.

"It got pretty bad," I told him, "but, you know, I walked away. That's all over now."

We were both quiet for a long moment. Then he asked me what was next for me. I smiled and handed him the job posting for parking control attendant. "I want to come back to the PD. I was hoping to talk to you about it."

He smiled back, and I could tell he was genuinely excited. There was a lot we both wanted to say, but instead he handed me back the paper. "I think I might be able to help you out with that."

During breaks, I began meeting Osuna at the PD **for coaching**. We pored over traffic codes and statutes, which he knew by heart, and he hammered on the concepts of the job. He grilled me on scenarios he knew would be part of the test and quizzed me on **department protocol**. He had sat on a lot of job boards, so he ran me through mock interviews, stopping to tell me to sit up straighter or make more eye contact. "Look every one of them in the eye, and don't stop doing it. Eye contact demands attention from the listener and makes you appear confident."

....

civilian life life outside of the police and military
for coaching so he could help train me
department protocol police rules and codes

All of it reminded me of when Osuna had pushed me to get my GED. His belief in me made me demand more of myself, and, just like that, I felt like I was moving forward in life again.

I took the test and a week later ripped open a letter **with city letterhead** and read the news: I was the fourth candidate on the list. I wasn't sure if that was good news or bad, so I dialed the information number listed at the top. The woman told me there were only two **posts** available, so I didn't get the job. My heart sunk, but then she said that I would be **in line for** upcoming jobs. A few months later, my turn came. The same woman called and asked if I would be able to start right away.

....

with city letterhead from the city
posts jobs
in line for chosen for

BEFORE YOU MOVE ON...

1. **Comparisons** Reread pages 219–221. How was Mona treated at the shelter? How was she treated at the welfare office?

2. **Conclusions** Reread pages 222–223. Why did Mona go back to Frank?

LOOK AHEAD Read pages 236–255 to find out why Mona learned that it was hard to escape her past.

~ Chapter Twelve ~

THE WALL

I loved the new job. I was outside all day, first of all, which made me less restless than working **the stacks of** the city library. On the days when street **sweepers would plod** up and down the neighborhood streets, I was one of the parking control officers who darted ahead and behind of the big rig to ticket the cars left in its path despite the "no parking" signs. Other days, I worked the busy downtown commerce area, driving a Pinto with a police **decal** that had a steering wheel and half-door on the left side so I could lean out and chalk the back tires of cars. An hour later, I would sweep back by and leave tickets on the windshields of cars that had been left too long in the crowded, narrow streets. A lot of people weren't happy to see me, of course, and some people even argued or insulted me, but overall it was good work. The sun on my face and the hours of independence were like a fresh start on life.

It was January of a new year, 1986, and I was back in uniform and free from Frank after five painful years of marriage. I had my

....

the stacks of inside
sweepers would plod cleaners drove
decal sticker

three kids with me and a new job that was both challenging and part of the law enforcement world, a world I saw **rife with** opportunity. Everything was **on course** and moving forward. It would have been easy to sit back and smile about my busy new life. I might have done just that if I didn't get a crushing reminder that some people will never let you distance yourself from your painful past.

We called the supervisor Hoops because he was so demanding that everyone felt like they were circus animals **jumping through his hoops**. He was a terse and gruff man, but that didn't bother me. He was fair to me during my first week, and any criticism he had of my work was **constructive**, and that's all that mattered to me. That changed one afternoon, though, when he caught a glimpse of my tattoo for the first time. Up until that moment, I had instinctively hid the mark when he was around by folding my arms, using my ticket book as a shield, or shoving my hand deep in my pocket. I hid it because I thought it would make things easier. I was right.

Hoops rolled his eyes when he saw the tattoo. "I need to speak with you in my office," he snapped.

He sat behind his desk and folded his hands. "Why didn't you tell me about that tattoo?"

"What?"

"The gang tattoo on your hand. Why didn't you show it to me earlier?"

My voice had an edge when I spoke. "I didn't think it mattered. I didn't think it had anything to do with my job."

He took the response as a challenge to his authority, and he

....

rife with full of

on course going well

jumping through his hoops doing what he wanted them to do

constructive helpful

237

responded with venom in his voice.

"Listen, if it were up to me, I wouldn't allow you to work here. I don't think you're right for this job or this department. You belong out on the streets."

I was stunned. My mouth was open in shock. I couldn't believe my boss was tearing into me because of a tattoo I got years earlier. He didn't see ink on my wrist, though, he saw a symbol of a life that he despised. Now he despised me, too. He told me to get out, but he gave me one last thought to chew on.

"Your career in this department will be over before mine, if **I can help it**."

He was smart; he told me all of this with no one else around. No one would believe me if I said anything. I was still **on probation**, anyway, and any trouble would cost me my job. I swallowed my anger, and kept my voice calm: "You don't even know me, but you're judging me. All I want is a chance to prove myself. If I don't **give you the highest stats** in this position, you won't have to get rid of me—I'll quit on my own. What do you say?" His faced scrunched up in surprise. He said my offer sounded fair, but he reminded me he would be watching. I felt like I had won a battle. I knew there would be more to come.

My sister Roni had gotten into Christianity about the time I gave birth to Vincent, and she had been **after me to look into** her new faith as something that might also help me. I had been resistant. I had turned my back on God when I first fell in with the gangs. The

----

I can help it I have any control over it
on probation a new employee
give you the highest stats do a great job
after me to look into bothering me to try

world was unfair and bad, I had told myself, so why should its creator be any different. I had also had a bad encounter with a Catholic priest in the early years of my marriage, when I had wandered into a church looking for guidance and advice. A crotchety old priest had dismissed me and basically told me my problems were **of my own doing**. I stormed out, pushed even further from the church. Then, after I talked to the marriage counselor about divorce, I learned that the church could seemingly change its rules whenever it wanted to. I thought the whole religion scene was a scam, a way to make money off sick and old people who needed something to make them feel better. If you needed real help, some real advice, or a shoulder to lean on, well, that's when you saw **the true face of the church**, I told my sister.

But Roni was persistent. Her church was different, she told me, with a different attitude. Finally, I gave in. It was Eagles Nest Church, and warm smiles and upbeat music greeted us at the door, far different from my childhood recollections of the somber Catholic services. The place didn't look like any church I had ever seen. It was a new congregation, and they gathered in a place that looked like a meeting hall. There were no crosses or candles. I was confused by the whole scene.

An older woman handed me a sheet at the door and leaned toward me with her arms out. I jerked back, startled by her **invading my space**. I realized that this woman, a complete stranger, was trying to hug me. She read the discomfort in my face and smiled again. "You've been through hell, haven't you?"

....

of my own doing my fault

the true face of the church how the church really felt about things

invading my space getting too close to me

239

It was the last thing I expected someone to say to me at the door of a church. I didn't know what to say, so I just stared at her.

"I can tell people have hurt you. You don't trust others now. But you're safe here. Everyone here cares about you."

It was strange, and I didn't know how to react. The woman seemed to have this quiet air of confidence about her, a contentment. The whole thing had me **off balance**. I had planned to come along and keep **everything at arm's length**, but now I wasn't sure I could do that. I walked in and sat down, telling the children to hush and pay attention.

I looked around and was surprised to see people of all races and backgrounds. Whites, Asians, Hispanics, old and young, rich and poor and middle-class. Everyone seemed to be getting along. Even more surprising, there were a large number of gangbangers in the parish. *Veteranos*, some in wheelchairs, dotted the crowd, and no one was looking twice at them.

The whole service was completely unlike any I had seen before. I was used to solemn ceremonies, where people were quiet and respectful. But everyone here was smiling and singing along, seeming to have a good time. It was a warm atmosphere, but it also felt a little wrong at first. Everyone just seemed too . . . happy.

The sermon included a talk about battered wives. At first I wondered what he could know about it, but the words he said rang true. It sounded as if he were talking straight to me, and I found myself leaning forward, **hanging on** every word. The pastor, a small man with a vibrant smile, spoke about treating yourself with respect

....

off balance feeling confused

everything at arm's length what was going on in my life a secret

hanging on listening very closely to

and he described the feelings that battered wives cope with, feelings I knew firsthand. Afterward they had some one-on-one counseling, and I walked into one of the small rooms while my sister looked after the kids. I was **skittish** at first, unsure of what to say or do. The counselor was a soft-spoken, middle-aged woman who told me to think of the Bible as a guide to life, not some dusty book or a story about saints and dead people. She quoted some passages and talked about the beauty of God and the need to have **divine answers in a complex world**.

I listened to her words, but I still held back some. She was a white woman, and at that time I had a deep mistrust of white people. But she spoke openly and warmly, and I began to loosen up. Then she told me she had been a battered wife years earlier.

"It's okay if you don't trust me," she said, startling me. Again, someone seemed to know what I was thinking. "You've been through a lot, I know, and it's going to take time for you to get over that pain. It took me a long time, too. But the healing begins with faith in God."

She handed me some literature, some brochures that had pictures of mothers and their children. Inside were quotes from the scriptures and advice on coping with difficult relationships.

"Read these and think about the messages you find there," she said. "The Bible can help you with the decisions in your life. Do you have a dream? Is there something you want in your future?"

I told her I had dreamed of being a police officer all my life. I surprised myself when I said it: I had not planned on opening up to

....

skittish nervous and afraid

divine answers in a complex world religion in your life to help you deal with difficult problems

these people. I went on to say that I had destroyed that dream with bad choices. I couldn't believe I was telling her all this. I described my time in the gang, leaving school and getting pregnant, marrying Frank. "I've made so many mistakes."

"But you're so young!" she said. "There's nothing you can't do. But you do have to believe in yourself. If you do that, you can achieve anything you want. The Bible will help you. Just read it."

I thanked her and left. My legs were wobbly under me, and I was drained. I had the same feeling that I had when I met the women at the shelter. There were actually people in the world willing to help, people who seemed to care. It was just a matter of finding them. And her words, could they be true? Maybe she was right. Maybe my mistakes didn't destroy my dreams. Maybe they just **delayed them**.

I started going to church every week.

It had been months since the final breakup, but Frank would still not **let me be**. He would wander by my house, stumbling from the booze and whatever drugs he and his buddies had enough money to buy. Often he came by in the morning, after a wild, sleepless night built up his anger, bravery or **syrupy sentiment**. Each time he came by, I wondered which speech I would be hearing—the profanity-laced rant about how he was going to teach me a lesson or the pleading to get back together, to give him another chance.

I knew the real reason he came by had nothing to do with me; it was all about him, his needs and his reputation. Life wasn't as pleasant without me around to pick him up and feed him, and he

....

delayed them kept them from happening right away
let me be leave me alone
syrupy sentiment sweet, romantic words

missed that. More than that, though, he hated the way the *vatos* tore into him for letting me **show him up**. It was a humiliating putdown for a homeboy to be **bounced** by his wife, I knew, and Frank's friends were not the sort to let it go quietly. I could hear their insults echoing in Frank's voice, a voice that was growing increasingly unfamiliar.

"Mona, you don't want to see me no more?"

A shiver straightened my back. I was at my front door, key still in the lock, and he was standing just off the porch, watching me. I hate when people sneak up on me.

"No, I don't. I don't want to see you, and I don't have time for you." I stormed off toward my car, wanting to get away. But I didn't want him hanging around my house either.

"I want to talk to you, it won't take long." He was wearing a sleeveless undershirt and some grungy jeans that bunched up over his work boots. His hair was slicked back and his unshaven stubble **added a few years to his face**.

"No. You're not part of my life anymore, and I got nothing left for you. I hate you! Do you hear me? I wish you'd die. Leave me alone or I'll call the cops and send you back to a cell."

He tried to laugh it off, but his grin **didn't survive my glare**. He knew I meant it, and, for the first time, so did I. There was nothing left between us. He looked lost for a moment and very tired beneath the early morning sun. Then, like a light switch flipping on, his anger returned. He lunged at me before I could slam the door and his fingers wrapped around my throat. I fought him off and told

....

show him up embarrass him

bounced left

added a few years to his face made him look older

didn't survive my glare disappeared when he saw my anger

Frankie Jr. to go across the street and tell Grandma to call the police. My son took off like a bolt, screaming, "Daddy is hurting Mommy!"

I pushed Frank away and he stood there panting for a heartbeat, then turned to see his son running into my mother's house. "Screw this." He waved goodbye sarcastically and took off down the street, pulling a cigarette from a crumpled pack in his back pocket. He looked back as he lit it, shook his head and rounded the corner. A patrol car pulled up a few moments later. A hulking, black cop named Marshall jogged up to my doorstep and asked if I was okay. I told him I wasn't hurt, just **shaken**. He asked where my attacker was, and I pointed down the street, "I'll **take a few laps** around the area and see if I can find him. Call if he shows up here again."

I suddenly remembered I had to get to work. I threw my stuff in the car and headed to the station after leaving Frankie with my mother. I was trying not to cry. I didn't want anyone at work to know about my troubles. I hoped Marshall would stay quiet and I reminded myself to thank him for his help.

I was on the weekend downtown shift, so I would be able to **lose myself in my labors**. At the time, only one parking control officer worked the busy merchant district lining the narrow streets of downtown, and it was a shift that always promised lots of work.

I drive fast when I'm angry, so I was half an hour early. I was furious that Frank was still on the edge of my life. I didn't mind him visiting with the kids—they were his children, after all—but I resented his mind games. What did he want from me?

I needed help. When I got to the station, I saw that the

---

shaken scared

take a few laps look, drive

lose myself in my labors forget about my problems as I worked

supervisor on duty was Cpl. Lucas, a cop who had always been kind and open with me. We worked together a lot, but I had never told him about my life away from work, just as he had never confided in me about his personal life. I didn't know him very well, but he seemed like someone I could trust. I asked him if I could talk to him about a personal problem, and he shut the door and asked me what was wrong. Before I was done, I was choking back tears. His face grew stern as I described Frank's antics, and I could tell he was sympathetic. I wasn't sure I had done the right thing by opening up, but just talking out my problems gave me some relief.

He asked where I lived, and I told him. He jotted down my address, which he said **fell within his patrol district**. He promised to cruise by to check up on me and to listen for my address on the radio. "And make sure you tell the dispatcher who you are when you call, Mona," he said. "We take care of **our own**."

Lucas was good to his word. Every day he would slowly drive past my house and flash a spotlight on the window. If everything was okay, I would lean out the door and wave. If he didn't see that signal, he would come up the sidewalk. It was incredibly comforting, but I wondered if it was really necessary. That question was answered one night when I went out for a drink with some of the women from work.

It was a rare and refreshing night out, and I was **in buoyant spirits** by the time I got home. Then I saw the police cars in front of my house. When I pulled up, I saw my parents standing on the lawn. My heart was pounding. I didn't see my kids. I spotted Lucas and

....

fell within his patrol district was in the area he worked

our own people who work for the police

in buoyant spirits feeling very happy

he flashed a smile and a wave that calmed me down. "Don't worry, Mona, everything's fine," he reassured me. "You just had a visitor."

Frank had tried to break in. A neighbor across the street saw him **prowling in** the yard and called the police. Frank tried to tell Lucas that he lived at the house and had only broken a window because he had lost his keys. When Lucas told him he knew he was lying, Frank had slipped into his angry *vato* mode.

The way Lucas told it, Frank had threatened to kick his ass if he stopped him from going into the house. Lucas chuckled when he recounted the story. "I told him to do what he had to do, and that I would, too, and, when it was all over, I'd clean him off the sidewalk and take him to jail."

It was the first time a cop had taken my side, the first time an officer had stepped in and told Frank straight out that he would get in trouble if he hurt or harassed me. All the other times, Frank had gotten his way. Frank didn't like the change, Lucas said.

"I told him to take a walk. I also told him to get used to seeing me around." Lucas said Frank marched off into the darkness, cowed and fuming.

After all the excitement, when the patrol car was gone and my parents had left, I **tucked the kids in** and read a book for awhile. Soon I shut off the light, thinking about my workday, the evening on the town and **our newfound security**. I drifted off to sleep, smiling.

Work was going well, and my beautiful daughter, Vanessa, was now walking and talking. Frankie was a little man, eager to help me with Vincent and Vanessa, and our new rented apartment started

---

prowling in sneaking around

tucked the kids in put the kids in bed

our newfound security the fact that we were now being protected

to feel like a home. Hoops had done nothing to follow up with his threats at the PD, and I felt like I was in a good groove with the work I was doing. Everything had turned around for me, but I wanted more. I needed a better job to make sure my kids would have the future I wanted for them. I certainly couldn't expect any financial help from Frank. I also wanted to give myself something I had always dreamed of: a career.

I was ready to **raise my sights**. Now that I was in uniform, I knew the PD was the place I wanted to be, despite the **odds stacked against me**. I began taking criminology courses at a local community college to educate myself about the complex world of law enforcement and criminal justice. I also began working on myself: I began lifting weights to become stronger and, for the first time in my life, I began running to improve my stamina and fitness. The range master at the PD had once offered to show me the basics of firearms—safety, marksmanship, cleaning a weapon—and now I took him up on his offer. I was pretty quiet about my goal, but I was pulling the pieces into place. I was going to make my dream come true. I was going to become a cop.

When I saw the guy running up from behind me, I locked my eyes forward and tightened my face. I was in training and I had no time for **racetrack Romeos** trying to make a move on every young woman they saw alone. It had happened a few times before and most guys got the hint, and the ones who didn't I told flat out that they had no chance. "I'm training for my future," was my usual response,

"I'm not interested. Get lost." My marriage had left me **gun-shy** when it came to men, and now that I had a goal to strive for I had even less interest in starting some new romance. I think most guys could read it in my face. But this runner, a *vato* by the looks of him, wasn't taking the hint.

"Hey, what's your name?"

"Look," I said, "I'm not interested."

"Interested in what? I'm just making conversation."

"I'm not interested in meeting guys. I'm here to run. I'm in training."

"Hey, same here. I'm training, too." He started to shadowbox, his thick arms snapping at the air in front of him. "Sometimes it's easier to keep going when someone is running beside you. That's all."

I looked over for the first time. His nose was flat and crooked, obviously a boxer's nose, and his body was lean and muscular. He was wearing gym sweats with "Westminster Boxing" written across them. His face was familiar. I realized he was a guy named Sal, a street-famous member of the Second Street Sharkside Gang, a gang that split off from the Troopers and claimed the west end of Second Street. The Sharksiders were **renowned as brutal old-timers**, as tough as they get. Sal was a guy everyone knew worked his whole life to become a professional boxer. He always seemed on the edge of that success and his **long string of** victories in the ring added to his gang's street reputation. Sal could kill someone with his fists, everyone knew, but he wasn't a bully or a mad dog. Maybe it was because he had no fear, but Sal was always kind and fair, **reserving his temper for**

....

gun-shy afraid, mistrustful
renowned as brutal old-timers a famous group
long string of many
reserving his temper for only getting angry at

people who crossed him or his homeys.

He squinted at me, tilting his head as his arms pumped. "Hey, I know you, right? You from around here?"

I told him my name and my cousins and he said he thought he had seen me around before. His tone was friendly but not forward, and I relaxed a little. I didn't think he was trying to **pick me up**, and we fell into a shared pace as we circled the track. He was right: Time goes faster when you run with someone. As my kids watched us circle again and again around the community college oval track, Sal and I talked about the neighborhood and, eventually, about our goals. I knew his already—to become **a champion in the ring**. When asked what I was pushing myself for, I told him I wanted to wear a badge and make a difference as a cop.

"What?! A cop?" He almost stopped running, and he scrambled to catch back up.

"Yeah, a cop."

"You're gonna sell out the barrio and become a stinkin' cop?"

I didn't take the words personally. A lot of people in the barrio see cops as the enemy, including myself in my younger years. That was part of the reason I wanted to become a cop, and I told Sal that, along with my goal to help women and kids, usually the first victims of crime, by my experience.

The muscular *vato* shook his head in disbelief and shared his view of cops. He listed the encounters he had with cops in the past, the ones who **hassled or dissed** him. His voice got louder as he recounted his beatings at the hands of officers who called him scum

....

pick me up get me to date him
a champion in the ring a great boxer
hassled or dissed hurt or disrespected

and worse. "The pigs **keep the people down**, and that's the truth."

The run was over and we went to pick up our gear. I told Sal he was wrong, that the badge was only as honorable as the person who wore it. I would do a good job, I told him. I would be a cop who made life in the barrio better. He chewed on that as he jogged off toward the chainlink fence and the street beyond. "Alright, Mona," he said, his voice still skeptical. "I'll see you tomorrow."

The debate continued that next day and for months after, as Sal and I met almost every day for our afternoon runs. Five miles a day, seven days a week. Our friendship grew, but never left that oval track or the shared ritual of pushing ourselves toward our goals. We debated cops and the barrio as we sweated, and we talked about our failed marriages and unlikely aspirations. He talked wistfully about the feeling of throwing a great punch, the ability to master himself and his opponent. He began to understand my dream better, too, and softened his view of cops.

"Do you know good cops, or are you gonna be the first?" he joked one day.

I told him about **my role models**. He **conceded** that they sounded like good people, dedicated people. He even admitted that, when he was young, even he had met a cop who treated people with respect.

"There was this one guy, he treated me like a human being, y'know? He busted me a few times, but never insulted me or tried to hurt me for no reason. He gave me his card and told me that if I ever wanted to go straight, he would help. Is that what you're going to be like?"

---

keep the people down make life harder for everyone
my role models the cops who helped me
conceded admitted

"Yeah."

"Well, let's say you get a call, right? Say it's a gang activity call, and you get there in your police car and you see me. You gonna pretend you don't know me? Would you act like some tough cop who don't **associate with** homeboys?"

I told him I would never forget where I was from, who I was, or the people who knew me. Those things, I told him, will make me a better cop. Then he asked me what Frank Ruiz thought of my ambition and I snapped that I didn't care what he thought or what he did anymore. "He's not part of my life or my kids' lives, not anymore."

He said even if there are "a few" good cops, that overall the PD was a bad thing for the barrio, a group that brought more pain to the neighborhood than help. I shrugged. "I think you're wrong, Sal, but couldn't you say the same thing about the gangs? You're an old-timer: Don't the gangs bring more pain than they're worth?"

He just smiled at that one and stared down at his stopwatch and his feet pounding on the track. Some days we would barely speak, lost either in our own thoughts or in the ache in our legs. Slowly, day by day, he not only understood my dream, he became one of my biggest supporters. He would badger me about filling out applications on time or about my study habits. He **was hungry for** details about my training, and soon began offering lessons from his world.

"Someday, you'll meet a guy as tough as me, or almost as tough as me," said Sal, his dark eyes smiling. "You got to know how to

....

associate with talk to
was hungry for always wanted

251

throw a punch."

He showed me how to **step into a punch**, and where to hit people to bring them down fast and hard. He reminded me that everybody **is armed** in the barrio, not like the old days, so if you **get in a tight spot**, you got to be ready to kill somebody. "Don't hesitate," he said, "because they won't." He also told me his best tactic as a fighter, the secret of his success:

"Never show fear, Mona. I've beat guys bigger than me 'cause I never looked scared. Just look trouble in the eye." He glanced down at his stopwatch and counted to himself, checking his time. "Remember: Take everything head on, with your eyes open."

I knew I would have to approach my dreams in the same manner, with my eyes open and aware. As I had several times before, I turned to Osuna when I was ready to put my improvement plan into action. For six months, the running, schooling, and training were making me stronger and better. Now, walking into his office, I was looking to take the next step. Osuna had continued his rise through the ranks at the PD and he was, by that point, the commander of the entire Traffic Division for the city. He was my boss and he was my mentor. I hoped he would support my wild plan.

"Can I close the door?"

"Sure. What's up? Everything alright?"

"Oh yeah, fine. Uh, I want to ask you something."

I looked him in the eye, as he always told me to do, and announced my dream. "I want to become a cop. I want to become a police officer."

------

step into a punch use my body as I punched

is armed has a gun or a knife

get in a tight spot are in danger

It was an old ambition, of course, but now I considered it realistic. Maybe I was wrong, but somebody was going to have to prove it to me.

Osuna eyed me warily, **gauging**, I think, how seriously I meant what I was saying. He said nothing. "I'm serious," I continued, desperate to fill the uncomfortable silence. "I want to know how I should get started."

That moment seemed **like a lifetime removed** from the day, back when I was a clerk, and Osuna had handed me a college catalogue with law enforcement classes circled. At the time, I knew he considered my aspirations a long shot. That was before my marriage and three kids, before I sacrificed five years of my life to violence and despair. I knew he thought I must be crazy, and I half-expected him to say so.

He didn't.

"You can do it, Mona. But do you know how much work it will take?" I nodded. He was surprised, I think, to hear how much I had done already. He told me that he would help me as much as he could, but he warned me not to take on the commitment lightly or underestimate the labors ahead of me. He reminded me how far I had come and he called me a survivor, someone who could make this dream come true if I focused.

He stood up and leaned over his desk, his hands flat on the tabletop. He nodded lightly and sighed. "Well, then . . . I guess we'll just have to get you into **an academy**."

....

gauging trying to figure out
like a lifetime removed so far
an academy a police training school

I knew everything was stacked against me. It was tough for women to make the force, both physically and because of the closed, fraternity-like atmosphere of the station house, and I had my background with the gangs working against me, too. But I was **hell-bent on trying**, no matter what. I was determined to keep all my regrets in my past. If I fail at this, I told myself, at least I have the satisfaction of knowing I tried.

There are a number of ways to get the training you need to become a cop. The easiest, most direct route is to be sponsored by the PD itself, meaning it sends you through the academy, picking up the bill. Sponsored recruits even draw a paycheck, with the academy considered to be on-the-job training. I tried this avenue first. Early one Saturday morning, I went to take a series of written and physical tests. The written exam was difficult, and I realized there was a lot more to learn about the law and police work. The physical test was even more of a wake-up call. I couldn't get over the wall in the obstacle course, so I couldn't complete the exercise. I didn't have to wait for the scores to be tallied to **have the door slammed in my face.** One of the instructors told me flat-out that I "was not **Santa Ana material.**"

Osuna had cautioned me that I might get turned down. He was quick to point out that there were other ways to go, but the other paths were difficult. Without the sponsorship, I knew I could not afford to quit my parking control job and go through the academy full time.

....

hell-bent on trying determined to try
have the door slammed in my face know I failed
Santa Ana material good enough to be a Santa Ana police officer

The best option, I decided, was unfortunately also the most grueling one. A one-year basic academy. I would have to work all day and then, in the evenings, put in the long hours at the academy at Golden West Community College in Huntington Beach. **On top of that**, of course, I had to juggle the responsibilities of being a full-time single parent of three.

Osuna warned me about what I was planning. He talked about the academic and athletic rigors, the long months of long hours.

"That's a major commitment, Mona. That's a tough pace to keep up. Are you sure about this?"

I told him I was. I had survived so much, put up with so many negative things, I was willing to walk through hell now to make life better for myself and, more important, my kids. I wanted to show them that they could attain any goal they wanted, and the best way was to present myself as a model.

Besides, I told Osuna, how could I live with myself if I didn't try?

....

On top of that In addition to all of this work

BEFORE YOU MOVE ON...

1. **Cause and Effect** Reread pages 237–238. Why did Hoops judge Mona differently after he saw her tattoo?

2. **Argument** Reread pages 250–251. How did Mona convince Sal that becoming a cop was a good idea for her?

LOOK AHEAD Read pages 256–268 to see if Mona was finally able to get rid of Frank.

A year after Cpl. Lucas had sent Frank walking off into the night, I heard from my ex-husband again. It was about 10 P.M. when the phone rang. At first there was no one there. Then I heard his voice.

"It's me. Hey, I just got out, y'know?"

"Out of where, Frank?" I knew before he answered.

"The Orange County jail. They had me locked up on some bullshit burglary charge. Hey, look. I want to come home."

"Then go home."

"No. Home, there. You know, I want to come back and be with you and the kids."

"You don't live here, this isn't your home," my voice was trembling with anger. I was so sick of these games.

We talked in circles a while longer, and I told him I was going to hang up.

"All right, all right, you hang up. But I don't care what you say, I'm coming home, Mona. Nothing you can do about it."

I slammed the phone down. I started racing around the house **locking the place up**. I called the station and asked for the watch commander. It was someone I didn't know, but he was helpful and tried to calm me down. I knew Lucas had been transferred to the Narcotics unit, so he wouldn't be able to help me, and I didn't know any of the cops on patrol in my neighborhood. The **WC** told me he would advise the units in my area that I might need some help. He took Frank's description and told me to call 911 if things **got dicey**.

I sat by the window and waited, wondering if he would show up.

....

locking the place up shutting and locking all the doors and windows

WC Watch Commander

got dicey became dangerous

Maybe he's bluffing, I thought, maybe he's just trying to scare me. No such luck. An hour and a half after the call, he came walking up the driveway. I quickly called the emergency dispatcher.

Frank was still banging on the door when the squad car pulled up. Two cops got out, a fresh-faced rookie and a chubby old sergeant I recognized as one of the crusty old-timers. The cops split up, the sergeant cupping his hand around Frank's elbow and pulling him to the center of the lawn. The younger cop knocked on the door and smiled at me when he came in.

"Are you okay?"

"Yeah, thanks.

I showed him the restraining order I had on Frank and I explained the situation, how my ex-husband had called from jail, how I hadn't heard from him in a year. The rookie said he would write up a citation for violation of a restraining order if I was willing to sign it.

"Yes, I'll be happy to."

I was relieved that things were going to **go by the book**. My experiences had prepared me for the worst, but this time it looked like it was going to be different.

I couldn't have been more wrong. When the rookie went outside, I could hear his sergeant barking at him, telling him to shut up and put his citation book away. I was standing in the doorway and couldn't hear everything they said, but I could read Frank's body language: Hands on his hips, he was pleased with the way things were going.

I walked toward the trio, thinking I had better set things straight, but before I could say anything, the sergeant was pulling me

....

go by the book follow procedure

by the arm.

"C'mon, you're **hitting the street**, sister."

"What the hell are you doing?!"

He tugged me toward the house. "Get your things packed."

"What? Why? This is my house!"

"You're leaving. He pays the bills, right? So it's his house. You can talk to him about coming back when you cool off."

I was in shock. The rookie cop was **flabbergasted**, too, but stood silently next to the patrol car. It was the **nightmare days** all over again, but this time I refused to be a victim. I locked my knees and yanked my arm away from the rotund cop, accidentally elbowing him in the side with the maneuver.

"LISTEN! This is my house. I pay the bills! He just got out of jail, he's on parole and he DOESN'T LIVE HERE!"

All three were staring at me, **struck mute by my fury**. "I don't know what he told you, but it's a lie and if you just check, you'll find that out."

The kids were in the window of the house, wailing and scratching at the glass. They thought I was being arrested, probably, and they were confused and scared. So was I. As usual, the sidewalks were beginning to fill with the neighborhood's curious onlookers.

The sergeant started calling me names. He told me to shut up, and he grabbed hold of me again. I pulled out the restraining order and waved it in front of him, but he slapped it out of my hand. "I don't want to see anything you got. You do what I say!"

I couldn't let it go any further.

....

hitting the street leaving
flabbergasted completely shocked
nightmare days same horrible experience
struck mute by my fury surprised by my anger

"Look, I was trying to do this the right way. I didn't want to tell you who I am, but this is out of control. I work for the Santa Ana Police Department. I'm a parking control officer."

The sergeant's face was twisted in a look of skepticism with a hint of apprehension. He thought I was lying. He hoped I was lying.

"Do you want to see my identification? Or maybe you should just call the watch commander? I talked to him an hour ago, and he told me to call back if I needed help."

The old-timer looked **stricken**. Frank saw the look of panic on his advocate's face, which made his grin fade. The rookie, who had been too nervous to **get a word in**, whispered something into the sergeant's ear. I don't know what he said, but you could see the change in the older cop's face.

"Well, why didn't you say that in the first place? You should have told us that at the beginning," he said. He was talking fast. **Damage control.**

"I shouldn't have to say that! I shouldn't have to be a police employee to get you to listen," I screamed at him. I was enraged, as mad as I had ever been. My arms were waving over my head and all three of the men looked surprised. "I did everything by the book, and YOU were going to throw me out into the street **on his word**!"

The cop was back-pedaling. "Well, you should have told us who you were. I didn't know. I can't read minds."

That was it. No apology, no explanation. The sergeant told the rookie to cuff Frank and write him up for a restraining order violation and trespassing, then he waddled off and sat in the car while

---

stricken terrified

get a word in say anything

Damage control. He knew he was wrong.

on his word just because of something he said

the younger officer leaned over to pick up the court document and take all my information. He told me he was sorry for the way things went, then told me to trust him. He would make sure this didn't happen again.

They pulled away from the curb ten minutes later, Frank grimacing in the back seat. I was glad to see him carted off. But that didn't calm me down. What if I had just been a law-abiding citizen who didn't happen to have a job at the police department. Was the law only for its enforcers?

The next day I called Osuna and told him everything. I knew the sergeant would be panicking. He had screwed up pretty badly. Osuna suspected the sergeant would try to preempt any departmental complaint I would file by submitting one of his own. He was right. The sergeant had **fabricated a false and flimsy account of** what happened, portraying me as a vindictive and unreasonable ex-wife looking for special treatment that would target my former husband. The supervisor then took the complaint to **the next rung on the command ladder** in Traffic—which was Osuna himself. It was all ridiculous. I wondered what the rookie would say if someone asked him what had happened. No one would, though, because the whole incident was about to **hit a brick wall**.

Osuna told the supervisor about my account and also said he had no plans to write me up. "You tell the sergeant that he can pursue this if he wants, but I suggest that he might not want this incident examined any further."

....

fabricated a false and flimsy account of written several lies about

the next rung on the command ladder his boss

hit a brick wall end

I never filed a complaint of my own. I was about to enter the academy, and I knew that any sort of controversy would hurt my chances. I had enough stacked against me, and I seriously doubted I would be able to win any kind of confrontation with a supervisor-level officer. The whole matter faded away, but not before it earned me one more enemy on the force. Another lesson learned.

When I arrived at the police academy at Golden West College in Huntington Beach, I saw a group of fellow recruits in the parking lot. It was an odd group, with different ages of men and women from a variety of backgrounds. Some were former military, others were mechanics, salesmen and housewives looking for a career as a cop. Some graduates of the academy were there to meet and help all of us **green** recruits. They showed us how to wear our Sam Brownes (the traditional name of a cop's gun belt), line up the buttons of our shirts and, for the women, how to put our hair up. They explained how we would have to stand at attention and march right away. They also told us to expect blistering attacks from the instructors, a group of cops from nearby cities who would be like drill sergeants with a new group of buck privates. I could see some of the other recruits were nervous when they heard all this, but I sort of shrugged it off with a smile. After what I'd been through, I told myself, I could take someone yelling at me.

I was dead wrong.

When we assembled in the courtyard near the academy's classrooms—an area called The Blacktop—we could hear the

---

green new

instructors laughing at us from the open-air corridors behind us. As soon as some recruits turned toward the voices, the instructors tore into us all. Face forward, they shouted, stand at attention! There were six instructors, and they started weaving through the rows of stunned recruits, stopping to scold and insult each person for the way they stood, looked or acted. I was near the rear and I braced myself and tried to hear all the questions given to the recruits ahead of me.

When it came my turn, all three instructors surrounded me and started **railing** at me. One, a female cop from Fountain Valley, tore into me about my hair, which was not **put up to her satisfaction**. She was asking me if I thought I was special, but before I could answer, a Newport Beach sergeant was right in my face, quizzing me.

"What is a 459?" he shouted at me. I searched my memory but nothing turned up. I didn't know what the code meant. It didn't matter, he was on to the next question. "What are the elements of a felony? Well?"

The third drill sergeant was off to my left. He was a veteran cop from Garden Grove, a department with a longtime rivalry with its eastern neighbor, Santa Ana. "So you want to join the Santa Ana Police Department? What, you don't want to join a real department? What's wrong with Garden Grove?"

I felt like I was trapped in a tornado. The voices **were relentless**, shouting and badgering and questioning. Finally, they moved on to the next victim. I was shaking with fear and anger. Maybe, I thought to myself, this isn't for me after all.

There were about one hundred recruits the first day. About

....

railing screaming
put up to her satisfaction the way she wanted it
were relentless never stopped

twenty never showed up for day two. I didn't quit, though. I pushed forward. The classwork was hard, with about seven books to study, and the hours on the blacktop were grueling. I learned to march and stand ramrod still at attention. I learned to never be late. I also learned how to think with people screaming at me, how to **keep my cool**. The stress was amazing, but each session ended with an exercise regimen, which gave me a way to **blow off my steam**. We ran five miles every day, and I could feel all the pain and pressure flowing out as my arms pumped the air. I felt myself getting stronger in almost every way. The people at the PD were extremely helpful as I made my way through the academy program. They lent me textbooks, equipment, even a **service revolver,** to help **defray** the costs of the academy training. When I ran and studied, I was doing it not just for myself, but for all those people, my kids and my family.

Not everything I learned was in a classroom or on the practice field. A fellow cadet approached me one day and told me a friend of his wanted to talk to me. The friend was a journalism student and a reporter for the campus newspaper.

"Your background makes you interesting, so he wants to do a small story on you," the cadet explained. I was reluctant, but the cadet laughed and said, "Don't worry, he won't burn you."

I was uneasy from the start, but the interview seemed pretty painless. When I picked up the new issue of the paper, though, my eyes widened in panic with every sentence I read.

The reporter was new in his field, I guess, just like me, so mistakes were only natural. But besides the inaccuracies, the whole

....

keep my cool stay calm
blow off my steam release my energy and anger
service revolver police gun
defray lower

tone of the article made me sound like some hardened gangbanger. Maybe the writer had seen too many movies or something, because he wrote my quotes up in street slang style and **peppered them with expletives** I knew I had never said. The story was dramatic, but it just wasn't true. Our training officers had already warned us to avoid reporters when we made it to the streets—they called them vultures who would do or say anything to get a story—and now I wished I had heeded that advice on campus, too.

Standing there with my nose buried in the paper, I dreaded what all my friends and teachers would think when they read the story. Some copies would make it to the PD, it occurred to me with a sick, sinking feeling.

I was surprised that some people were happy with the article and supportive of me getting recognition for making it so far. But I would have none of that thinking. There were too many people at the PD already against me, and now they had more **ammunition**. Sure enough, I saw a copy of the story tacked up on a station bulletin board. In the margins, nasty remarks and cartoons depicted me as ignorant street trash. I was sick at heart. There were people in the PD who hated me, I knew, but now I had a firsthand view of their sentiments.

Rereading the article again and again, I couldn't blame my peers and the older cops for resenting the person portrayed in the article. That Mona was a stereotypical gang girl with no respect. That wasn't me, but suddenly that was **my persona** to a lot of people. One cop who knew me told me it was even worse than I knew: Cops in other

....

peppered them with expletives added curse words
ammunition reasons to dislike me
my persona who I was

departments in neighboring cities were making snide remarks about **the slipping standards** at the Santa Ana PD and, because of the article, my name was often cited as an example.

I wanted to hide. I wanted to quit. Instead, I lowered my head and tried harder. I also pledged that I would never trust another reporter.

Just like the day I tried to gain sponsorship for the academy, the portion of my training that was the hardest to overcome was the wall in the obstacle course. I spent hour after hour at that wall, trying to beat it.

I remember one afternoon, I was breathing hard and my legs felt rubbery. I started to wipe the sweat from my forehead, but I stopped when I saw my palms were a bloody mess with splinters. The wall was there, down the short dirt runway, taunting me. It was a weather-beaten fence, old and worn so much it was hard to tell the color of the paint anymore. There were no handholds on it. It stood six feet tall, but it could have been sixty. I couldn't get over it.

There was some shorter hurdles put in just before the six-foot wall on the obstacle course, which made it hard to **get up the running head of steam** someone like me would need to get up and over it. The spacing was done that way purposely. This was a test of upper-body strength, which made it, traditionally, the most difficult feat for the female recruits. Not to say it was **a breeze** for the men either; more than a few trainees of both genders failed the test because of the dreaded wall.

....

the slipping standards the poor quality of people being hired

get up the running head of steam run long enough to get enough speed that

a breeze easy

My kids were sitting on the grass watching me hurl myself against the wall for more than an hour. It was getting dark. "Can we go home?" Frankie Jr. asked and I nodded. "Yeah, let's get out of here." I turned and stared at the wall. I'll see you tomorrow, I thought.

I learned different approaches and handholds and then, one day, I made it over. I let out a yelp of pain and excitement, and immediately went to the start of the approach path to do it again. And again, and again. I had finally won. It was only a few days before the academy finals, and if I didn't make it over the wall, all my work would be for nothing. Thrilled and exhausted, I headed for home. The limp didn't start until I hit the parking lot.

My triumph had a price. I had twisted my ankle badly and the throbbing, like my **jitters**, was relentless, keeping me up for much of the night before my run through the obstacle course.

I didn't tell anyone about my bum ankle. At that stage, if I backed out or a supervisor disqualified me for a health problem, it would mean redoing a large part of the program and adding months to my stay at the academy. I would go through with it, no matter what.

Out of one hundred recruits or more, there were just a dozen of us there at the end. I was the only female. As a crowd of students, past graduates and friends watched from a grassy field, we ran through the obstacle course. I pulled the heavy mannequin, swung beneath on the overhead bars and darted my feet through the row of flat tires. As I rounded a pylon and headed for the dreaded wall, I was too **pumped** to even feel my ankle. I hit it as hard as I could, planted

....

jitters nerves
pumped excited

my arms and pushed up and over, landing with a burst of pain on the other side. I made it, I screamed inside my head, I made it.

Santa Ana Police Chief Paul Walters pinned badge No. 1725 on my crisp blue uniform on graduation day, December 16, 1989. Then, Osuna repeated the pinning for me, honoring me as my mentor and dear friend. I had finished seventh in my class, **flouting all the doubters and cynics**. My family surrounded me and snapped photos, hundreds it seemed, and I felt a sense of achievement that I had never tasted before. Nothing meant more, though, than my father's whispered words to me after the ceremony. **Walking tall** despite his weary and bent back, he hugged me and put his mouth next to my ear. He told me that he loved his little girl. "I am so proud of you today. So proud."

A few days later, my fellow parking control officers and other friends at the station **threw me** a surprise party to celebrate my graduation. All around me were the people who had supported me, donated equipment and cheered me on. I was blushing from the attention and delighted by the gesture. We all laughed as I opened gag gifts and read a greeting card cluttered with signatures and words of encouragement. Some clerks rolled in a cake shaped like a huge Santa Ana PD badge, with white filling and sweet navy blue icing. I carved it up into ragged slabs for everyone. I'm going to be

---

flouting all the doubters and cynics proving myself to everyone
Walking tall Looking proud
threw me had, planned

a cop, I thought to myself as I looked around the station and at my friends and colleagues.

I felt like crying, but laughed instead. All around me, thanks to the cake, I saw a dozen blue grins.

BEFORE YOU MOVE ON...

1. **Evidence and Conclusions** Give 2 examples from pages 256–260 that show that Mona became stronger and more determined.

2. **Summarize** Reread pages 263–265. How did other police officers react to the story in the paper? Why?

LOOK AHEAD Would Mona succeed as a cop in Santa Ana? Read pages 269–300 to find out.

~ Chapter Thirteen ~

DIRECTIONS

After the grueling pace of the last few months at the academy and the flurry of excitement surrounding my graduation, I suddenly found myself face to face with doubt: Can I really do this?

I had managed to put aside a lot of those anxieties while I was climbing toward my goal. But then after the victory and the celebration, I was staring at myself in uniform, with a polished badge gleaming on my chest like some jewel. I thought back to the rookie cops I saw when I was a Trooper Girl and I wondered if I would look the same as them, gawky and uncomfortable on the street. I promised myself that wouldn't happen. These were my streets, the place where I grew up. These were the streets where I belonged, even in a new uniform.

I was assigned a training officer (T.O.), a guy nicknamed The Commander by the rookies because of his **imperious**, military attitude. All rookies get three T.O.'s and spend a month with each. For all three of those months, the training officers **grade out**

....

imperious bossy, strict
grade out give grades for

everything the younger cops do, evaluating them on everything from the way they use the radio to their knowledge of state statutes.

I slid behind the steering wheel of the patrol car and winced as my gun belt pinched my side. It's an acquired skill to be able to sit in a car with a **full-gear Sam Browne** around your waist. I put the key in the ignition and tried to be calm. I was petrified. I hoped the T.O. would say something that would put me at ease.

"First of all, I don't think women belong out here," The Commander said as he locked his seat belt. "That's nothing against you, now. That's just how I feel."

Great. He leaned into his coffee cup, and I took a deep gulp, turned on the engine and backed out. We pulled out of the garage, passed a sign that says "IT'S SHOWTIME!" and flopped up onto southbound Ross Street. Over the next few hours I listened while my T.O. talked. He wore a sour expression the whole time, and I wondered if it was permanent or just for me. I didn't really mind what he thought about women as cops; I just hoped he would give me **a fair shot**. His attitude was his own problem. I just hoped it wouldn't become mine.

My first T.O., I learned through the grapevine my first week out, was supposedly out to prove the PD had made a mistake by **bumping him down to corporal** after he transferred over from a sergeant's post at Los Alamitos, a far smaller department. I knew during our rides that he **was a stickler for protocol**. I also knew he had a wealth of things to teach me. His fuse was short, though. He would rattle off a long list of facts and orders, and then tell me to parrot

....

full-gear Sam Browne belt carrying all the equipment
a fair shot a chance
bumping him down to corporal giving him a lower position
was a stickler for protocol liked to do things by the rules

them back. If I missed anything, he would glare at me.

"Are you stupid?"

I bit my tongue. I could feel **the heat rising in my face**. I was angry, flustered and self-conscious, but I wasn't going to lose my cool. In the academy, they berated you until you felt like your nerves had been whipped raw, but the lesson was not to crack.

"I'm not the fastest learner in the world, I know that," I said, trying to use measured tones. My voice was quaking with anger, though. "But I try hard and when I do learn something, I don't forget it."

"Sometimes there's not enough time on these streets for slow learners, officer. Santa Ana is a tough place."

"I know. I grew up here."

He shot me an icy look. "And now you're a cop. So get the job done."

His scrutiny and harsh judgments made me more nervous, which, of course, meant more mistakes. We were from different worlds, too, which didn't help. We even saw the city differently.

I knew the streets that crisscross Santa Ana from two decades of roaming them daily. I knew which streets **were dead ends** and which **were shortcuts**. I knew the fastest way across town and every freeway exit. I could find every school campus and knew by heart the invisible boundaries of the city's gangs and drug dealers, the way a soldier knows an old battlefield. If I ever learned the concept of north, south, east, and west in school, I had no memory of it. The words were vague to me, as odd as that sounds, the same as a lot of other schoolbook

....

the heat rising in my face my anger
were dead ends ended suddenly
were shortcuts streets got us somewhere faster

concepts. School had never been my strength or my focus. I was embarrassed when The Commander saw the blank look on my face every time he pulled out the map, but what could I say?

"God, what did they teach you in the academy? You did go to the academy, right?"

"I can get anywhere you want to go."

"Okay. Tell me what the cross street is for 1300 Bristol."

I shrugged. If he had told me the name of the store at that spot, or asked what intersection was closest to Mater Dei High School, I could have told him the answer was Edinger. But the **grid system**, and even **cardinal directions**, meant nothing to me. I knew the city, not the numbers.

"When you're answering a call, you don't have time to look for the address on a building or drive up and down the street until you find something. You need to hear an address and know where that is. Understand?"

"I'll learn it."

"You shouldn't even be out here."

"I said I'll learn it."

I wasn't as confident as I sounded, which was part of the problem. Math had never been my favorite school subject, and my anxiety about past failures made it harder to learn. I had to overcome self-doubt, and it wasn't easy with a mentor **putting me down**.

When I didn't learn the grid system in a few hours, he grumbled something about female cops. I sighed and glanced at my watch. It was going to be a long day.

....

grid system way the roads connected
cardinal directions North, South, East, and West
putting me down who kept insulting me

Just as I was gathering some confidence, my **standing** in the department was in doubt again. And the worst part of the new crisis was that it was something I had no control over.

I was riding with The Commander when the 997 call came over the radio: An officer-involved shooting, and an ambulance was needed. I recognized the address. It was the house where my cousins lived. We weren't among the units that responded, and the next few hours I was tense and found it hard to concentrate. What if one of them is dead? Did they hurt the cop? I said absolutely nothing to The Commander. That could only **bring me grief**. It had been three years or more since I had seen Jesse James Elizalde. That day, I wondered if I would ever see him again.

Jesse was indeed the one shot, but he did not die. Later, he was found guilty of assaulting an officer and of other charges. This is the account, according to Orange County Superior Court records, given by the officer who fired the shots: He and his partner had been driving down Daisy Street when a grey Cadillac made a wide turn as it exited an alley. He caught a glimpse of the driver and thought it was a parolee who had fled police earlier when they had questioned him about drugs. The two factors—the looping turn and the presence of a suspicious person in the car—prompted the officers to stop, turn and **bird-dog the Caddy**. The two officers both testified that they did not turn on their lights or sirens while following the car.

Jesse was the driver of the Cadillac, and he floored it when he saw the patrol car behind him. (He had been in the Myrtle Street

....

standing place, position
bring me grief make things worse
bird-dog the Caddy follow the car

cul-de-sac area, **a den of** bangers and dealers, and I have no doubt he was **up to no good** there.) When Jesse hit the driveway of his house on Franklin, he bounded for the door. The cop that would shoot him called out for him to stop, and ran up to the house when Jesse went inside anyway.

The two ran all the way through the house. When Jesse reached the enclosed patio behind the home, he slammed shut a gate behind him and held it tight so the cop couldn't pursue him further. The two were nose to nose, with only the gate separating them. At their feet was Jesse's dog, barking madly at the cop, who drew his gun, aimed it at the pet and threatened to shoot it if Jesse didn't let go of the gate. The wily *vato* did let go, and he raced toward the back of the patio. He didn't get far.

The cop swung his baton at Jesse, who caught it before it could land a blow, and the two of them struggled with one another across the patio. What happened next **is a point of contention**. The officer says Jesse grabbed at a heavy pipe. The cop, fearing he might get his head bashed in, drew his weapon and **popped off four rounds, point-blank**.

The Elizaldes scoff at that version. The pipe Jesse grabbed was actually a pole cemented into the ground. They say Jesse reached out for support as he fell. "He woulda needed to use a jackhammer before he could use that pipe to hit that *jura*," one of my cousins said. Their take on the shooting was that the cop was a cowboy who either panicked or got angry enough to cap Jesse.

My view on the incident? It's hard to say. Events are blurry and

....

a den of an area filled with
up to no good doing bad things
is a point of contention depends on who you ask
popped off four rounds, point-blank fired four shots

bullet-fast in battle, and I would give the officer the benefit of the doubt and accept his statement that he perceived a threat to his life. Some other officers say he should never have been on that porch in the first place, but I'm not going to question him without knowing all the facts.

No matter what, though, Jesse was **asking for trouble** by refusing to surrender when he first arrived at his house. The two versions of what happened are classic examples of the vast distance separating the perspectives of cops and gangs. Both sides contributed to what happened and both sides refuse for a moment to even consider the possibility that the opposition might be in the right on any issue.

The shooting led to a short-lived lawsuit against the PD and a new set of headaches for me. I wanted to distance myself from the whole thing and try to **ride out** the controversy. The cop who pulled the trigger never talked to me about what happened that day, nor did he ever really speak to me again.

While The Commander thought I was an idiot, others on the force viewed me as a threat. I had been on duty less than a month when I found out that I had inspired a variety of colorful rumors. An old favorite had resurfaced, one I had heard while I was a clerk: I was a spy for the Santa Ana street gangs, an undercover banger with a badge who was collecting intelligence on the PD. Whoever **cooked it up** certainly gave a lot of credit to this mysterious network of *vatos* I was serving. The homeboys I had seen growing up could barely organize the collection for a keg party. And, again, I was never sure

....

asking for trouble putting himself in danger
ride out suffer through; survive
cooked it up made up the rumor

exactly what type of information they thought I could be passing on. I wasn't in the Gang Unit (and that elite group operated far from the eyes of a rookie patrol cop) and I was **hardly privy to** any plans for major operations or busts. I would have laughed the whole thing off, but as a probationary officer, I was too worried that even a rumor might be enough to hurt my chances of building a career with the PD.

The other rumor was just as lame but, because it fell within the realm of the believable, it was far more damaging. The word was that I was wired. I wanted to burn cops, the story went, so I had a hidden tape recorder or microphone meant to catch **off-hand racial or sexual remarks**.

Other female officers have been the subject of similar rumors, I know. The world of cops is still a difficult place to navigate if you are a woman. Many of the old-timers automatically label women daring to wear their blue as **hateful interlopers or hopelessly inferior**. Also, the slack a rookie male officer might expect is seldom available for a female counterpart. I learned that through firsthand observation. In the eyes of many of the old guard, a female cop has to perform twice as well as a male peer to get half the credit.

But all that, just like the rumors, was part of the new life I had chosen. I knew the deal when I walked in, and whining about it would only make my critics happy. Still, I was stunned by the hostility that greeted me. If I didn't know what I was getting into, well, there were people always willing to educate me.

"When I first saw you, I thought you looked like you belonged in

....

hardly privy to not told about

off-hand racial or sexual remarks comments that would get the police into a lot of trouble

hateful interlopers or hopelessly inferior people who do not belong or are unable to do the job well

the back of the squad car, not the front," one senior officer told me. He said getting to know me changed his mind, but I wondered how many others weren't fair enough to give me that shot.

My reaction to the barbs and threats was to harden my face and, in effect, **bare my fangs**. I resorted to my old habit of wearing a mask to survive the hazing of my peers. The same as in a gang, everyone seemed to be jockeying for position and sizing each other up. If the game was a mean one, then I would be hard and mean, so I would win. Looking back, with age and hindsight to sharpen the view, I probably came on way too strong and not always with the right people during those months. If someone looked at me funny (or even if I thought they might have), I would stop and ask them what the hell they were looking at. If someone said something I didn't like, I would **call them on it**. Part of me knew even then that it might be better to keep my mouth shut until I could get some **time under my belt** and learn my way around. Instead, though, I was starting to believe it was me against the world, and for a cop that can be a deadly attitude to wear on the streets.

My first month was over after what felt like a year. I was relieved to be leaving the withering glare of The Commander, but I dreaded the evaluation he would give me. What I feared more than the words was his stern belief that I was not fit to be a cop. Was he right? He raised a lot of doubts in me. Maybe I wasn't fit to wear the badge, after all. My spirits were lifted though when I heard more about his reputation around the PD. A lot of cops viewed him as a blowhard, someone with a short fuse and none of the patience

....

bare my fangs to act tough and threatening
call them on it confront them about it; start a fight
time under my belt more police experience

needed for teaching.

I knew things had to get better with my second T.O. After all, how could they get worse? My jaw dropped, though, when I read the name next to mine on the new assignment sheet. Sonny Coberly was my new teacher. I had already been around long enough to hear the stories about Coberly, the imposing old-timer everyone called The Godfather, although not to his face. The nicknames reminded me of the gangs, like a lot of things in the PD culture. The two worlds were not far removed, I had learned often, but the similarities still surprised me.

Everyone spoke with respect when they mentioned Coberly. He talked in a hushed, almost gentle voice and he moved with a measured grace. His thick arms suggested power, but he wasn't a showy or loud guy at all. His name and face were well-known on the streets, even when I was a kid running with the Troopers.

One of the tales that circulated about Coberly told of how he **fended off a pack** of armed homeboys that ambushed him one night. When it was over, The Godfather was the only one standing. His reputation wasn't just from his fighting prowess. He **lost his sergeant's stripes in a dispute with the brass**. He had stood by the officers under him, refusing to **make them the fall guys**. I, like a lot of other younger cops, didn't even know what this mysterious infraction had been, what he took the blame for. It didn't matter, really. The demotion made him a folk hero to the rank-and-file cops, who hold loyalty above all else. Even the sergeants and lieutenants praised The Godfather. "If you're going to be in an alley fight, and

---

fending off a pack fought a group

lost his sergeant's stripes in a dispute with the brass was demoted after an argument with his boss

make them the fall guys blame them

there's one guy you can have with you, it'd be Sonny," Osuna once told me.

I wasn't sure what to expect from this **taciturn local legend**, but I worried that he also might not respect female cops. I was beginning to think it was a generational thing.

When he finished his bran muffin, The Godfather lit up his first Pall Mall of the morning, sipped his steaming coffee and asked me how things had gone with my first T.O. I told him it had been rocky.

"I think **I rubbed him the wrong way**," I said, watching for his reaction. I didn't want to say the wrong thing, to **get off on the wrong foot**. He finished the cigarette and tossed it out the window.

"I've been a cop for twenty-four years. Twenty-four long years. And I can pick 'em and I can throw 'em back."

His voice was soft. He wasn't trying to scare me, not like the first T.O. Everything was straight and up front.

"I will watch you this week. I'll pay attention to your performance and how you handle yourself. I'll try to tell you things you need to know. I won't criticize you. And, at the end of the first week, I'll tell you if you have what it takes to be a cop or if you should just become a janitor or something."

I was so jittery I wondered if I would be able to get the squad car out of the garage without wrecking it.

All my worries evaporated, though, when Coberly began teaching me more than I had learned in a year at the academy. I was so focused on storing away all the lessons that he was providing, I forgot to be nervous. Patiently, he would repeat explanations two or even three

---

taciturn local legend quiet, famous hero
I rubbed him the wrong way he did not like me
get off on the wrong foot upset him right when I first met him

times until they sunk in. He even asked me questions, trying to tap into my knowledge of the neighborhoods that had passed by his car window for better than two decades. I suspected later that the questions were just a way to make me feel more confident and at ease. If they were, it worked.

"Listen, I'm like your dad for a month," he said. "Come to me with your questions. I know you're jumpy. That's because of that academy bullshit, all the drill sergeant stuff. That was fine then, but now you're **out here for real**. Try to stay cool. What they teach you in the academy will only take you so far."

He taught me how to search a car by dividing it up into sections, like a pie. He told me about the **stash spots** that slip past the eyes and flashlights of a hasty cop, and he said that dividing it up in sections would help me write my reports and testify in court with more precision.

He guided my hand as I drew up a mini-map with just the city's major streets, a small sheet I could study to get used to the grid system that had been so hard for me to nail down. Starting simple made it easier to **get a grip on it**. He picked up the radio and told the dispatcher that we were 10-6 on training, meaning we were unavailable for calls. Then, for a full day, we just made laps across the city's dense neighborhoods and business districts. Back and forth we went, while I sat and rattled off the name of every street, road, avenue, lane, and boulevard. We did that until I knew most of them and could see the patterns and progressions that **had eluded me** before. The system, when presented to me in a calm and logical way,

....

out here for real no longer in training and out on the streets
stash spots hiding places
get a grip on it understand
had eluded me I did not understand

was suddenly fairly easy to grasp.

For two days, he monitored the radio for a variety of calls. He wanted me to get experience with as many different types of situations as possible, from car theft to domestic disputes to gang activity. After each, we would discuss the performance of every cop on the scene, dissecting and grading each move.

"Tell me what you saw," he would say, and I would replay the whole encounter, searching for the perceived cues and responses that made up every cop's performance. Sometimes I **cited minor departures** from policies and procedures. My knowledge of the books didn't impress him: He wanted the common-sense answers.

"Remember, what they teach you in the academy is all clear-cut, it's all printed out on the page. Life isn't like that. There are a lot of different ways to do this job, some good and some bad. Watch for the cops that do the wrong things, and then make sure you do the right things."

Common sense was a key component of Coberly's lessons. So was observation and playing it cool.

"Listen to the call that comes over the radio, first of all," he said. "And make sure you understand it. And don't be in such a hurry to get there that you don't keep an eye on the traffic headed toward you."

After a crime is committed, you know the bad guy will be leaving, which means he might be headed straight toward you. A cop in a hurry to get to the action might drive right past it. He told me to listen, too, to the number of units **en route** and where they're

....

cited minor departures talked about small changes
en route on the way to a crime scene

coming in from, so I'd know about my backup and when to expect them. "Don't get tunnel vision. Think about **the big picture**."

When Friday rolled around, I had butterflies in my stomach. I kept wondering, have I done well enough? Every mistake I had made during the past few days was running around my mind, each magnified by the dark cloud of doubt that surrounded my head.

Just before lunch, The Godfather smiled. "Oh yeah, by the way, I think if you keep working this hard, you're gonna make a helluva cop."

I almost ran a red light. I was ecstatic, but I wanted to play it cool. I couldn't keep a huge smile off my face.

Coberly shook his cigarette pack, emptied out the last Pall Mall and lit it. "It takes most cops five years to learn what you already know about the streets," he said, pointing through the smoke toward the storefronts passing by his window. "You'll be just fine."

He said nothing else. It was back to work, learning today's lessons. On the agenda, he said, stumping out his cigarette, was the interviewing of witnesses and learning more about controlling a crime scene. "First of all," he said, "don't let your witnesses sit in the same place. Keep them separate so they don't **compare notes and mess up everything in their heads**."

I was listening, but it wasn't easy. I wanted to pull over and jump up and down on the sidewalk. The Godfather said I was going to make it.

The stamp of approval from The Godfather carried a lot of

....

the big picture everything that is happening

compare notes and mess up everything in their heads talk
to each other and change their stories

weight around the station. Probably more than any other single event, his blessing changed the way other cops viewed me, especially the old-timers. It gave me some instant respect in their eyes. If I was okay with Sonny Coberly, well, maybe, just maybe, I did belong in that Santa Ana police uniform after all.

My third T.O. was another name I had heard around before, but for different reasons. I knew the name Cabrera from his past on the streets, the stuff he did before he ever donned a police uniform. Mikey Cabrera was a former F-Trooper, just like me, but he had run with the branch of the gang based in his hometown, the city of Orange, which lies across Santa Ana's northern city limits. He had pulled off the magic trick I was attempting, going from **predator to protector**. I couldn't wait to meet him.

We **hit it off** right away, although neither of us mentioned our Trooper days at all during our first week together. I didn't want to be the first to broach the subject, so I concentrated on learning everything he had to teach me.

The first day, he told me he had heard I had a hard time with The Commander. The **book on me**, according to The Commander, was that I was dismal on officer safety and had poor judgment about dealing with the community.

"Tell me what you went through," he said. "Tell me your version of what's happening. I've heard a lot of stuff, but I want to hear it from you."

I took a deep breath. My first instinct was to say nothing, but then something told me I could trust Cabrera.

....

predator to protector criminal to cop
hit it off got along well
book on me problem with me

"Well, I had a **major personality conflict** with the guy, right from the beginning." I briefly described some of my **run-ins** with The Commander, but I tried not to bad-mouth my former teacher. I was certainly not blaming him for any lapses in my performance.

When I was done, Cabrera nodded and told me not to worry. "Everything I grade you on, good or bad, will be based on your performance with me, not with what somebody else says about you."

That was all I could ask for.

Cabrera was patient, like Coberly, and willing to go over things again and again if it helped me learn. While the two shared that trait, their demeanor was completely opposite. Where The Godfather was **deliberate**, with no wasted movement, Cabrera was a bundle of energy, always looking to race off on a new mission. More than once, if we had a suspect in our sights, my T.O. would be gone, sprinting off without warning or notice. After one of those mad dashes, I started calling my mentor Rabbit, and, laughing, he promised he would try to give me a clue the next time he was going to take off. Because of our backgrounds, we had great communication, both with each other and with the people we policed on the streets. The culture, the language, even just the feel of the streets, was all part of who the both of us were. I was increasingly proud of my performance, and, while I still felt lost sometimes, my confidence was building. Every day, I felt like I took some new lesson home with me.

One day, Rabbit **locked on** a guy sitting on the bumper of an old car and reading a newspaper.

"Pull over, there's something here you need to take a look at,"

---

major personality conflict bad relationship
run-ins problems
deliberate very careful
locked on noticed

Rabbit said. As the car drifted to a stop, Rabbit was out and walking, and I scrambled to catch up. Rabbit was asking the middle-aged guy questions as I trotted up to both of them. I **cast an eye** behind and around us (I was backing up my partner, and general safety is always a concern. I wanted to check out our surroundings and situation.) and then I studied the guy with the newspaper. I didn't see an obvious problem. Did Rabbit recognize him? I could tell Rabbit was waiting for me to explain why we stopped, but I wasn't sure. I shrugged and waited for the new lesson. In Spanish, Rabbit told the guy to hold his newspaper up higher.

"Tell me, Ruiz, when was the last time you saw someone read a paper that was upside down?"

It turned out the guy had been busted in the area a week before on drug sales and told not to return unless he wanted to face deep trouble. When he saw the patrol car, he grabbed a paper from the street and held it high in front of him, never noticing the headlines and photos were all flipped. Later, back in the car, Rabbit told me to always look skeptically at the world I see outside. Take a moment to study the things that might seem normal with just a glance, and sometimes you see something unusual. Investigate, and every once in a while you'll get lucky, he said.

He also shared insights into the way suspects **ditch evidence**. If you bust somebody on a sidewalk, look in the crooks and roots of nearby trees, behind car tires, in paper cups that looked like innocent litter. The kids liked to use the plastic bubbles that gum and trinkets are sold in from quarter vending machines or ice-cream trucks, and

....

cast an eye looked
ditch evidence get rid of things that can link them to a crime

they weren't afraid to ditch them in wet, nasty, or remote places and worry about fishing them out later. Rabbit also taught me to **read the body language** of the *vatos* and thieves and dope dealers who were thinking about bolting when confronted with capture. "They get this 'Oh man look' and then they look in the direction they're gonna run," Rabbit said. "Watch their eyes, and you can predict which way they'll go and **cut them off**." He showed me the way to question people, the tone to use and some of the questions to ask. A lot of times, especially with the junkies, they'll admit their crimes if you ask the right way and stare them down. He told me when to ask "yes or no" questions and when to ask more complicated questions that might force someone to **trip themselves up in a lie**. Rabbit also showed me, through example, how to talk to residents and street characters who were trying to get by and deserved our respect and protection. I knew the value of this already, but his example taught me even more.

Eventually, as the days passed and Cabrera and I grew more comfortable with each other, the squad car discussion turned to a shared history, to the Troopers.

Rabbit had been a *vato* in a gang called Cypress Street Boys, and when they hooked up with the fledgling F-Troop in the '70s, they changed their name to F-Troop Orange. By the 1980s, that group had broken off again and taken to calling itself O.V.C., but when F-Troop was at its most powerful and largest, the contingent in Orange was second only to the original *clica* in Santa Ana.

He told me that one of the reasons he and his friends formed the

---

read the body language pay attention to the movements
cut them off stop them
trip themselves up in a lie reveal they lied

gang that would eventually become the Orange branch of F-Troop was for protection.

The Latinos in his school were a small minority then and **vulnerable to** other types of gangs, although they weren't called gangs—they were the school's athletes, called the Sportos, and a group of tough white kids who loved cars and wearing jackets, the type of kids we later called Bikers. When there was trouble, when a Latino kid was getting beat up on, Rabbit would go to a school official. "Take care of this. Or we will," Rabbit would say.

Often the gangs would be a policing arm on the streets, **dispensing street justice**. Sometimes it was fair, sometimes it wasn't, just like every other system, Rabbit said. All that changed as the '70s wore on and the drug flood hit, along with **gun proliferation**. There have always been losers and killers in the gangs, but never as many as now.

Cabrera enjoyed using his past to startle the young *vatos*. To the homeboys, nothing is quite as unsettling or intimidating as a *veterano*-turned-cop. Rabbit would tell them that he never left the gangs, that he had just changed membership. "Now I'm in the Ross Street Locos, ese," he would rasp as he cuffed the junior homeboys. Ross Street was the site of the PD. "You never heard of us, man? Sheeeit, *ese*, we're the baddest. We go in any barrio we want, we got our colors and guns . . . you sure you never heard of us?" Rabbit would laugh all the way to the station.

After finishing up with my training officers, it was time to

---

vulnerable to in danger from
dispensing street justice punishing people who broke their rules
gun proliferation a huge increase in guns

request an assignment. First, though, I had to return to the streets with The Commander for a ghost ride. A ghost ride is the final step in the T.O. process: The trainee rejoins the first of the three T.O.'s for a weeklong patrol, but this time the T.O. is in civilian clothes and remains a silent observer, watching and noting the young officer's progress. The trainee is either given a passing grade or sent back for two more weeks of training, which is followed by another ghost ride. Sure enough, the sullen Commander sent me backward for two weeks, and I was worried that he was going to do it again. He was like the wall in the academy—an unforgiving foe who threatened to block my path until I could prove I could get past him. I wasn't sure that was his intended role, but that's what he had become. I was shocked when the news came down that he would not be **the ghost peering over my shoulder** for the second ride. Later I learned that Rabbit and The Godfather and some others went to the training office to say I deserved a fair chance with someone **impartial**. They said they were sure I would do well, and they were right. I passed my second ghost ride with The Commander out of the patrol car. I moved on to a one-year probationary term and on to the streets. It was thrilling to be accepted.

I was still on probation—it lasts six months—and I knew everything I did would be watched and graded, but I opted to ask for duty in the highest crime area in Santa Ana, the central area that included the neighborhood where I had grown up. The department **was short of manpower**, so it was never guaranteed that you would get the duty you requested, but I lucked out and got assigned the area

....

the ghost peering over my shoulder testing me
impartial who did not dislike me
was short of manpower needed more cops

I wanted. It may sound odd, but I was really relieved to be working the most troubled streets. I had known other young cops who got assigned to low crime areas and spent their first year writing traffic tickets and doing little else. There's nothing wrong with that, but I wanted to be where the action was, and I wanted to be where I could make the most difference. I wanted to be where I was needed, and that was on my home streets.

Nothing special happened my first day solo. I think I took a bike theft report and helped with some traffic accidents and a burglary call. It was one of the best days of my life. It felt right. Cruising on my own, I felt like I was part of the streets again, and I remembered the old **taste of adrenaline** and risk and the new flavor of responsibility. I always liked the edge, and now I was a protector walking that edge. There's a feeling of being really alive that comes from being in the middle of things. I felt at home. And it was a relief to be away from the microscope of the training officers.

I got **a commendation** after a few months on my own for a burglary investigation and for recovering stolen cars, good police work that my supervisor noticed and drew raves from Osuna. I knew what cars looked out of place in the neighborhood, and I knew how the *vatos* acted when they drove a stolen car. I didn't tell anybody that it was pretty easy.

A year later, I got selected for a directed patrol operation in the central district. Cpl. Ann Vickers was assigned to the detail as well. She was well known for her **expertise in narc work**, and she also had a number of years in the Central District directed patrol.

....

taste of adrenaline feeling of excitement

a commendation an award

expertise in narc work experience in arresting drug dealers

A directed patrol is when some uniformed officers are assigned to work problem areas. Other officers still work the area, responding to the daily calls for service, but the directed patrol members focus on the **hot spots**. The assignment to work with Vickers sounded tremendous, and I jumped at the chance to help out.

Our assignment was to crack down on the high drug trade moving through a section of the barrio near Center Park, very close to the old stomping grounds of Jesse James, Little John and all their cronies. The streets we focused on—Myrtle, Wood, Shelley, Walnut and others around them—were bristling with dope and banger activity. It was a rough place to be trying to raise a family, and I felt a lot of sympathy for the hard-working people who lived there. I was eager to make a difference in their lives, and add some misery to the lives of the people who were responsible for their neighborhood's woes. I wanted to make an impact and, one of my first days there, I found a way to **announce my intention**.

I was halfway down Myrtle when I heard a series of pops and a crash. A rock had thudded into the side of the patrol car, then a bottle had skidded across the trunk and shattered on the pavement. I slammed on the brakes, lurching to a loud stop. If the *vatos* were watching, and I knew they were, they expected my next move **to be a hasty retreat**.

I knew some young *vatos* had thrown a challenge at me, and they were expecting me to turn tail and run. Most cops wouldn't wander into the gang-heavy Willets cul-de-sac without backup in the first place, and they had no reason to expect different from this new face.

....

hot spots areas where crime happens the most

announce my intention let the *vatos* know I was serious and here to stay

to be a hasty retreat would be running away

I flipped on the radio's public address switch, "Hey chickenshit," I barked into the mike, "why don't you come down out of that tree and face me one-on-one. I'll leave the gun in the car . . . c'mon, you and me . . . I'll kick your ass right here, right now."

I knew the number one rule on the street was never to back down. Show weakness and the predators come after you. All along the stoops and sidewalks that lined the street, homeboys and the neighborhood's **beleaguered** residents were staring with their jaws dropped. I cruised up and down the street four or five times, calling out challenges that echoed throughout the block. "Hey hey, come out and play . . . Officer Ruiz is here to stay . . ."

For weeks after that, homeboys I busted in the area would tell me that **the word on the street was** that the new cop, Ruiz, was crazy. "They think you're, like, insane, that you'll go off on somebody," one nervous kid told me after I busted him for a dope charge. I, of course, did nothing to change that view. A healthy amount of fear and respect could only make my job easier.

I was using what I had learned from driving through Minnie-Standard with Rabbit. Everyone we passed in that ramshackle complex would call his name, from the surly dope dealers lurking in the doorways to the waving grandmothers leaning out their windows. He had made **his presence felt**, and let his reputation build. "You got to get close up, let people see you," he told me then. "And that way you can see them, too."

I wanted everyone to know my name, too, in part so I would

---

beleaguered tired and worried
the word on the street was everyone was saying
his presence felt sure that everyone knew him

recognize people that weren't residents. That was also the way to earn respect and also develop lines of communication with the community. A lot of good police work is done by people who never wear a badge. If an officer can reach out enough so that the **eyes and ears of** the neighborhood report to him or her, then that officer will **be plugged in** when the bad stuff goes down.

Tips come from different places. A lot of people are mad about the crime in their neighborhoods. Others are shady characters who have been done wrong by another shady character, maybe in a soured drug deal or a skirmish. Lots of times someone will **drop a dime on** a drug dealer who has gotten their brother or sister or child hooked on drugs. One of my best snitches was a young guy who would throw his basketball toward my car. I'd slow down, lean out, pick it up, and wait for him to casually step up and give me the latest scoop. Another kid would yawn when I drove by and his stretch would end with him pointing at someone. I'd walk up to whoever he pointed to and, every time, it was someone carrying dope or stolen goods.

I handed out business cards, subtly, so people wouldn't see my prospective snitch being recruited. A lot of people who didn't want to risk a face-to-face meeting would call up with information about dealers or bangers. Crimes that otherwise would never have been reported or detected were coming to me through this network of citizens and street characters. Another part of the directed patrol effort was a simple but great idea: Officers in the field were given cellular phones and they directly took all of the area's drug-related calls to the department. We got tips, complaints, and calls for help in

....

eyes and ears of people who know what is happening in
be plugged in get tips; know
drop a dime on tell the police about

a matter of seconds, and we were able to act fast and effectively.

The quick turnaround helped me build my reputation with the local troublemakers. For a while, I seemed to be there every time they turned around. And, because I had seen every **scam in the book** growing up, I was usually pretty effective at seeing through their games and excuses. One of the *vatos* told me he thought I was psychic. "It ain't fair if you're reading my mind, y'know?"

As I grew more comfortable and gained experience wearing the badge, I felt, for the first time in my life, that I was where I truly wanted to be. The hours for a cop can be tough and the harshness of what you see every day takes its toll, but the work is, I believe, honorable and a real service to the community. I go home weary, but proud. The role of single parent, as many people in our society have learned, is also challenging and draining. I was raising three great kids, each special in a different way, but **keeping after them** and holding down an intensive job wasn't easy. Still, after so many years of feeling my life was falling apart and lacking direction, the stress of holding things together was a welcome labor.

Work was especially satisfying. After moving past the difficult rookie stage, I felt a growing confidence in myself. I was careful to remember the negative things I had seen cops do when I was younger, and I held on to those memories as valuable reminders of the right way to do things.

I tried, for instance, to never speak to people in an insulting way. I knew from experience that some young people, if treated like street thugs, will respond **in that fashion**. In other words, if people talk to

....

scam in the book trick that there was
keeping after them paying attention to them
in that fashion like street thugs

293

you like you're a criminal often enough, sooner or later you start to believe it a little, or at least you begin **playing the part**. After I joined the force, I think I understood better why those situations occur. Officers learn a lot in training about having a "command presence," a way of speaking and presenting yourself that gives you a firm handle on your dealings with people. The goal is to keep situations under control, the first step in officer safety. I didn't know about that when I was younger, but it certainly made sense as I learned police skills. The problem, though, is that some officers take command presence in the wrong direction. They think that they have to intimidate or belittle the people they deal with to keep them in line, whether they are suspects in a crime or not. It's a defense tactic, I know, but I think it can really **drive a wedge** between police and the community they serve, especially in a city like Santa Ana, where most residents are Latinos and most cops are white. For good or bad, I know what it's like to be treated rudely by police, and I made that one of the key things to avoid doing once I was the one wearing the uniform.

The next step in treating people with respect is offering them solutions and options to their problems that do not demean them. Not every call ends with an arrest; in fact, most don't. A lot of times, police officers are negotiators, helping to safely settle disputes between neighbors, spouses, and strangers. Growing up, I had seen officers bully or corner people in situations like that and force them to back down or **escalate the confrontation**. That doesn't help anybody. If you can find a way to deal with people that allows them to **walk away with dignity**, it can be the first step in a solution that

....

playing the part acting like a criminal

drive a wedge cause problems

escalate the confrontation fight back

walk away with dignity still feel good about themselves

lasts. In the long term, that approach can also build a bond with the community. People remember their dealings with officers, and it **colors** the way they and other citizens view the badge. If the dealings are respectful and positive, the community can help us become a lot more effective.

A lot of these ideas are part of a philosophy called community policing, which is active in Santa Ana and cities across the country. Basically, the approach builds bridges between officers and the community, and encourages citizens to help by providing information, resources, and support. It makes cops more **attuned to** the public and creates the teamwork needed for tough problems, such as gangs and drugs. I think it's a great way to approach law enforcement. It's hard for me to ever forget how frustrated I was with police officers as a teen or, later, as a battered wife. They weren't there to help me, and I hated them for it. I think things like community policing remind officers of what's important and who we are trying to serve.

All that sounds pretty easy, but it can feel practically impossible on the streets. I and other officers have to deal with people that really get on our nerves, and remembering to keep your cool during a tough shift isn't easy. The job is rough, but sometimes the extra things you do come back around when you least expect it. Sometimes the community you serve gives you something in return.

I remember one afternoon when a robbery call came over the radio. The chase was **cold** and the suspect was **in the wind**, but I had nothing else going on. I decided to cruise in that general direction

....

colors affects
attuned to aware of
cold going badly
in the wind well-hidden from the police

and see if I could help.

I knew the gang members there, and they knew me. Maybe I could **get a lead** (or hit it lucky and drive by just when the fleeing suspect **came up for air**). An officer was already handling the call and two others had helped by taking a few laps around the area, but they had turned up nothing. Still, I knew the area better than just about anybody, and there was no harm in trying.

As soon as I pulled up, I saw a group of homeboys at curbside, waving their arms and hopping up and down to catch my attention. I cruised up slowly, wondering what they were up to. "Officer Ruiz, hey!" There were five of them, all early high school age, although they probably spent more time in front of a television than a classroom blackboard. They were all talking at once, and I had to calm them down to understand what they were saying.

"You looking for a robber? He's over there!" The tallest one was pointing down the block, but I didn't see anything at first.

"We'll help! What do you want us to do?"

"Yeah!"

I wondered if I was **walking into the scam of the day**. "Since when are you guys police cadets?"

Howls of laughter. They gave each other high-fives and stomped with delight. Then the tall one was speaking again: "We ain't no cadets. This guy's a punk, though, an outsider. And he messed up my cousin, y'know, Juan. That ain't cool."

Juan was a young kid from Mexico who had come to join his family in Santa Ana. He was a nice kid, not real bright, but friendly

---

get a lead find something out

came up for air stopped hiding and tried to run

walking into the scam of the day being tricked

and willing to work hard. He handed out a free ice-cream treat to his regular customers when business was good. He was part of the neighborhood. The robber had pissed off the locals by sticking up a local guy.

"Okay, then . . . where's the bad guy at?"

They took off running, looking back and waving me on as I coasted up the block behind them. One of them, his pants so baggy that you couldn't see his knees bending as he ran, stumbled every few yards and had to keep a hand fixed to his waist to keep the trousers up. I radioed in that I might have a possible location on the robbery suspect based on a "citizen report." I almost laughed when I said that one.

When I turned the corner onto Myrtle, there was a crowd gathered, maybe fifteen homeboys and locals, all in a circle near a chainlink fence. I pulled to the curb, called in **the block number** on my radio, and stepped up to the group. I recognized a lot of the people (including some of the *vatos* who spun on their heels and took off upon seeing my blue uniform), but the face in the center of the commotion was a **strange one**. He was a Hispanic male, late twenties, maybe early thirties, and he was a sad-looking sight, sitting with his elbows on his knees with a dazed look on his face. Blood was streaming down from his nose and a shiny red welt was rising on his cheek. He squinted up at me with an odd look of relief.

One of the *vatos* emerged from the crowd and, with a broad and satisfied grin, stretched out his hand, slowly presenting me with a .38 caliber handgun, barrel down.

....

the block number my location

strange one face I did not recognize

"Here's his gun and here's the money," he said, producing a small wad of five- and ten-dollar bills. He handed it over like a grade-school student presenting an apple to his favorite teacher. "We done good, huh?"

The suspect watched all this with sagging shoulders. He shook his head, muttering. He dabbed at his swollen nose. "Ahg . . . ah-assholes."

He glared at my unlikely group of **vigilantes**. I thought of Rabbit and his stories about the origins of his gang, how they used their numbers and fists to bring fairness to their neighborhood. They had caught the bad guy this time, but these were also the same *vatos* responsible for mayhem and mischief throughout the barrio. What was I to do with these kids? I was tugging the robbery suspect toward my unit and asking witnesses to the crime to stick around when I heard the sirens signaling the approach of patrol cars and, by the sound of it, a lot of them. I wondered if I had missed a radio call for some local **calamity**, but later I found out I was the reason for the streaking squad cars. The people leaning out windows of the apartment buildings lining the block had seen me with the group of *vatos*, a lone officer seemingly surrounded. They called for help, and now help was on the way.

The units came up at full throttle, screeching in close. I was waving them off, telling them everything was all right.

"Everything's **Code 4** . . . Got our **perp** right here," I called out, pointing to my cuffed arrestee. The suspect had his eyes tightly shut, like he was hoping everything would go away when he reopened

....

vigilantes law-enforcers, helpers
calamity disaster
Code 4 just fine
perp criminal

them. The cops smiled or muttered as they got back in their units and headed off. A few lingered and asked me how everything went down. Their expressions were priceless when I explained how my "junior detectives" had performed a citizen's arrest on the bad guy.

The best look was on the face of the lead officer, the one who was working the robbery to begin with and had called off the pursuit when the trail got cold. He bounded up to the scene as things were calming down, his face red with anger. It was an old friend: The Commander, one of my training officers.

"What the hell are you doing down here, I told you not to come down here alone!" He was yelling and had a hand on one of his hips. He had **surveyed the scene** and assumed that I had been in trouble, in need of being rescued. Before I could shoot back an explanation, one of the other cops did it for me. "She didn't need us, the neighbors called in. She already had the guy **in the bag**."

I smiled at The Commander and tried to **clamp down on** any sarcasm that might tint my words. "Hey, don't worry about me, everything's under control," I told him as I pushed the still groggy robber forward. "By the way, I think you were looking for this."

After the incident with the robber I would jokingly call the Myrtle Street gang members my "Citizens on Patrol." While the *vatos* knew I would never cut them slack if they were breaking the law, they also knew I would always treat them like people, too. Some were and would always be criminals, but many of them were

....

surveyed the scene looked around
in the bag arrested
clamp down on control

unsupervised kids looking for mischief. Act like you expect good behavior out of them, and many will respond. And, at least once, they might even be heroes.

BEFORE YOU MOVE ON...

1. **Cause and Effect** Reread pages 293–294. How did Mona's gang life affect her police work?

2. **Conclusions** Reread page 299. The Commander assumed that Mona was in trouble. What does this show about him?

LOOK AHEAD Read pages 301–321 to see what dangerous new assignment Mona took on with the police.

~ Chapter Fourteen ~

PC 187

At one point, I worried that my efforts to establish a strong presence in the Myrtle Street district might **backfire**.

The directed patrol was working with the Narc Unit on a series of undercover drug buys in the area, a quick-hit effort aimed at forcing the area's brazen drug dealers to **rethink** their busy sidewalk commerce. The drug market in the area was a tough **nut to crack**. The dealers served other gang members almost exclusively, so anyone who didn't look local had no chance of scoring. A network of lookouts up and down the street made the task even tougher. If they saw anyone that looked, walked, talked, or smelled like a cop, business would shut down along the entire avenue. The organizers of the directed patrol wanted **a fresh face** to try out undercover, and they thought my appearance and background made me an ideal choice. (I'm sure they didn't even know about my most extensive experience—Frank and his buddies were no strangers to the drug-dealing world, and I had heard and seen enough transactions to know

....

backfire have a negative effect
rethink stop
nut to crack problem to fix
a fresh face a new police officer

it well.) I jumped at the chance to work with the Narc Unit and its group of veteran investigators, but later some anxieties nagged at me.

The same reasons they wanted me for the job were the reasons for my concerns.

Despite having a huge Latino population, the city of Santa Ana has a mostly white police force. A Latino cop is noted by the barrio community, especially if he or she is local. And especially if she is a female officer, another relative rarity. I worried that those factors, and my aggressive efforts **to make a splash** in the Myrtle area, might make me too recognizable for an undercover job. I kept my fears to myself, though, and decided my disguise would have to be a good one.

After the nerve-racking experience of my first undercover assignment—the street purchase with Muñoz that was punctuated by the startling appearance of Little John—I ended up doing about a dozen more plain-clothes missions. Each **went off without a hitch**, and by the last one I felt almost comfortable with the dangerous work. I also had a lot more confidence in my disguises.

The quality of my makeup job was proved by the words of one frustrated drug runner I arrested. I had first seen the kid when I was on patrol in uniform one afternoon. I **did a field interview** after getting reports that he was dealing and, after getting his name and information, I let him go with a warning to stay out of trouble. The next time I saw him was a week later, as I leaned out of a beat-up old Monte Carlo and handed him a few twenties for some dope. I recognized his face, but he didn't **see past** my makeup, wig and *chola*

....

to make a splash to be known by everyone
went off without a hitch went well
did a field interview asked him some questions
see past recognize me under

appearance. He was arrested by other officers as I headed back to the station. I saw him there, a third time. I had scrubbed off the makeup and was wearing my blue uniform when I sat down across from him to fill out his arrest report. Only after I filled out half the sheet did a look of realization—and a wave of disgusted frustration—wash across his face.

"You're the cop I talked to last week," he said. "And you . . . and you're the one I sold to! Awww. I can't believe this . . . "

He covered his eyes with his palms and sagged back into the seat. I wanted to give him grief for his sorry situation. After all, I did warn him earlier. Instead I played it cool.

"I don't know what you're talking about," I told him. "Yeah, I saw you a week ago, but I've been here all day. I don't know who you sold drugs to." His face screwed up in confusion and he kept prodding me. "No way, it was you. I know it was you. It was you, right?"

I just smiled. It's always best to keep them guessing.

The special details like Homicide, Narcs, and Gangs are considered the **elite** assignments for cops, and many officers aspire to reach those areas. The thrills of undercover work and the **autonomy** given to investigators make those the **plum** jobs. I would love to work with the Gang Unit someday. I know firsthand how good our gang investigators are, and working beside them would be an honor and an education. But more than that, I would love to work full-time with the crime issue that dominated much of my life, the **death grip** the gang mentality has on inner-city Latino communities,

....

elite best

autonomy freedom

plum greatest, coolest

death grip powerful influence

such as the Santa Ana barrio where I grew up. I realized working on patrol, though, that the Gang Unit wasn't the only way to get a grip on the gang issue. If those special details are the elite arm of the department, then patrol is its powerful backbone. Patrol officers deal most directly and most often with the public, day and night, every day of the year. They see it all, and a lot of it is **not pretty**.

My time on patrol taught me to see the city of my birth in a new way, a view shaped, sadly, by crime and tragedy. Patrol cops know the alleys and streets and parks and schools, but they learn them as a list of crime scenes and crash sites. They know which intersections have the most car accidents, and which apartment buildings have been visited most often by the black van of the coroner's office. Instead of storefronts, cops see old burglary reports, and house addresses stick in their head for terrible reasons: That's where the widow lives, that's where that rape was, here's where we caught the kidnapper . . .

It's a struggle for cops to sort through **that catalogue of horrors**. **Getting jaded** might be the worst part of the job, worse even than the risk of injury. A lot of times you can live with wounds to the body, but your soul is difficult to mend. When I talk to some of the old-timers, they rattle off the worst of the worst (shotgun suicides and drowned babies, moldering bodies and torture crimes—everything has happened in Santa Ana), passing on the stories that horrify and, for some reason, fascinate all of us. The thread that connects the worst of these stories, the ones that left the deepest scars, is a feeling of helplessness for the cops. There is nothing worse for people who put on a badge than the feeling that they can do

....

not pretty disturbing
that catalogue of horrors their awful memories
Getting jaded Becoming an uncaring person

nothing when things go wrong.

In September 1992, I was surrounded by death and pain and a feeling of helplessness that made me sick with grief. The papers called it the deadliest car crash in Orange County history, and it left a huge impact on our city and our department.

The Ford van was packed with people, eighteen total, all on the way to a Sunday evening church service. Many of the women and children in the back were sitting on wood benches that the minister had **fashioned and set across the rear cargo area**. For a year, the preacher had made a habit of picking up his Spanish-speaking **congregation** at their homes several times a week and driving them to services. The benches weren't bolted down, and there were no seat belts.

About 6 P.M., on September 21, the van passed through the intersection of Flower Street and Civic Center Drive. At that same moment, a speeding Chevrolet pickup ran the red light and plowed into the side of the van, sending it into a spin that threw open the back doors. A witness said the passengers flew out like pilots ejecting themselves from an airplane. The bustling Civic Center streets were littered with bodies, like a war zone. Eight were dead, including a pregnant woman, two teens and two children. Eleven others were injured. The blood and body parts were everywhere, including a decapitated head. Rosaries and children's toys were scattered across the asphalt. It was a massacre.

The driver of the pickup truck got out, saw this unbelievable **carnage**, and he ran. He ran like a coward. Beer cans littered the

---

fashioned and set across the rear cargo area made and put in the back of the van

congregation church members

carnage death scene; gore

floor of the truck. Later, a friend identified the driver as a twenty-three-year old cook from Riverside. The friend said the driver had bolted to Mexico, but promised to "make up" for what he had done. He may have been smart to run. I saw the look in the eyes of officers searching for him on the day of the accident. I have never seen such fury.

I cannot describe **adequately** what I saw when I arrived at the accident scene on that fall day. It was the worst thing I have ever seen.

I was called to the scene, along with many of the officers on duty that day. The accident scene was large and difficult to manage, but we had to make sure people stayed away from evidence. It amazes me how people are drawn to gruesome crashes, craning their necks for a view. I have seen too many. I wonder how many a person has to see before he doesn't want to look anymore. Because I speak Spanish, the officers running the accident scene investigation called on me to help talk to witnesses and injury victims who did not speak English. I also helped separate all the witnesses, shuttling them to different patrol cars so they didn't talk to other people about what they had seen. It may sound cruel to pull apart people who have just gone through a tragedy together, but when witnesses talk with each other, it can **taint their recollection** of what they actually saw. They take scraps of each other's stories and merge them together. It's always **a priority** to keep the witness accounts pure and separate.

When I had guided four witnesses to squad cars, the lead investigator on the scene assigned me a second job, a chore that sent chills through my body.

....

adequately completely
taint their recollection change their memory
a priority important

We needed to identify the dead as quickly as possible. Many did not have ID's on them or even own one. The only way to get a handle on who the victims were—to begin the process of contacting their families as soon as possible—was to **get a visual identification of each corpse**. The driver of the van, a minister named Octavio Valentín, had **escaped harm**, and only he knew every one of his passengers. He agreed to walk through the carnage and list the dead.

Large tarps, thick and yellow like heavy raincoats, covered the corpses, but not completely. Arms and legs jutted out and it was clear, too, from the shapes beneath the tarps that some of the bodies were badly mangled. I walked with the minister, propping him up by his elbow, as he sobbed and wailed. I thought he might faint with grief. When we came to the first body, an officer asked him if he was ready, and the minister nodded. He nearly collapsed when the covering was pulled back to reveal the bloody body of a pregnant woman. He told us her name and said that she had her two children with her in the van. My eyes darted to two small forms nearby. Tiny hands and feet stuck out from beneath the covers. I swallowed hard. I wondered if the minister could handle the sight. I also wondered if I could. I did not want to see those small faces. I didn't have to. Just then, the supervisor called me to translate for some more witnesses and a different officer took the arm of the minister. As I jogged over to my new duty, I could hear the preacher's wail of misery and grief as, one by one, he visited the gruesome remains of his congregation. It was a nightmare.

Some days I have a hard time remembering the names or faces

....

get a visual identification of each corpse have someone who knew them look at each body

escaped harm not been hurt

of old friends, or the look of places I visited just a few years ago. But I have never forgotten the sights I saw that day, or the sounds of that minister's pain. The images are **seared into** my memory. I wish I could wipe them away forever.

I also wish I knew what to say to the victims I meet. As cops, we know what to do with the bangers, pushers, felons, and violent suspects; that's the easy part. But what do we do for the people who suffer at their hands, the people who remain behind after the **flashing lights** go away?

Tragedy surrounding or involving children is especially hard for me to handle. I guess everybody is that way. Little ones are innocent and vulnerable, and to see their potential and sweetness wrecked by the evil in our world is the greatest loss of all. It's hard to cope with and impossible to forget. That's probably why I can still hear little María's voice.

I met María and her mother in October 1991. For weeks, the eight-year-old had barely eaten or slept. When she did sleep, she would wake up crying and shaken from relentless nightmares. María would not tell anyone what was bothering her. She would only bite her trembling lip and keep her fears inside. Her mother was confused and worried. Then, when María began complaining about pain in her private parts, her mother reached a sickening conclusion. Her daughter had been molested. She thought she knew who might have done it, too.

Pancho was a cousin by marriage. The forty-three-year-old was **rootless**. He mostly drifted between his native Mexico and Orange

....

seared into a permanent part of
flashing lights police
rootless a wanderer; homeless

County, where many of his relatives lived. When his travels took him to Santa Ana, he worked at a downtown bakery making ice cream. Pancho loved children, he would tell people, and he always **doted on** the kids in his extended family. In recent months, his behavior had raised some suspicions. When María's mother heard the talk, a cold fury gripped her. She asked María if Pancho had ever touched her in a bad way.

The eight-year-old broke down and burst into sobs. Her distraught mother called police and soon I was sitting in their living room. Talking to strangers is never easy for shy little girls. It's practically impossible for a youngster who has experienced the kind of trauma that María had suffered. I spoke to her quietly and tried to ease her mind. I think my uniform frightened her and my mind flashed back to my childhood when I saw the blue suits and feared them. She asked her mother a question that almost broke my heart.

"Am I in trouble? I'm sorry, Mommy . . ."

I felt angry at her attacker and powerless to help this poor child. Her mother and I just kept reassuring her and, eventually, **slivers** of her story started emerging. Pancho had touched her on several occasions. Later, he raped her. Each time, he warned her that if she let the secret out, something terrible would happen to her and her mother. He made her feel guilty and terrified. Using a basic sketch of a child's body, María hesitantly circled the places she had been touched. She described in child's words the sex acts that were so difficult for her child's mind to understand. She was very brave.

I knew Pancho was a danger to every child in the neighborhood.

....

doted on spoiled; paid a lot of attention to
slivers parts

María's mother began making calls to friends and relatives to find him. Word came back that he was at a relative's home visiting children. My gut clenched. We had to get him right away. María's mother called the house and I talked to her relative, a woman who took the phone into the bathroom to speak to me without Pancho overhearing. I told her to stall Pancho but not to leave him alone, especially with the children. Within minutes, patrol cars were pulling up to the home, and we took Pancho into custody. The case was solid and others **stepped forward**. Pancho was **put away** for a long time, which means the neighborhood is a little safer for children. Maybe someday that will mean something to María. Maybe she will be able to clutch to the fact that she helped put her attacker behind bars and save other youngsters. I think about María a lot. I haven't handled many child abuse cases, and I'm thankful for that. It was a wrenching experience. I knew the dangers that awaited young people out on the streets, but until I heard María's voice, I never fully understood the threats that could terrorize them right in their own homes.

By 1993, I had a new assignment and a new partner, a big, hulking guy named Marshall. Cpl. Dave Marshall was like me, a "homegrown" from the Santa Ana streets. He ran with the gangs when he was younger, too, and we even had vague memories of seeing each other on opposite ends of the gang scene when we were both at Valley High. Marshall was in the Westside Gang, also known as Dogtown (a longtime F-Troop rival), as a kid, and he grew up tough, like any black kid who grows up in the barrio. Santa Ana's

....

stepped forward told the police that he had molested them, as well

put away sent to prison

African American community is tiny, and Marshall saw few faces like his own while growing up. He earned the respect of the Latino homeboys, though, with his fierce attitude and tenacious personality. Becoming a martial arts fighter didn't hurt either. As a cop, he enjoyed the advantages of being a street kid, just like me. We often compared notes, and chuckled at the scams and stories the *vatos* would try to put over on us. We had heard it all before and, in some cases, we had even tried it before ourselves. It was the little things, too, the things you can only know if you have been on the other side. For instance, Marshall was the only other cop I've met who knew to put a hand over his badge when he tried to sneak up on somebody on a dark street. If you don't, a glare will catch on the badge and your quarry will take off. We both knew because, when we were kids, we were the ones doing the running.

Marshall had selected me as his partner because he thought our mutual background would help with his new assignment: trying to squelch the flood of graffiti **washing over** Santa Ana. Graffiti had been a part of the gang scene for years. Blocky, Old English-style writing was often used to mark the boundaries of gang turf and send messages to rivals. But as the 1990s began, the culture of **taggers** swept through the barrios and beyond. Taggers were often not gang members, although they shared many of the same fashions and language. A tagger's goal is to spread his name and street acclaim by covering everything with his "tag"—a nickname, usually an abbreviation or short word, scrawled in a distinctive style. Their targets were freeway signs, school walls, homes, stores, streets, even

....

washing over being painted all over
taggers graffiti artists

cars. Their logic was that the bigger or better the target, the greater the audience and the acclaim. The risks were not obvious to many of them. (I remember one case where a tagger in Orange County fell to his death while writing his **moniker** on a sign above a busy freeway, and another where a homeowner shot a kid spray painting on his property.) Tagging attracted a lot of kids who were **enamored** by the gang scene but did not want to plunge into the violence of banging. They figured that writing on a wall with spray paint and running away was enough of a criminal thrill.

Marshall and I were assigned full-time to tracking the city's growing population of taggers, and trying to put the **most prolific of the graffiti bandits** behind bars. The job got increasingly difficult as the tagger crews and the city's entrenched banger gangs began an odd relationship. The tagger crews had a lot in common with banger gangs, of course. They shared the same city and schools, attended many of the same parties and crossed paths often. The taggers embraced many of the banger traditions, but altered them somewhat. For instance, a potential member of a tagger crew had to prove himself (that often meant competing with other candidates to see who could most effectively spread their tags) and might even have to go through the jumping-in process. The rival crews also fought, too, but their battleground would be the walls and signs of the city. A tag war between two large crews meant that hundreds of people would wake up the next morning to find spray paint scrawls dotting their property and neighborhood. Soon, the number of tagging crews and free agent taggers competing for notoriety and

....

moniker nickname

enamored fascinated

most prolific of the graffiti bandits taggers who made the most graffiti

space made things uncomfortable on the streets. The battles between rival taggers turned more traditional: Guns and knives and fists replaced aerosol cans. Tagbangers were born. Now, all this new activity in the barrios didn't sit well with many of the traditional gangs, especially the older bangers. They were not pleased to see their neighborhood—and their own turf graffiti—covered by this relentless tagger attack. They hit back hard, and many of the kids who had embraced tagging as a non-dangerous way to be outlaws abruptly found themselves with more trouble than they could handle. The bangers' distaste for tagging and taggers was most evident when a shaky truce was **brokered** one summer by Southern California gang leaders. No drive-bys, the truce declared, and no random violence. The only exception? It was still **open season on** taggers.

That truce, and others like it, **was always short-lived**. There were too many bangers and too much bad blood on the streets. The gang population had exploded into the thousands in Santa Ana by the 1990s, just as the city had exploded in population. Everything was on edge. The gang violence claimed a life every week, it seemed. Marshall and I and other cops had a front row seat to the mayhem. Death was everywhere. One night, we stared it right in the face.

It was Halloween night 1993, and there may have been more cops on duty within the city limits of Santa Ana than ever before. Officers from agencies across Orange County were helping with a massive operation aimed at snuffing out the heavy cruising traffic that had been attracting bangers to Santa Ana in unprecedented numbers for weeks. Traffic on the major streets would slow to a crawl

....

brokered agreed upon
open season on okay to shoot
was always short-lived never lasted long

as low-riders from places like Whittier, San Diego, and Riverside would join the local homeboys for a **parade with no destination** and plenty of potential for trouble. In October of that year, there had been a murder, drive-by shootings and robberies, all tied to the *vato* migration to Santa Ana, suddenly the new cool cruising spot. The merchant community was **hammering** the PD brass for action. Parking lots, like the one at the shopping center on Edinger and Bristol, were being taken over at night by masses of homeboys, their girlfriends and the curious, all watching the slow march of muscle cars and low-riders. A good number of the participants in this curbside spectator sport were looking for a fight, too, **throwing hand signs** to announce themselves and provoke others. The merchants were both afraid and furious. Sunday nights were probably the biggest cruising night, which made it hard for the cops on patrol to do much about the huge, spontaneous gatherings. Police staffing levels are probably at their lowest on Sunday nights. A handful of cops who tried to break up a crowd of five hundred juiced-up homeboys would only create trouble and put themselves in extreme danger. It was a matter of numbers. So, when we saw that Halloween night would fall on a Sunday, the directed patrol came up with a plan to stifle the cruising and, hopefully, **diffuse a potential powder keg**. Nearly every Santa Ana cop was on duty that night, and they were joined by officers from neighboring cities, along with parole and probation agents. The plan was to spread out and be visible by posting cops at every intersection on some streets. We wrote up tickets, did warrant checks and kept the traffic moving as briskly as

....

parade with no destination drive with no place to go
hammering bothering
throwing hand signs making gang signals
diffuse a potential powder keg stop any violence

possible, stopping anyone who tried to slow to a cruiser's snail pace. The number of cops and bangers in one place made for an uneasy night. It was made stranger by the Halloween atmosphere. We stopped cars with vampires, superheroes, and monsters.

By midnight, Bristol Street and the other main **drags** were quieting down. Marshall and I were beat. We had talked to dozens of kids during traffic stops and while breaking up sidewalk gatherings. Tempers among the kids were high. They had come looking for a good time, but everywhere they turned they saw a cop. They didn't believe it, but keeping them from bunching up on the side of the street was for their own protection. Marshall and I had been hearing rumblings on the street about some planned paybacks. Anybody hanging out in a group was a potential target, whether they knew it or not. We saw a lot of the same faces throughout the night, people we had warned again and again. Sometimes, the job can be really frustrating.

When we cruised by Serrano's Taquería on Edinger Avenue near Sullivan Street, we saw a group of familiar faces gathered on the restaurant's patio. The bangers were from the Sullivan Street gang, and they had **an entourage** with them. There were always kids who orbited the gang members in their neighborhood, eager to be near the excitement but not part of it. They didn't know that **flirting with** danger and actually being in danger are the same thing in Santa Ana. These kids were all tempting fate. They were boldly gathering for a good time in an area where they would likely run into their Sullivan Street rivals.

....

drags streets
an entourage a large group of supporters
flirting with thinking about; being near

We drove past, but then circled up through an alley across the street and blacked out the car so we wouldn't be seen. I could hear the asphalt crackle beneath the tires as we slowly edged the patrol car up to the parking spots next to a mostly empty strip mall. With a full moon overhead, we **had a clear line of vision to** the taco stand, but the patrons could not see us. Marshall and I **scoped out** the crowd, scanning for faces we might have seen on fugitive bulletins. We planned to get a good **bead on** who was in the group, then pull up and drive right across the street to break up the gathering.

I was exhausted. I looked at my watch: It was past midnight. My eyes were sagging and my back hurt. It's hard to sit in a police car with your gear and vest and not get sore. I was watching a girl dancing on one of the red and white concrete benches in front of the taco stand. She was surrounded by her friends as she laughed and tossed her hair from side to side. Marshall and I were talking about two bangers sitting in the rear of the group when, out of the corner of my eye, I saw the two cars cruising up.

The cars were headed east on Edinger, a path that would bring them between our patrol ear and the open patio of the restaurant. It was a blue Honda and a Caprice, I remember, and my eye left them for a moment and returned to the girl dancing on the bench. A sound like a baseball bat breaking jarred me, but my eyes never left her figure. Her neck jerked with the impact of the gunfire. It had caught her in the rear of her head, right there in front of me. Everything started moving in slow motion. I could see her crumple to the pavement, obviously dead before landing. Marshall and I were

....

had a clear line of vision to could easily see
scoped out looked at
bead on idea of

stunned, but quickly **slammed into action**. He gunned the engine and reached for the radio as the car lurched forward. Marshall called in the description of the cars and asked for backup, and I kept my eye on the path of the suspects.

"We have a drive-by, with a female Hispanic taking a shot to the head . . . we need paramedics . . . we are **in pursuit of** suspect vehicle, eastbound Edinger . . . request backup units, 10-3 . . . "

I yelled out their direction each time they turned, and Marshall repeated the information into the police radio. There was no time to think about the grisly sight we had seen. I was forward in my seat, thumping on the dash with anxious energy. There was no more fatigue, just the pounding of blood and adrenaline in my head and chest.

On the radio, we could hear other units chiming in with their location and the dispatcher assigning them to assist us. Sirens in the distance started filling the night air, but not ours. We were in such a rush to follow the two cars, we never hit the lights or siren. The streets were mostly empty as we raced up behind the cars as they turned on Sullivan Street and then Borchard Avenue, stopping at one of the first houses on the street. The two carloads emptied and the homeboys gathered for high-fives in the driveway as we skidded up and hit the spotlight. They never saw us behind them. The expression on their faces was total shock. Marshall and I had our guns aimed at them, and we shouted for them to freeze. We had two suspects in our sights and spotlight, but two others had already bolted toward the house.

....

slammed into action reacted
in pursuit of chasing

Marshall leaned into his field radio to rattle off a description of the two suspects in front of us. My eyes were locked on the palms of their hands and the darkness over their shoulders. We knew these guys were armed, and we didn't want any surprises. All around us, we could hear patrol cars pulling up and car doors slamming, along with the sound of shotguns being **racked** by our backup officers. The radio traffic told us **a perimeter was** being set up around the neighborhood to **box in** the remaining suspects. With the extra help, we focused solely on the two *vatos* in the spotlight. If the pair had thought about gambling with an escape or **resistance attempt**, the sheer number of cops now on the scene changed their minds. We told them to walk backward, one at a time, toward the sound of our voices. We made each do a slow circle so we could check for weapons in their waistbands. We then ordered them down to their knees and told them to cross one leg over the other, a position that puts a suspect in an awkward position to resist. Finally, we told them to lock their fingers behind their backs before cuffing them and putting them in separate cars. On the radio, we could hear the officers at the scene of the shooting. There were two victims, the girl we saw shot in the head and a boy hit in the buttocks. The girl was en route to UCI Medical Center, but was likely to be dead on arrival, I heard. I wondered if the suspects heard it, also. I wondered if they cared.

Up at the house, meanwhile, officers were surrounding the yard and, over a bullhorn, ordering anyone inside to come out with their hands up. They repeated the order in Spanish. The guy that came out wasn't one of our suspects, and he was hostile. Officers asked

....

racked loaded
a perimeter was police officers were
box in trap
resistance attempt trying to fight back

who else was in the house, but the guy only wanted to argue. "What do you want? I haven't done anything! Why are you doing this?" He said all of this loud enough for the growing crowd of neighbors to hear, of course.

The suspects had fled through or around the house, and were either in the backyard or beyond. Marshall and I joined the hunt. A police helicopter was now overhead, shining a bright, wobbly spotlight on the overgrown backyard. I was with a K-9 officer and her dog in the house's kitchen, watching as **a SWAT-trained officer** slowly made his way into the dark yard, right behind the police dog. The place was a mess, junk everywhere and plants that made it impossible to see more than a few yards. There's somebody down there, the helicopter pilot said over the radio, we're getting something on the **heat sensor**. The officers shouted that the police dog would be sent to find and attack if the suspect didn't surrender and, as usual, that coaxed the bad guy out of hiding. He emerged from the brush with his hands up, but denied having a weapon.

Marshall went back to the crime scene after the bust, while I stayed at the arrest site to assist in the search for the guns. "I'll find out about the girl," he said as he turned to go.

Her name, I found out later, was Isela. I had seen her around the barrio before. She had never been in any real trouble. She just hung out with a rough crowd, just as I and all my sisters had. Tramping through the dark, overgrown backyard of the suspects' house, I couldn't help thinking back about a different night, a different girl. My neck seemed to throb, reminding me of the party where I felt

....

a SWAT-trained officer a Special Weapons and Assault Team officer

heat sensor machine that senses body heat

the slash of the bullet that **took the life of another**. I was Isela, and she was me. I felt as if I had watched myself die. This time my head was a little to the left and, instead of a burn on my throat, I was dead, lying in the flower bed while my sister and a woman with holy water hovered above me . . .

The flash of a spotlight from a police chopper close overhead **snapped me out of the vision**. I used my nightstick to move aside some plants. We had to find the gun.

I knew the shooting had **shook Marshall up**, too. He had a story remarkably similar to mine. He was at a party when a shot slammed into a close homeboy of his who had been standing within arm's reach. When Marshall spun around, his friend was on the ground, blood pumping out of his throat. Sometimes it felt like everyone in Santa Ana had the same story. Marshall's version, at least, had a better ending than mine. His friend lived (and even had a grim reaper tattoo drawn around the bullet wound), but the incident had shaken him badly and led directly to his departure from the gang world. All that was awakened by Isela's death.

Marshall was mad when he brought the squad car back to a screeching halt in front of the suspects' house. It would be the next day before he told me what happened. When he arrived back at the *taquería*, a couple of cops were milling about the body, cracking jokes about the corpse and **making slurs** about her background. Dark humor is a staple of cop life. It's a way for officers to distance themselves from the daily carnage, but Marshall was infuriated by the crude jokes. He looked down at the body and saw a little girl who

....

took the life of another killed Oso
snapped me out of the vision brought me back to reality
shook Marshall up affected Marshall
making slurs saying terrible things

was dead for no good reason, and he thought about his own family, who lived just a few blocks away, close enough to be awakened by the shots and sirens. He kicked at an alley cat that kept trying to get to the body, and he turned on the chuckling cops.

"You better shut your mouth," he said, grabbing one of the cops. "My family lives here, I have nieces and nephews here. If you can't have any respect for these people, why don't you just quit? Why are you even working here?"

"Back off, Marshall," one of the other cops said. My partner turned to go and saw the cat again trying to reach the body. He sprayed it with Mace, got in his car and drove off.

More frustrations awaited back at the house. A dozen cops peering past plants and poking bushes with their billy clubs could not find the guns. It would be six hours later before Marshall and a gang investigator found both weapons, an Ml Carbine and a .45-caliber handgun, in that backyard jungle. They succeeded only after retrieving a metal detector from the station to scan the heavy ivy along the yard's fence. The guns produced prints that led to the ID of the two shooters. They faced a charge of PC 187, **homicide** in the first degree, along with attempted murder for the injuries the boy suffered. The three arrests that day were followed by a fourth before the year was **out** and two more in the following months. The case is still **winding its way** through the court system now, in 1997.

....

homicide murder
out over
winding its way moving

BEFORE YOU MOVE ON...

1. **Summarize** Reread page 301. Why was Mona perfect for undercover work with the police?

2. **Paraphrase** Reread page 320. What did Mona mean when she said "I was Isela, and she was me"?

LOOK AHEAD Why would Mona risk telling her story to a reporter again? Read pages 322–338 to find out.

~ Chapter Fifteen ~

SURVIVORS

Isela's death left me emotionally weak and pondering my own mortality. Was her murder a message for me? Oso's death was a warning to escape the gang life, so I wondered if this latest tragedy was a sign that the badge was too **costly to carry**.

Marshall and I were like zombies in the days after the drive-by, and the stress had us snapping at each other and anyone else who caught us at the wrong moment. It seemed every call took us past that *taquería* or the house where, we now knew, Isela had lived. A lot of people at the PD had congratulated us on the quick action to collar the 187 suspects, but I knew Marshall felt the same way I did: We didn't do enough on Halloween night. Neither of us could come out and say it, but we were angry with ourselves for not preventing the shooting. The scenarios played out in my head again and again. What if we had gone over to the *taquería* sooner to send the crowd on its way? Or what if we had realized what the two carloads of homeboys were **up to** a little quicker? We could have turned on our

....

costly to carry dangerous
up to planning to do

sirens and scared them off. . . . All the different things we could have done haunted me. That kind of logic had me **beating myself up pretty bad**. I was skittish and edgy on the job, which can **be an invitation for** disaster. Luckily, I found some help. His name was Blum and I had never met anybody quite like him.

Larry Blum was a psychologist who worked with police officers all over Southern California. He did not look like my image of a psychologist. He was burly, with broad shoulders, and he had a mustache and close-cropped black hair, like a lot of cops. He lifted weights so all the officers called him Dr. Deadlift. He told me he ran with the street toughs back in his old New York neighborhood, and he had this loud, Bronx voice, like a bullhorn. He wasn't the first counselor I went to in the weeks after Isela's death. The department is good about getting us help following traumatic events, but the so-called experts they had lined up for me did little. I left each office **scratching my head or rolling my eyes**. They all talked about focusing and breathing, but they didn't understand the things I had seen, the feelings I was going through. I decided Blum was the last one I would try.

His office was covered with police department patches and hats, mementos left behind by former patients. Blum sat down across from me, and we talked about ourselves, our backgrounds and mutual friends. I liked him right away. He seemed honest and straightforward. He pointed to my tattoo and asked me the story behind it. I explained about the Troopers and my life with Frank, my relationship with my father and his dream for me to be a cop.

....

beating myself up pretty bad blaming myself for what happened

be an invitation for easily cause a

scratching my head or rolling my eyes frustrated and confused

As we met several other times, I told him about my kids and my career. I shared the painful old memories that still haunt me, and the fresh, haunting image of Isela . . . I had never really opened up to any person like I did with Blum. I had shared many things with my sisters, friends, and people like Osuna, but never everything, not the whole story. It was a great relief, for some reason, to **lay it all out**. Blum listened to my story and told me I could not allow myself to feel guilt for Isela's death. "You caught the bad guys," he explained. "You're not superhuman. You can't save the world, and if you **try to hold yourself to that standard**, you will never succeed and you'll never be happy."

The most valuable thing I got from Blum's advice was to look back on my own life with pride. I had been carrying a lot of shame around with me about who I had been and where I had been. But he told me the climb I made in my life would only be worthwhile if I were brave enough to turn back to see **the distance covered**. I had to acknowledge my past. And I had to embrace it. "You should tell people your story," Blum told me. "It will help the people who listen. And you should listen to it yourself."

I first noticed the reporter because he was the only one without a gun. There were about ten cops circling in around the house, which is a lot for arresting a lone tagger, but it was one of the city's most dangerous blocks. One or two cops trying to drag out a suspect might find themselves surrounded by curious homeboys from up and down the avenue. The guy we were arresting was a tagger named

---

lay it all out talk about everything

try to hold yourself to that standard blame yourself for every mistake you make

the distance covered how much I had accomplished

Kaya (street slang for pot, taken from a Bob Marley song), and the charge was a felony. He might have been the most prolific tagger in all of Orange County, and cops from three cities were **on his trail** for thousands of dollars worth of damage. I guess that made Kaya **newsworthy**, because a reporter for the *Los Angeles Times* was along for the ride. I saw him standing behind a tall palm tree in the front yard as the cops banged on Kaya's front door. The bust went off without a hitch, and I headed straight for my patrol car, pretending I didn't see the reporter's waves. I didn't want anything to do with him—I had learned my lesson with the reporter back at Golden West College—but he tracked me down afterward and asked about my tattoo.

"Most cops don't have those," he said.

I just shrugged.

He badgered for a few more weeks and sent me some stories he had written. They seemed fair and straightforward so, after checking with Osuna, I agreed to meet him for an interview. Blum's advice was the primary reason I decided to gamble on another **brush with the media**. He told me to tell my story, and now there was someone who wanted to hear it. I shared a lot about my past with the reporter over lunch at a steak restaurant on Bristol, although I told him very little about my marriage to Frank, I couldn't take my eyes off the small, spinning wheels of the tape recorder sitting on the table right in front of me. I hoped I was doing the right thing.

A few weeks later, I was stunned to see the story on the front page. The first sentence stuck in my head: "Mona Ruiz carries the

....

on his trail trying to arrest him; after him
newsworthy worth writing about
brush with the media interview with a reporter

weight of two badges." Right above that was a picture showing my tattoo and my police badge. Osuna was a big part of the story, explaining my path to becoming an officer, and Marshall was even quoted. A criminal justice professor at a local college was interviewed, too, and he talked about how rare it is for someone to escape the gang scene but remain in the barrio. The professor was himself a former **Crip** from Los Angeles. He said it was "incredible" that I had become a cop.

At first, the attention I got from the article was dizzying, but then I realized that it had a huge impact on young people. I was asked to speak at schools and colleges, and in the neighborhood, boys and girls on the edge of the gang scene would come to me for advice. Blum was right. People were finding help in my story.

I always surprise people by telling them that, in some ways, my life isn't that different from when I was in a gang. I love the streets, the danger and excitement of it. A lot of cops won't admit that, but it's why they get in the business. That attraction may **wane** through the years as the tragedies and injustices **mount**, but that same thing happens to *veteranos* from the street gangs. The crazy life takes a toll on everyone who runs the streets, good or bad. Veteran cops and veteran *vatos* have the same look in their eye, and, sadly, more than a few share the same coldness in their heart.

I am not proud of many of the things I did in my youth. Too often when I was young, I **took the wrong road**. I could try to blame it on a lot of factors, I suppose, like economics or foolish youth

....

Crip gang member
wane fade
mount keep adding up
took the wrong road made bad choices

or the influence of the people in my neighborhood and schools, but really **it all comes down to me**. Everyone is responsible for their own actions, and I have to live with what I did. Sometimes that isn't easy. Like my cousin Eddie says: The bad you do doesn't end with the act, it **lingers on** like an echo, or a dark stain on your soul. All you can do is try to balance it out by creating good in the world.

I think a lot about a woman I beat up once, a woman I caught sitting in my car with Frank in front of Little John's house. Frank and I had been married two years by then, and the abuse had me edgy and desperate. Oddly, the fact that they were sitting there in my El Camino, the car I had bought and rebuilt with my father, is what made me maddest. Instead of venting my anger on him, I yanked the homegirl out by her hair and threw her to the ground. We scuffled briefly. I was on top of her then, punching her with all my strength. She was unconscious when I was done. I turned and left her there like that, vulnerable and hurt and half-dressed, I didn't lash out at Frank for some reason. Maybe my anger was spent. I just shoved him to the passenger seat and drove off. The last thing I saw in the rear-view mirror was that girl lying there in the middle of the street.

I feel more regret for that act than just about anything in my life. I victimized her completely. She may not have even known Frank was married.

My cousin Eddie and I were talking recently about the old days, about the people who made it and the ones who **live on only in our memory and** in the grainy photos of picture albums, forever young and forever lost. We started talking about karma, and the weight

....

it all comes down to me I can only blame myself

lingers on remains

live on only in our memory and died and now are only seen

we both carry from the things we did on the streets. "I feel bad, you know, I mean . . . I did some bad stuff, mean stuff that wasn't even necessary or nothing," he told me, looking off over the roofs of houses along my parents' street. "Sometimes I think about it, the people I hurt and robbed . . . it's hard to live with now."

I don't know which things in Eddie's past haunt him now. Like a lot of *veteranos*, he doesn't want to speak about his dark days—he just wants to **try to set them aside**. I told him about that girl I left in the street, and he just nodded. Eddie said all we can do is try to be better people and be grateful that we were among the survivors. Eddie barely made it out. When he told me about his final days in the gang scene, I realized again how narrow a difference there is between death and living another day.

It was in 1989, not long after his brother, Jesse, was shot by the cop who chased him through his house. Eddie was living a frantic life, bouncing from crime to crime to pay the bill for his drug addictions. When the cops tried to stop him one afternoon, he bolted, afraid that there were outstanding warrants or a good beating waiting for him once the cuffs closed on his wrists. The chase wound through the backyards and alleys of the barrio before the officers caught up to him. Eddie says they had a message for him once he was sitting in the rear of the patrol car. One cop took a pencil and leaned close to Eddie. "I'm sick of your attitude and your family," the officer said, according to Eddie. Then he traced an X on Eddie's forehead. "You're next. That's where I'm going to put the bullet."

The next week was a rough one for Eddie. He tried to steal some

----

try to set them aside forget them

drugs from a young, nickel-bag dope dealer over on Myrtle, but he **got cold-clocked** by the guy's buddy. Eddie never saw the guy with the pipe come up behind him, and he was in a fight for his life when other dope dealers jumped in to **dogpile** him. Eddie had made a steady habit out of scamming and robbing the area's younger dealers, and they all wanted a piece of him. He made an escape, bricks and bottles flying over his head, but he was hurt badly. Broken bones were showing through his wounds. After a night sleeping in his truck, he decided to finally ditch the gang scene. He sold his gun for some coke and one hundred dollars, but his bad luck continued when the guy he sold it to immediately loaded the weapon and started shooting at Eddie. The guy wanted his money and dope back. Eddie ran again. A few hours later, the cops were on his tail. It was all too much. Hiding out at a friend's house and watching the **blue suits** run by the window, Eddie vowed to get out. He took his money to the bus station, and they told him he could get as far as Colorado.

"I got off the bus the first day I got there and people said hello to me. I bumped into somebody, and they said, 'Excuse me,' " Eddie said, still sounding surprised by the way people act when they don't live on the mean streets. "And I said to myself, this is the place for me."

He's been there ever since.

I saw Little John once more after the undercover operation, when I arrested him **on a vagrancy charge** and possession of drug paraphernalia. This time, he was so far gone I didn't even recognize

---

got cold-clocked was hit on the head
dogpile attack
blue suits police officers
on a vagrancy charge for living on the street

him, Little John was living in the empty, concrete flood channels most nights. The residents whose homes rubbed shoulders with these long, narrow basins were sick of the **transients** climbing up to their yards when they needed a bathroom or settling their heroin squabbles with fistfights in the streets. The incidents terrorized young kids, who thought these toothless men in rags were like trolls beneath a bridge. In some ways, I guess, they were.

The neighbors pointed out the troublemakers when I arrived and I climbed down into the channel. One of the guys everyone identified saw me and started to amble off, but I pulled him back with the sound of my voice and the slap of my nightstick against my leg.

"I mean it, get back here . . . You really don't want to make me come after you." I didn't want to, either. The stink was unbearable down in the channel, and I wasn't thrilled by the idea of **locking up with** a guy who probably hadn't seen a shower in six months. In the car, I looked up at the mirror to inspect the haggard face in my back seat. He had a heavy beard and his hair was long and stringy. Nobody I knew. During the drive, the guy finally spoke, asking, "Don't you recognize me?"

I stared for a moment, searching the eyes. Then I realized it was Little John again. I gasped at how far down his slide had taken him. He used to be feared and followed, the guy who led the way, either to a fight or the next party. Now he looked eighty years old. I despised the needle. At the station, I sat him down to fill out booking forms. I typed his name and birth date without asking. When I looked up at him, he was staring at me and beyond. He looked sad but serious.

....

transients homeless people
locking up with fighting

"I'm glad for you," he said. "I'm glad you made it out, y'know? You can help those kids out there. They know where you've been and they're **tripping on** who you are now. Don't ever change, Ruiz. Don't let them end up like me."

The charges that day only got Little John into Orange County lock-up, where he got a shower, a meal, and forty-eight hours off the junk. I hoped he would get into some intensive counseling program to **pull him out of this nosedive**, but deep down I suspected it was already too late for that. Still, I would check the channel beds for his hunched figure for weeks. I never saw him. Little John got busted on a felony drug possession charge a few months later. News came from my cousins that he would not be coming back out. Someone **gutted him with a shank up** in prison. I checked my street sources and sent out word that I wanted some information on what went down. Nothing came back. No one knew who stabbed Little John or even would say if he really got stabbed. He died **faceless** in a place where he was called by a number. A lot of people were surprised when I told them about the stabbing, but not because of the act itself. Many assumed Little John was already dead. In a way, they were right, though. Like every hype, he traded his life for a needle. He hadn't been alive in years by the time the knife came. Even so I never forgot what he told me.

His buddy, the great Jesse James Elizalde, seems to be on the same path. In the 1980s, he got tired of the cops and gang foes, and walked up to the Trooper leaders and said he was leaving. Instead of quietly ducking out, as most people did, the gang founder was

....

tripping on completely amazed by
pull him out of this nosedive help change his life
gutted him with a shank up killed him with a knife
faceless without anyone knowing him

open and public about his desire to ditch the *clica*. The stance did
not sit well with the wild-eyed leaders. His *vatos* **gave him a brutal
farewell**. His arm was torn up so badly the doctors had to put metal
rods in it. Jesse married for a time and had kids, but it went sour.
For a decade, he wrestled with heroin. He **made it to methadone** a
few times, and even moved away from the neighborhood more than
once. The usual magnets dragged him back. I heard he hoped to
make it to Colorado like his brother. He wanted to move to a place
that seemed like heaven after tasting Santa Ana's most hellish life. He
called me up after the newspaper story on me. He congratulated me
and told me I should write a book. "If you do," he said, "tell people
that gangs aren't what they used to be. We didn't shoot little kids,
y'know? It was different in the old days. We had respect. A lot of
people don't understand it, but you know we had respect. Now . . .
now everything's crazy."

Frank Ruiz's shadow still touches my life.

Every child must have a father, I believe, and I cannot deny
my kids a chance to have Frank as part of their lives. Frankie Jr.,
especially, has found a need to build bridges to his father. At my
son's prompting, the two shared some letters when Frank was in
prison. The sight of the envelopes and their return address filled
me with dread, but I tried to stay positive when Frankie Jr. spoke
about the written conversations with his dad. Later, when Frank was
back in Santa Ana, I would let the kids visit with him on weekends,
as long as it was at the home of my former mother-in-law. I think

....

gave him a brutal farewell attacked him for wanting to leave
the gang

made it to methadone tried to quit using drugs

the visits were good for everyone, to help answer the questions that must be in the minds of my children. I'm not sure it was enough for Frankie Jr., though. Vincent and Vanessa do not remember when their parents lived together, but Frankie Jr. does. I can't imagine how my old life looked through a little boy's eyes. I think he wants love from his father and **feels cheated by** the way things turned out. I hope he can find the answers he needs. It has been difficult for both of us. Frankie has been a strong-willed young man in recent years, stubborn like his mother and aggressive like his father. The traits have taken him into some troubled areas, even to the point where his actions got the attention of people at the PD.

Like a lot of young people today, he is mesmerized by the street style created by rap music. The message of the rap and dance culture today is sex, drugs, and gang fashion, and I worry that it glamorizes the same wrong paths that nearly **sidetracked** my entire life. Despite what rap videos suggest, guns and drugs and gangs don't make men, they destroy them. I think, too, that young men are especially **susceptible to** these images if they don't have the guiding hand of a father to show them how to become men. I cannot show Frankie how to be a man. I worry that he will try to **fill the voids** in his life with what he sees around him. These problems have not really existed with Vincent and Vanessa, who are, of course, younger. But I think it's not just the age factor. Vincent and Vanessa have always been very close to me, and I have always been a big part of their lives and interests. Frankie Jr. has always been more independent and forceful, traits that could help or hurt him in his future.

....

feels cheated by is upset about
sidetracked ruined
susceptible to affected by
fill the voids find meaning

In the past two years, Frankie Jr., like any teen at his age, began questioning everything around him. The tension between us built, though, when his questioning turned into something more serious. In the summer of 1996, I took a drastic step to, hopefully, provide my eldest son with some **sort of compass** that might help him **sort out the direction of** his life. I don't think he took my promise seriously until we were actually on the shuttle bus headed to the airport. I could tell his anger was **giving way to** the nervous fear any fifteen year old would feel when faced with the unknown. Frankie had never been further than San Diego, and the military school I enrolled him in was in a hot, rugged stretch of Texas near Corpus Christi. He was silent most of the plane trip. We could see the Marine Military Academy base from the airport when we landed, and on the drive over we passed a replica of the Iwo Jima monument out front, along with flags and imposing gates. Inside, a registration office was crowded with families dropping off their sons and grandsons. A lot of the boys were wide-eyed and on the verge of tears. The drill sergeants said everyone should say goodbye before the boys walked past a set of doors to the inside. I knew why from my academy days: On the other side of the doors was the equivalent of The Blacktop. The screaming and criticism would start the moment the boys hit the other side, and there would be no more mothers and fathers and grandparents, only discipline and officers. I hoped that Frankie would find himself in this difficult regimen, just as I did. I hoped he would fill some of the voids in his life. I told him on the plane that sometimes you have to leave home to grow up, and I prayed I was

....

sort of compass sense of direction

sort out the direction of decide what to do with

giving way to being replaced with

right. But I missed him terribly in the meantime.

Frankie Jr. was like a different person when he returned to Santa Ana. He had grown some and the rigors of the 4 A.M. drills and all-day exercising had added muscle to his small frame. He was promoted to sergeant in his class during the summer, and the responsibility had shown him some things about leadership and pushing himself. He said he actually missed having someone yell at him during the day. After such an intense experience, he found himself missing the driving personalities of the camp leaders. Frankie had talked to his mentors, I knew, about subjects more complex than push-ups and the shooting range. The **base minister** had counseled Frankie on his complex feelings toward his father. One of the first things Frankie wanted to do when he got back home was arrange a weekend visit with his father, both to rightfully brag about his new accomplishments and to clear the air between them. I don't know what happened between them on that weekend. I hope that my son has found some satisfaction. No boy should be without a father.

The relationship between my ex-husband and myself is now **an oddly quiet exchange of space**. I don't press him, either about our past or his present, and he doesn't bother me or the life I've created with my children. I don't hate him anymore because hate is a waste of the spirit.

I saw Frank Ruiz in 1995 when he came back to Santa Ana. His face and voice seemed oddly unfamiliar to me. He had heard talk in prison that I was thinking of writing a book about my Trooper days,

....

base minister military school's religious leader
an oddly quiet exchange of space peaceful

and he was not happy about the idea. He told me about a new job he had, but then he said he didn't expect to have it much longer. The bosses weren't pleased with him. The job was as a worker in a huge haunted house that sets up at Knott's Berry Farm every year around Halloween. Frank was one of the monsters or ghouls or something, but the supervisors weren't happy with his performance. I wondered if he had been caught high at work or something like that, but I didn't ask. Frank joked that they were going to make him **turn in** his costume because he wasn't scary enough. I smiled and felt a little bad for him. I realized I would never be frightened of him again, either. I wished him well and told him it was time to go.

What have I learned? When I speak to the school classes or neighborhood groups, I tell them that the streets are the toughest school in the world, and that you have to learn if you ever want to make it to a **saner** life. I learned that people can't be judged by where they are from, what they look like, or the uniform they wear—whether it is police blue or gangbanger baggy. I also learned that prejudice is part of our culture, and to deny it defeats any chance of changing it. I know that many cops and gang members are more alike than either would like to admit, each sharing a thirst for action and an expectation that they deserve something more than the people who share the streets with them. I have learned, sadly, that women are the first to be victimized in our society, and, even more tragically, many of them pass on the pain and abuse to their children. I have learned what death smells like, but I have also seen my three

....

turn in give back
saner safer and happier

336

beautiful babies come into the world. I have felt love and trust, but I know those feelings fade in the face of betrayal. I have learned that no street, barrio, or gang is worth dying for, but that sacrifice is worthy in the name of justice and family.

Maybe most important, I have learned that you can never give up. There were so many points in my life where I could have surrendered and let myself **sink down**. At certain times, I did allow myself to slide, and I'm not proud of that. But faith, and the help of key people, helped me turn my life around. Almost everyone doubted that I would ever become a cop, but the only skeptic that mattered was myself. As soon as I believed, things began to happen. Nothing has been more important than that.

Sometimes, I find myself studying the fading tattoo on my hand. The blood is not as bright now, the flames are pale, but the symbol of my past and my path is still impossible to miss. To this day, every time I meet a new cop, their eyes are drawn to the tattoo on my wrist, the **brand** that marks me as a former *chola*. I watch their eyes to see how they react. The cops I get to know pretty well sometimes ask me if I ever think about tattoo removal. That's a big thing these days in Southern California. Lots of former bangers have their old tats removed with laser surgery to make an easier transition into **mainstream** life and jobs. When someone asks, I usually answer that I don't want to go through the medical procedure—too expensive, I say, or too painful. Sometimes I tell them I want to keep the tattoo so I can do more undercover work in the future. But, to be honest, those answers aren't the real reasons, just the easiest to explain.

....

sink down give up
brand symbol
mainstream ordinary

The truth is I often feel a sense of pride about the tattoo. Maybe it's the same for a soldier who brings back **a battlefield memento**, even though, to other people, that object or uniform might seem like a painful reminder of the horrors of war. Some people think of my tattoo as a mark of shame. But when I look down at the dagger and heart with the name of my ex-husband written across it, I remember not only the pain and mistakes of the past, but also my triumph over them. The *Times* reporter called it my second badge, and a burden. Blum might tell me it is part of that complicated, valuable view I see when I look back on where I've visited during my climb to a new life.

These days I tell people that the "Frank Ruiz" written on my tattoo is for my son, Frankie, not his father. I cannot separate myself from who and what I was before, and I can't erase the things I have done that are wrong—they are permanent, just like the image on my wrist. For better or worse, it defiantly shows where I have been and who I am. The image is a pierced but undying heart and it coils down my wrist. It is my past, and I am it.

....

a battlefield memento a souvenir from a war battle

BEFORE YOU MOVE ON...

1. **Cause and Effect** Reread page 326. What effect did the news article have on Mona's life?

2. **Conclusions** Reread page 333. Why was Mona concerned about rap music?